MILTON
AND THE
ITALIAN CITIES

Minturno to the Apennines
The Language of Natural Description in
Eighteenth Century Poetry
On A Mask Presented at Ludlow-Castle
On the Poetry of Spenser and the Form of Romances
Dante, Michelangelo and Milton
The Art of Shakespeare

MILTON AND THE ITALIAN CITIES

JOHN ARTHOS

BARNES & NOBLE Inc
NEW YORK
PUBLISHERS AND BOOKSELLERS SINCE 1873

First published in the USA by Barnes & Noble Inc, 1968
Printed in Great Britain by W. & J. Mackay & Co Ltd

CONTENTS

ILLUSTRATIONS

To the memory of
Edith P. Hubbard
so true a flame of liking

Preface

When Milton left England at the age of thirty to travel on the Continent he had already written some of the most beautiful poems in the literature of the world. There was nevertheless still, and there was to remain, considerable uncertainty about his future and about his profession. As it turned out, his stay in Italy was richly stimulating, and at one point in his travels, in Naples, he came close to fixing his ambitions on writing an epic poem in honour of his nation. But as the years passed he gave up that idea, and for some time it might even have appeared that he had been cut off from literary accomplishment. Considering all this, one must suppose that the chief result of his travels was an enrichment of his experience and even of his talents rather than a definitive settling of his intentions—chiefly a deepening and extending of his knowledge of himself and of the potentialities of poetry in the current state of Europe.

That much certainly. Italian culture was adding to his already superbly cultivated nature and mind. It continually introduced him to new ways of using verse and language. It offered him other glimpses into ideas about epics and about tragedy. It helped him in his thinking about Protestantism. He says all this in as many words, although what it all signified we understand in reading the poems that were to come, better than in his too brief reminiscences.

Accordingly it has seemed to me worth while to attempt to re-create something of the quality of the Italian environment at this time, to look somewhat closely at the particular interests of Milton's friends and at the society and the civilization they were part of and that he was enjoying at first hand. Looking, too, at some of his work against that background, we may come to a fresh view of some of his deepest interests.

*   *   *

Milton left England in the spring of 1638. He was assured
of an extended time for his travels and he was free to make
his plans as he went. He was attended by a servant, one supposes for the entire journey, and he had at least one travelling
companion for a while—between Rome and Naples—but we
know of no others.

He was to spend most of the fifteen months or so of his
journey in Italy, and while he might have gone on to Greece,
at a certain point he decided not to, and after travelling as
far south as Naples he returned north, staying again at the
cities that apparently offered him the most—Rome and
Florence. He visited friends in Lucca, he stayed about a month
in Venice, he stopped off in Geneva, and he then came back
again through France, to arrive home perhaps in July of 1639.

It is not possible to conjecture closely the duration of his
stays in the cities that attracted him the most. It is he himself
who said that each of his visits to Florence and Rome was for
about two months, and that the stay in Venice was for one.
His letters certify a couple of dates and there are the records of
his attendance at some meetings of an academy in Florence.
Making the best use one can of these indications, one comes
out with something like this:

He spent at least several days in Paris in early May 1638.
Some time later he began the journey to Florence, going by
way of Nice, Genoa, Leghorn, and Pisa. There are a couple
of records that could signify that he was in Florence in late
June or early July, but these offer grounds for only the most
speculative hypotheses. It is more probable that he came there
towards the beginning of August. This would mean that his
travelling from Paris would have lasted nearly three months,
in the loveliest time of the year, and this is almost all we have
to think of in reflecting on the slow pace of his journey.

He was in Florence until September 16th at least, then
making the passage, by way of Siena, one supposes, he spent
October and November in Rome. He would then have been in
Naples for much of December, returning to Rome again for
January and February. (The only date recording his presence
in Rome is of his taking dinner at the English College on
October 30th.) There are several records of his stay in Florence

in March. March and April, then, would make up the two months of the second visit to Florence, and that would leave May for Venice. On June 10th he was writing a note in Geneva. Then there was the way back through France again, and so home.

It must have been a splendid tour. He seems to have loved Florence especially, he made several friends there he continued to cherish, and he was ever to remain stirred by the thought of Galileo's achievements. In Rome his three little poems to Leonora Baroni speak of an uncommon joy. In Naples the friendship with Manso led to talks in which he was able to speak of his dearest ambitions, and Manso encouraged him as he desired to be encouraged. He was made welcome everywhere, and as in the years ahead a letter here, a reminiscence there, a point in debate called up some incident of remembrance, it is always with an evident pleasure that he returns in thought to that time.

*   *   *

I am very glad to acknowledge the aid that a Fellowship from the American Council of Learned Societies has afforded me in the preparation of this work, and I wish also to express my appreciation for a grant in aid of publication by the Horace H. Rackham School of Graduate Studies of the University of Michigan.

Part I

Florence

When Galileo returned to Florence in 1610 as 'First Mathematician and Philosopher' to the Grand Duke of Tuscany he had already made some of his most famous discoveries. And in 1633, when he moved to Arcetri, just outside the city, to live there under house arrest, he was more than ever in the eye of everyone. One of his clerical admirers had called the *Dialogue on the Great World System*, which had been printed in 1632, the greatest book in the history of the world,[1] and others were linking his name with Dante's. The achievement appeared to many as truly stupendous—the Copernican view of things had been greatly strengthened, the old conceptions of solid spheres, of the crystalline heavens, of the earth as the fixed centre of things, were now all but disposed of, and in their place were to be perceived systems of mechanical operations.[2]

The effects for religious thought were equally startling, and in Arcetri as the prisoner of the Inquisition Galileo had become the obvious sign of the magnitude of the trouble. Continuing the Counter-Reform, the Church was indeflectible in imposing the authority and rule of faith, and now, in Florence, the Inquisition was displaying the terrible strength of the defence of orthodoxy.

At his villa Galileo continued his investigations, and in 1638 he was publishing in the north of Europe his greatest work, *Discourses on Two New Sciences*. In this he avoided polemics, but he was all the same pursuing his habitual reasoning more extensively and profoundly than ever.

In the same year he became wholly blind. He was to die in 1642 at the age of seventy-seven, and while in those last years he would suffer still other afflictions, he continued his correspondence and he received the homage of those who were permitted to visit him. In his abjuration he had sworn never again to put forward the doctrines that had been condemned, and the ecclesiastical authorities were vigilant in keeping him from seeing such heretics as were suspected of wishing to further the Copernican theory.[3] His conveniences and comforts were provided for, and once for a few months in 1638 he was allowed to take up residence in his house on the Costa di San Giorgio in order to receive the medical attention he required, and he was even allowed to attend a near-by church for mass. His other requests to move to the city were denied.

In 1634 he had suffered the inconsolable loss of the daughter who had been closest to him in his tribulation, but a son and another daughter remained, and in the last years a devoted young disciple came to live with him in his villa. Indeed, it looks as if when he was well enough to receive it he did not lack company. And there is the charming anecdote Carlo Dati related long afterwards that gives a certain support to all those pictures artists were to paint as they imagined the circumstances under which the young Milton would have been received by him: 'Many, many years ago there came to Florence a gentleman from beyond the Alps, no less rich in the goods of fortune than of virtue, extremely anxious to make the acquaintance of Galileo, whose reputation had caused him to revere and love him dearly. He had hardly dismounted at his inn when he asked how to find where the old man was living, and learning that it was outside the city it was with the greatest impatience he waited until the next morning, and at the very break of dawn he set out for Arcetri.'[4]

But even before the imprisonment one could not say that Galileo by being there had made Florence into the kind of capital it had once been. It had for sometime ceased to be the city from which a new sense of the beauty of life had radiated, and there was no such concentration of talent as had once made it the centre of centres. Nor had it become a city in which the university was pre-eminent, not in Italy and certainly not in the world. The presence of Galileo did something, of course, to call attention to its congeniality to the most advanced speculation in philosophy and science but he himself discouraged the setting up of anything like a school. He had come to Florence from Padua partly in order to be free of the obligations of lecturing and of so much else that went with university life. At times the Grand Duke arranged meetings at which he and

others read papers, and he himself on occasion permitted this or
that friend to present his views at meetings of the academies.
But he seems to have preferred disciples to pupils, intimate
conversations to formal meetings, and he would hold forth in
the garden of the villa of his friend, Filippo Salviati, at Lastra,
or in the park of one or another of the villas of the Grand Duke.
The coming and going of scholars he enjoyed enormously, but
he rejected a settled organization.

He laboured at his correspondence and gave to this the kind
of effort another might have given to setting up an institute.
Like the early humanists, he poured out his life in letters, the
Republic of Letters was his Academy, and for all that Florence
meant to him Galileo cared more to communicate with the
learned by that means than by identifying himself with the
life of a court or a city or a nation. And so on all the innumerable matters he gave his mind to—astronomy, the basis of the
passions, the substance of light, the mechanics of music—he
engaged in that vast system of correspondence that seemed
sooner or later to embrace half the leading minds of Europe:
Mersenne, Naudé, Gassendi, Heinsius, Hobbes, Descartes,
Grotius, Mansus, Torricelli. Inquiries passed from one to
another, and the most careful and elaborate presentations of
experiments were communicated. It would be several years
before academies would print their transactions and take over
this charge.

So it is that one might say that Galileo's care was more to
participate in the life of Europe than in that of Florence. With
him there was a particular consideration that made this almost
inevitable. His temperament and disposition were highly
polemical. Again and again, from the earliest times, he had
thrown himself into controversy. The defence and justification
of Copernicus he regarded as a war he would lead on many
fronts, most especially against the fiercest enemies of all, the
Aristotelians. Florence, he had gambled, would give him his
base and liberty. He would attack in Padua, in Pisa, in the
Low Countries, and in Rome. Wherever the ancient, stubborn
errors and obscurantism maintained themselves he meant to
bring the truth. His heart appeared to be as much in this as in
his studies themselves.

After the condemnation he continued his correspondence, and as the years passed he came to express himself in his letters with great freedom on precisely that matter he had been ordered never again to forward.[5] In the city itself, in his conversations, in any of his communications there he could not, of course, make a public declaration. His son, his disciples, his friends, were members of the growing number of academies, but now there was no possibility of his using their offices for the presentation of his ideas. He no longer had the kind of position in the city in which he could guide and govern study had he wanted to. At one time, however much he cherished his release from the requirements of lecturing, he would have encouraged others to follow up the results of his studies, and by his very prestige he would have stimulated the most various and vital speculation. And now it was his own presence that compelled the exclusion of these matters from public discussion.

The repression was not wholly the work of the enforcing agencies of the Church, nor in Florence did it effect itself through mere deference to the Grand Duke in his official if not personal concurrence with ecclesiastical policy. The most intimate enforcement was effected through the necessities of piety itself, in the community at large, and in Galileo himself. All felt increasingly the awfulness of the dilemma, and almost all meant to maintain the supremacy of faith and the authority of the Church. The means of reducing the constraint had not been discovered.

Galileo's daughter, Virginia, living as Sister Maria Celeste in the Convent of San Matteo in Arcetri, was his most cherished support in his distress. It has been said that he almost clung to her, as if the role of parent and child had been reversed.[6] Her faith was deep and serene and in speaking to each other about their religion each of them expressed the tenderest and most perfect concord. Ordinarily not at all a humble man, Galileo seemed to beg help of her, and somehow, with the way she spoke of prayer, of reading the Psalms, of the intricacies of penitence, she gave him comfort. And with this sort of testimony of the value he set upon religious practice, I think we may glimpse a little of its importance to the life of the whole

city. The ardour with which Galileo advanced his speculation
was rooted in a more general passion, the love of what had made
Florence and Tuscany what they were, a life and a culture that
were not to be separated from its religion.

When Milton insisted in speaking on behalf of his beliefs
in Florence and Rome and Naples he was acknowledging the
energy and depth of the faith he opposed. He was opposing
Catholicism itself and also opposing the means by which the
Church of Rome was labouring to maintain its ascendancy. He
was criticizing its methods in repressing opposition, yet as events
were to show, he would be one with it in its fundamental
purpose while increasingly hostile to its methods. By whatever
ways he was to approach the problem of censorship, it does not
seem that he ever came upon a solution to the problem that
faced Galileo in advancing the Copernican theory. Milton
might justify liberty of speculation, yet he himself would hold
back when it came to committing himself to any astronomical
theory, and he did so, in *Paradise Lost,* because he judged it
more important not to allow controversy in this matter to
confuse the claims and authority of religion.

A few years after he had returned home from his travels he
put down something of what he had concluded about the life in
Florence. He allowed himself some exaggerations and some
omissions to make the point he wanted to make about the
effect of the silencing of Galileo upon the city, and he did not
attempt to get at the heart of the matter with his few words,
but he was exactly right in the point he was making—the
imprisonment of Galileo did more than divert some energies, it
stifled others.

I could recount what I have seen and heard in other
Countries, where this kind of inquisition tyrannizes; when I
have sat among their lerned men, for that honor I had, and
bin counted happy to be born in such a place of *Philosophic*
freedom, as they suppos'd England was, while themselvs did
nothing but bemoan the servil condition into which lerning
amongst them was brought; that this was it which had
dampt the glory of Italian wits; that nothing had bin there
writt'n now these many years but flattery and fustian.

There it was that I found and visited the famous *Galileo* grown old, a prisner to the Inquisition, for thinking in Astronomy otherwise then the Franciscan and Dominican licencers thought. And though I knew that England then was groaning loudest under the Prelaticall yoak, neverthelesse I took it as a pledge of future happiness, that other Nations were so perswaded of her liberty.[7]

In these years none of the leaders of Florentine life possessed minds of much original power. Giovanni Baptista Doni was the one with perhaps the best intelligence and the finest sensibility but in the 1630s he was almost always either in Rome or abroad. The chair in Greek at the *Studio* had been granted him in 1638, but he was not free to occupy it until 1641. Carlo Dati—to whom the same chair was to descend a few years later—was at this time a very young man, of good mind and a most lovable nature, and as time went on he was to make himself a name in many fields. His correspondence, it is said, would in itself provide a summary of the intellectual history of Europe for a large part of the century, and in his character as a citizen he was to make such an impression that his biography would be written more than once in the centuries to come. But when all that is said it signifies that although a man of admirable cultivation and energy, his talents were modest.

Jacopo Gaddi seems to have been the intellectual and social arbiter of the city, second in importance only to the Grand Duke himself. He possessed great wealth, he was unendingly generous and hospitable,[8] and prodigal in his support of every kind of learning. He had inherited wonderful collections of antiquities and paintings and books, he brought plants from all Europe and from Egypt to his botanical gardens, and he provided beautiful and lavish facilities for academic meetings. Yet neither he nor the Grand Duke was able to assemble the kind of talent the Barberinis in Rome were gathering around them, with Bernini, Borromini, Salvatore Rosa, and a host of musicians, to create models in every form of art for the emulation of all Europe.

But if there were no original minds in Florence to bring this kind of life forward, and if Rome and Venice and Paris were drawing away some of its talent, there yet remained a considerable group of men who set a high value on learning and the arts, and who were ambitious to maintain the traditional eminence of the city. That the presence of the imprisoned Galileo helped with other repressions to muffle their efforts is obvious—the absence of certain topics in the discussions of their academies and in their books proves that. It is as if the sciences had ceased to exist.[9] Yet it is clear that Galileo had led many to understand the scope of the new science as they would not have but for his leadership, and many were eager to continue learning. Here and there, in the visits of Torricelli to Florence, in the continuing studies of Viviani after his service to Galileo, in the homage Dati offered throughout a long life, one sees something of what had enough force to continue to contribute to the life of the city. And the fact of the adulation of Galileo—this is not too strong a word—during all the time of his imprisonment, the respect and love the young were coming to know he deserved, all this testified to a pervasive appreciation of his achievement. The long history of discussion and correspondence was not to be erased, however fearful the oppression. Meanwhile, Dati and Coltellini and Buonmattei and others Milton met[10] would have known, as well as we now do, that it was not only outside Florence, but outside Italy that the promises of science and philosophy were being taken up.

It must have been clear that Galileo's work had been nourished by the traditional Florentine humanism, and that that at least was still in honour. Visitors who were coming to a city where the example of Lorenzo and Ficino and Alberti supplied so much of the reason for their coming would be able to see how closely Galileo associated himself with the past, and if they were perceptive they would have seen how much of the ancient energies persisted even in the subdued intellectuality of these years. And Milton, I should think, in the reverence for Galileo would be honouring not only the principle of liberty but the historic sources that were sustaining him in his programme.

As one looks back over Galileo's writings, and especially over some of the letters in the early part of the century when he had begun to construct a defence even of the implications of his discoveries, a defence that included a view of man's place in the universe,[11] one can see how solidly he was founding his thought upon the reasoning of the great philologists and the students of philosophy. He presents himself as one among the Tuscan humanists, pious, advancing the standard of the liberty of judgement, and as confident in the power of the human mind as he is of the sovereignty and care of God. It must have been as such that Milton thought of him when he called him 'the Tuscan artist'.[12] Brought up in the discipline of the ancient languages, devoted to music, a thoughtful critic of the great Italian poets, again and again he returned for refreshment and support to the ancients.

Archimedes it has been said he admired above all others, but it was not alone through mathematics and philosophy that he came to the past—it was also in marvelling at the nature of language. He said this most impressively in a praise of the dignity of man nearly as eloquent as Pico della Mirandola's:

I have often considered with myself how great the wit of man is; and while I run through such and so many admirable inventions found out by him, in the arts as well as in the sciences, and again reflecting upon my own wit, which is so far from promising me the discovery of anything new that I despair of comprehending what is already discovered, I stand here confounded with wonder and surprised with desperation and account myself little less than miserable. If I behold a statue of some excellent master, I say with myself: 'When will you know how to chisel away the refuse of a piece of marble and discover so lovely a figure as lies hidden within? When will you mix and spread so many different colours upon a cloth, or a wall, and represent there with all visible objects, like a Michelangelo, a Raphael, or a Titian?' If I behold what invention men have had in parting musical intervals and in establishing precepts and rules for their management with admirable delight to the ear, when shall I cease my astonishment? What shall I say of such and so various instruments of that art? The reading of excellent poets, with what admiration does it not fill anyone who

attentively considers the invention of ideas and their arrange-
ment? What shall we say of architecture? What of naviga-
tion? But, above all other stupendous inventions, what
sublimity of mind must have been his who conceived how
to communicate his most secret thoughts to any other
person, though very far distant either in time or place,
speaking with those who are in the Indies, speaking to
those who are not yet born, nor shall be this thousand, or
ten thousand years? And with no greater difficulty than the
various collocation of twenty-four little characters upon a
paper?[13]

He must have thought that the language of man bore some
relation to the language of God. Galileo shared with many the
idea that the study of nature was the study of God's work, and
he came to think of Nature as a book, a book that God had
written, in His language, and so written that men should come
to know Him in reading it: 'God is discovered no less perfectly
in the effects of Nature than in the sacred words of Scriptures.'[14]
This being so, we might study and explore Nature without
fearing that the Bible would ever confute us: 'It seems to me
that in considering problems in nature one ought not to begin
by citing places in Scripture for authority but rather with
judicious experiments and the required demonstrations, and
this because, since Holy Scripture and Nature alike proceed
from the Divine Word, the one as the very utterance of the
Holy Spirit, the other as the faithful executor of the ordinances
of God.'[15]
We are not to think it impious to use the powers God has
given us in deciphering His works, and even the power of
doubt: 'It is clear that in philosophy doubt is the father of
invention, opening the way to the discovery of truth.'[16] He
made the claim as strongly as he could: 'But that that same
God [who has created all things] who has endowed us with
sense, with reason, and with intellect, should have wished us
not to use them, giving us by some other means the knowledge
that we could obtain through them, and in such a way that we
should be obliged to deny the sense and reason of what natural
causes or the sensations of experience and the necessities of

demonstration have revealed to our eyes and mind—I do not believe it is necessary to believe this.'[17]

He tries again and again to make the argument secure: 'It being clear that two truths may not contradict one another, it is the duty of wise expositors to labor to find the true meanings of the sacred writings, harmonizing them with those conclusions regarding the things of nature that plain sense and the appropriate demonstrations certify.'[18]

There could be no doubt what integrity required, and he showed that he understood very well how fiercely he could be attacked. He was well acquainted with the inexhaustible pugnacity of the Aristotelians and all the force that envy and discomfiture and entrenched position could bring to bear, and he seems also to have had some sense of what later was to be called the warfare of science and theology:

> If this of which we dispute were some point of law, or other part of the studies called the humanities, wherein there is neither truth nor falsehood, we might give sufficient credit to the acuteness of wit, readiness of answers, and the greater accomplishments of writers and hope that he who is most proficient in these will make his reason more probable and plausible. But the conclusions of Natural Science are true and necessary, and the judgment of men has nothing to do with them, so that one must be more cautious how he goes about maintaining anything that is false; for a man of an ordinary wit, if by good fortune on the right side, may lay a thousand Demosthenes and a thousand Aristotles at his feet. Therefore reject the hope that there can be any men so much more learned, read, and versed in authors than we, that in spite of Nature they should be able to make that become true which is false.[19]

Had the Enlightenment advanced to the point it was to with Newton and Kant the abjuration might be regarded as *il gran rifiuto*, the ultimate betrayel of honour. But because the doctrine of 'dare to know' had not yet made its most extreme claims for the adequacy of reason when supported by a comprehensive empiricism, Galileo could not be held to account by that standard. The abjuration was nevertheless categorical, and Galileo apparently could not press a principle that would justify him in refusing to make it. He had underestimated the difficulties for religion that the disinterested study into the ways of nature was offering, most especially that it would undermine the authority of Scripture, and he also failed where the Inquisition failed, in articulating a philosophical justification for subordinating his studies to his faith. He evidently believed in the unity of truth, and it seems that he hoped that the results of empirical study would harmonize with the faith of a Catholic. He could hardly more than hope for it, because the difficulties were so many and so great and were if anything multiplying, but he would have continued to argue that the humanist's sense of the beauty and power of the mind was part and parcel of that faith. Humanism would support him where empiricism might not, most especially at the point of the abjuration itself.

Despite so many of the ideas that the tradition of humanism would bring to support the study of nature, the point was clear that mathematical reasoning applied as Galileo was applying it was continuing the destruction of the traditional picture of the world and of man living at the centre of it. The imagining of the universe had itself been all but sanctified, and there was much philosophy to support that image. If mathematics could dissolve that, then, as a preacher in Santa Maria Novella said, mathematics was the work of the devil. A man of spirit, like Carlo Dati, could remark that just as it had been asserted that Galileo was not competent to speak on theology, so priests as such were not competent to speak on philosophy— that some indeed were capable of every stupidity and indeed enormity.[20] And however much Galileo would continue to affirm his own orthodoxy and his humanism, it is certain that he was no more able than his opponents to weigh properly the metaphysical matters his investigations were bringing forward for examination.

For the time, certainly, there was to be no resolution to the quarrel. Expression was restrained, and men who might have laboured to resolve the problems were pretty much obliged to take up other kinds of work. Very often they were drawn to pursue and explore the ways of piety itself, by those paths hoping to arrive at affirmations comprehensive enough to put an end to the growing divisions in men's minds. In their different ways, and by their own lights, men of letters in Florence would be attempting what Milton would be attempting in *Paradise Lost*, and this indeed is why it sometimes seems that Italy all but claims that poem for its own—it accomplished what Italy needed to accomplish for itself.

Most of the friends Milton made in Florence belonged to two academies, the Svogliati and the Apatisti. These met frequently, sometimes once a week, to listen to readings from works of the members and to discourses. They read poems and parts of plays, and papers on many matters, and in looking over their proceedings one is struck by the predominance of works supporting piety. Buonmattei and Chimentelli were priests, Coltellini was a Censor of the Sant' Uffizio, and there were other clerics besides who attended these meetings, but it was not their presence in itself that accounted for the emphasis on religion. Everywhere in Italian society laymen and clerics alike were increasingly absorbed in what for many years now had been among the chief interests of literary men, a more and more intimate mingling of devotion and the arts. These two academies were of a strongly literary cast, most of the members wrote verse, several wrote plays, and although the bulk of their most ambitious work was in scholarly and doctrinal writing, when they came together it was mostly to listen to poems and to hear discourses on religion and morality and decorum.

There were papers on theological matters and accounts of the lives of saints. Sometimes there were experimental essays in character-writing on the model of Theophrastus, the out-lining of virtues and vices in the generalized portrayals of men and women. Presiding over even such efforts, but still more pervasively over the verse, was the example and inspiration of Tasso. His way of conceiving of the heroic and the pious as the very substance of Italian sensibility all but possessed the imagination of the generation after him. It almost seems as if cultivated Italy could hardly wait for someone to take up where he had left off, to renew for them the power and wonder he had helped them know.

He had successors and they, too, were adored. Marino passed from city to city, fêted, and honoured in the public squares. He had died in 1625, and Chiabrera apppeared like another marvel to fix the admiration of the age. The pious and the heroic now appeared in other guises: on one hand there were the ambitions to imitate Pindar, on the other there were satires in the form of sermons. And through it all there continued to shine so much that had come into the language only with Tasso, some gleams of his incandescent religiousness and his equally incandescent luxuriousness. The balancing, or the truce, between these extremes was somewhat easier now to bring off than it had been for Tasso himself, the tension and the intensity seemed to have burned themselves out; perhaps this was because theology was winning its points and the poets were glad enough to give the intellectual and the abstract more play.

The revisions of the *Gerusalemme Conquistata* in the interests of orthodoxy demonstrated how Tasso finally thought poetry could be put to the service of devotion, and how thoroughly he had been persuaded of the overriding need to subordinate art to piety, and it was in a like spirit that Andreini and Chiabrera and Rospigliosi seemed to take it for granted that they would pursue their undertakings. For the countless lesser writers of the age this was a procedure that at its best promised access to the richest resources of sensitivity and magnificence; at its worst it would elaborate on the vogue for the grandiose.

Not long since, stories of Orpheus and Aminta and Silvio might in themselves have seemed to offer the widest opportunities for the play of imagination and meaning, and gatherings of literary men would be discussing theories on the forms such matter might take. The academies, in debating the requirements and virtues of tragedy and epic and pastoral, were weighing the relation of modern writers to antiquity, and trying at the same time to assess their relations to their own great predecessors, most especially Dante and Petrarch. With the passing of time the whole complex of relations continued to change. There were not only the transformations of style and shifts in critical doctrine to reckon with, there were the fundamental matters of belief and philosophy to face as the perennial questions were asked about the relation of writers of the Christian era and Catholic culture to literary models that had been perfected in the pagan world.

As the decades went by the changes in the ties to antiquity were as subtle as they were various. In the early seventeenth century in Italy imaginative artists continued to respond to the ancient myths and conventions as profoundly as Poliziano had in his time, but the uses to which they were putting them were, of course, greatly different. For one thing, they were being influenced by the energies and directions of the Counter-Reformation. In earlier times there may have been the mere determination to re-create the antique forms in their original character, as once also there were the efforts more simply to harmonize ancient and Christian meanings. Now there was coming into being the sense of an imposed obligation, as if the ancient forms and meanings must be incorporated in Christian sensibility and philosophy.

It was not only in Catholic Christendom that this effort seemed to be required. In *Lycidas* Milton himself had already performed a like service for what is in part a Protestant poem. Christian epics, Christian tragedies, Christian pastorals—in a baroque or mannerist or Arcadian style—these represented responses that were being developed throughout Europe, and in Florence, in the gatherings that Milton found so congenial, men were for the time being putting aside the prospects Galileo and his fellow scientists were presenting to them and pursuing others that must have appeared at least as important and perhaps more rewarding. For apart from serving the interests of religion, they were coming upon a new and wonderful beauty—new ways of combining elegance and strength, a certain formality in grace to set against the lyrical violence of Tasso, or even the exquisite delicacy of the century before. There was the wonderful excitement that comes with

the discovery and creation of a new style, a fresh and endlessly
intriguing classicism, no mere imitating the externals of
ancient art, but an imitation that consisted in abstracting
ancient ideals and infusing them with the most innocent and
unclouded of religions aspirations, even of ecstasy. Bernini,
Monteverdi, Salvatore Rosa were finding their way to
astonishing triumphs in a variety of forms, and it was in
similar undertakings that lesser figures were putting aside
the appeal of the developing sciences in order to mine such
wealth.

The controversies around Galileo could not be stilled and
were going deeper. The undercurrents of quietism were nearly
as strong in Italy as in France, and on all sides the Jesuits were
marshalling their forces. The unsettling and excitement,
directly and also indirectly, were affecting religious expression
and styles in devotion. A revolution was taking place in the use
of music in the churches. Theatrical elements were incorporated in the services even as church architecture itself was
adapting devices designed for theatres. Mythological and
pastoral conventions were being used to sustain dogma and
belief and not only in writing—the sculptured saints on the
façade of Santa Trinità in Florence were to resemble Guarini's
shepherds.

The orthodox everywhere were leaving the questions that
the study of nature had raised to resolve themselves if they
would, although occasionally this or that poet or tract writer
would try what writers in the previous century had attempted
as they took some of these same concerns into their view. They
attempted to extend the efforts that Du Bartas in *La Sepmaine*
and Tasso in *Il Mondo Creato* had made to enlist the knowledge of nature in the service of piety. For many years the new
efforts would be hardly more sophisticated than the first ones—
whether by Gasparo Murtola or Giles and Phineas Fletcher or
by Milton himself, and while there was often something close
to obscurantism in much of this, in the best there was the
intention to preserve the prior claims of humanism and
religion; their purpose was to continue the traditional dis-
qualification of the study of science as of much use to the
governing of human life.

But it must also have been that Christians throughout Europe were feeling the deepening need to strengthen the claims of faith in the face of the growing understanding of so much in the world that had seemed inexplicable and part of the mystery sanctified by religion. The study of nature was now clarifying much that had once been unintelligible, and it was becoming evident that the most sustained efforts would be needed to preserve the honour of what was to remain intrinsically mysterious and holy in the Christian faith. Philosophy as well as the conventions of ancient literature would be put to work in forming the expression of new tempers in religious faith.

The Svogliati and the Apatisti almost never discussed the subjects in astronomy or natural philosophy that were soon to be dominating the meetings of the Accademia del Cimento, although something of the uses of the telescope came into the epic poem on Amerigo Vespucci that its author, Girolamo Bartolommei, outlined to the Svogliati in 1636, and however much the problems raised by the reasonings of Galileo and his condemnation persisted in the very air of Florence, the academies were pursuing their labours with an almost ostentatious observance of the requirements of piety. There were times when the Svogliati met in the Spanish Chapel of Santa Maria Novella. San Filippo Neri was the patron saint of the Apatisti and his portrait looked down upon their meetings. But what tells most about the spirit of these associations, I think, were the terms used in constituting them. The statutes of the Svogliati, for example, begin with a general assertion: the members are being brought together by 'the inextinguishable light of nature that the eternal law has kindled in the mind'. They will be guided in their discourses by 'the light of reason which is the very soul of law.' And whereas Ficino had said of the members of his academy that the Divine Love bound them together, here it is said that the members of the Svogliati have become 'a mystical body'.[21] The language of Platonism has been transformed into the language of contemporary Catholic devotion, and it is to this rather than to the study of the Book of Nature, even as God's writing, that they will devote themselves.

At the same time the members of the academies wanted earnestly to continue the life of the mind their great predecessors had so superbly encouraged. The academic tradition in Florence from the time of the patronage and inspiration of the greatest Medici had provided the most vital energy in renewing the intellectual and the spiritual life of Europe. If the academies of the 1630s were to be no such nurseries, yet it would not be much longer before the Accademia del Cimento and the Accademia della Crusca would be spreading their influence well beyond the borders of Italy. In any event, the vitality of the idea of academies was rapidly increasing. They were springing up everywhere, even in the smallest towns. Old ones were being transformed, new ones were established, and it was into one of the new ones and one of the transformed ones that Milton was introduced.

Coltellini, who had founded the Apatisti on the remains of the Alterati, in a phrase very much like Milton's 'nothing but what is good and fair', seems to me to have struck the right note in characterizing the spirit as well as the style of these gatherings—'nihil nisi utile, & pium continet'.[22] As for the conviction that the eternal light of the law of the universe shone among them and the loyalty to classical standards that that included, Coltellini also put this well—he was writing in praise of a friend who had just died—'If we glance over the whole of his life we shall find that his every act was determined by reason.'[23] Piety, the control of reason, and something else— the air of grandeur. In their lives, as in their works and as in their piety, there was always the identification of reason with the authority of the literature and the imaginings of antiquity, and in their manner of conducting the academic meetings, in their writings, in the conventions they adapted when they thought of their roles in life, they took the postures of the ancient models—Icaruses rising in flight above the world, Dedaluses who never scorched their wings.[24]

When Milton met him Carlo Dati was not yet twenty years old. He was the warm and open person people were to love as long as he lived, and he was already establishing himself as one of the most ardent supporters of the city's academic life. Over the years he was to become a beacon for many who lived

in Florence and for many more who came to visit the city.[25]
More than a century later his memorialist could confidently
say that he had been the perfect exemplar of a man of letters
and a citizen,[26] but even in his lifetime Coltellini could address
a sonnet to him in which he would say that the ideals of aspiration as of duty had found their living form:

Follow the path intrepidly, Carlo, that ascends so steeply to
eternity, for there alone you will make yourself immortal,
there Fame and Virtue hold their sway. Nor let grandeur
here below—which has no value—ever hold back thy lofty
thought; riches, honor, beauty are frail things—false promises of good, only shadows of truth. Time and Fortune
overturn all those at will, and in an instant the inconstant
moon takes wealth away, an envious wind extinguishes the
brightness of glory, the beauty of the sun is eclipsed and
darkened. Only the light of virtue is never dimmed.[27]

Like Dati, Coltellini was to lead a long and valuable life.
Also a few years younger than Milton, small and frail, he was
boundlessly energetic. Encouraged in his studies by Giovanni
Baptista Strozzi and Buonmattei from his childhood, he was
guided unerringly by them to the love of Dante and the
purity of the Tuscan language. But he was also inducted into
the humanity of his teachers. He was learned in law, in Greek,
Latin, Chaldaic, Arabic, and Syriac, and one of the loveliest
of tributes was offered him—'whatever any desired to learn of
him, he would teach them'.[28] There is the like gentility in the
poem he wrote to his friend, Montalto, a Jew:

Montalto, the Great Lord who made the universe, and
whom you devotedly adore, I also adore. It is in this only
that we differ—that you, like your ancestors of old, still
thirst for the Messiah who is to come; and I, the off-
spring of Mary, not with the eye of a fox but in humble
faith perceive Him veiled in the white circles of the Host.[29]

Strozzi had introduced him to Galileo, and years later
Coltellini was to publish his praise of the astronomer, inci-

dentally interpreting in what was no doubt an orthodox way
the meaning of the abjuration, and of Galileo's very blindness
itself:

> The great Tuscan Lincean no longer surveyed the spots
> upon the sun, nor cared any more to study Jove and Saturn
> and the Bear. He put down his crystal lens and closed his
> eyes, and from the lowly earth, filled with the desire to
> behold lovelier things than these, with the wings of love he
> raised himself above the stars, the eyes of his mind fixed
> upon God.[30]

Alessandro Adimari would say of Gaddi, 'He penetrates to
the most secret temples of Theology, he looks into the most
concealed abysses of Philosophy, he scans the highest peaks of
sounding Parnassus.'[31] The conceits, the platitudes, the
extravagances, were all somehow serviceable to belief, and
in particular they would show how Christian and classical
ideas of virtue could cohere.

It is such ways of characterizing their own efforts that give
us a glimpse into the fineness and grandeur these men aspired
to, and that can give us an idea of the tone of their meetings.
And from what one can learn of the surroundings in which
they met as well as their procedures one judges that their
assemblies at times were conducted in the manner of royalty.
Gaddi indeed, accustomed to entertaining members of the
noblest houses of Europe, thought it proper for an academy to
invite kings into their deliberations, and once he allowed himself to imagine an ideal king establishing an academy within
his palace, meeting with it regularly to take part in its deliberations, asking questions and suffering correction when it was
called for, so intent on governing as perfectly as possible he
would accord to learning all fit dignity.[32] The accommodations
he himself provided for the meetings of the Svogliati were
incomparable—whether in the Paradiso Gaddi, the palace on
the *Piazza Madonna*, or in the adjoining gardens on the Via
Melarancio, or at the Villa Camerata near Fiesole, which was
now one of the most exquisite of all. The collection of books
and manuscripts he assembled, building on that of his ancestors,

in the next century became part of the glory of the Palatine Library. The dwellings and the open galleries facing upon the gardens included many remarkable pieces of modern and ancient sculpture, including a famous torso of a Faun. On view also were marvellous collections of jewels and medals, antiquities from Egypt, and paintings of Leonardo, Del Sarto, and others of the greatest Italians.[33]

The auspices in short were princely. And indeed throughout the records there is the pervasive sense of the necessary reliance of literature upon princes—as Dati put it, 'The patronage of the great stimulates letters, and letters make the great illustrious.'[34] It was indeed confidence in that bond that had brought Galileo back to Florence to serve under his former pupil, and this was the reality Lucas Holstein was to underwrite so unreservedly—since all Europe is afflicted by a 'barbaric fury', the only hope for restoring letters lies in the patronage of learned princes.[35] And these, in the nature of things, were as likely to be ecclesiastical as royal.

Sooner or later many of the papers delivered in the academies were printed, and they were offered as coming from them, indeed, in the not uncommon phrase, as their 'glories'. Sometimes to a modern reader these volumes have too much the air of self-congratulation, the commendatory praises of the authors themselves take up too many of the pages, but if one gets past that, even when the contents are commonplace, one is bound to recognize that the essays and poems spring from a deep sense of what is owing to society. It is almost ungracious to say that the collections of Jacopo Gaddi's papers or the *veglie* of Carlo Dati lack that combination of intelligence and timing that made the working of the Camerata in the century before so miraculously fruitful, or that, not many years in the future, were to cause the offerings of the Accademia della Crusca to be watched for throughout Europe. The assemblies of this decade in Florence were part of a movement in Italy that was growing more and more vigorous, a multiplication of academic gatherings in almost every community in the peninsula that meant to maintain its claims to cultivation. The idea of the dignity of learning was not only gaining strength as it became more widely celebrated, it was even becoming, as the Apatisti maintained, 'public'. In Florence there was the inescapable example of the most distinguished history, and the sense of what that city especially could offer the world contributed a peculiar ambitiousness to its productions.

Many of the discourses were eulogies—of the members' own ancestors, or of men of the greatest distinction—Farinata degli Uberti, Amerigo Vespucci. Often papers were read on general matters—the nature of magnanimity, the relation of ethics to politics. One poem bore the half-proud, half-rueful title, 'An invitation to the Florentine nobility to flee the luxury of the age and attend the meetings of the academies.' Comparisons of Dante with Petrarch were made constantly, partly because Petrarch was still so much to be reckoned with even in the very forming of new styles, partly because they were absorbed in measuring the character of their city, and also because Florence felt especially responsible for the preservation of the purity of the Italian language. Much of Buonmattei's study was directed to that end, and at this time he was at work on a treatise on the language. In corresponding with him Milton brought forth an argument the two of them must have spoken of, an argument he would know that the Florentine valued:

> Nor is it to be considered of small consequence what language, pure or corrupt, a people has, or what is their customary degree of propriety in speaking it. . . . I, for my part, would rather believe that the fall of that city [Athens] and its low and obscure condition followed on the general vitiation of its usage in the matter of speech; for, let the words of a country be in part unhandsome and offensive in themselves, in part debased by wear and wrongly uttered, and what do they declare, but, by no light indication, that the inhabitants of that country are an indolent, idly-yawning race, with minds already long prepared for any amount of servility?[36]

The point was one Milton was glad to make on any matter, but for the Florentines, as so much of Dati's own work was to show, the preservation of their language also represented the maintenance and nourishment of the peculiar savour of their city, *la fiorentinità*.

How to preserve that character and at the same time take up with the new modes of expression presented puzzling and difficult problems. One must say of the Florentines what one says of all Italy—their loyalty to decorum and their sense of a harmony in the manners of mankind was being put to a test by the pressure of changing circumstances. The effort to reunite the ancient and the modern worlds, the reordering of classicism under the auspices of the Counter-Reformation, was more easily effected in theory than in the forms of art, but there were successes everywhere none the less. A pervasive *concettismo* was one of the primary means of reaffirming the relation of the new age to antiquity. The academic writers particularly, aiming at grandeur and nobility and even ecstasy, may often have been perplexed by the difficulties inherent in the intention of merging the requirements of classicism and of orthodoxy, but there were many successes, some of them hardly to have been expected. As Ezio Raimondi has remarked in speaking of the achievements of Adimari and Chiabrera and some others, the new ways of transplanting classic forms were leading to some of the same effects that the *recitatif* in music was achieving;[37] like that, when it was employed upon the stage, they gave the fullest emphasis and éclat to the idea of a single personnage on display. The language that seemed to be called for was the language of the spectacular and the extravagant and, at the same time, the correct.

Poems like Gaddi's *De Herode Debacchante in Puellos Innocentes* or the Duke of Salviati's collection of sonnets, *Fiori dell' Orto de Gessemani*—one of these, for example, describing the Lord washing the feet of one of His disciples—exploit diction that in other circumstances would be both theatrical and luxurious. In these works, however, the irony of using the language of luxury in order to express piety underscores what is genuine as well as dramatic in the religious sentiment. This is a manner partly owing to the art of Marino, and *La Strage degli*

Innocenti—printed first in 1632—is not only crystallizing the imagery of devotion, it is fixing the manner of dramatizing.

The newer vogue for Chiabrera and for a classicism more hospitable to the abstract and general was also encouraged by the contemporary taste for the dramatic, even at the expense of the sensual. One sees this development especially clearly in many of the dramas composed for music that the Florentines were writing. Girolamo Bartolommei, who was present at one of the meetings of the Svogliati that Milton attended, wrote many such plays, some on classical, some on sacred subjects— *Il Natale di Minerva, Amore Gastigato, Il Sacrifizio d'Isac, La Vendita di Gioseffo*, for some of which he provided allegories. As he himself remarked, these are more like musical dialogues than dramas,[38] but one may go further and say that the characters seem to be addressing the skies rather than each other, and the point of it all is to make a pose in which the sense of the prestige of the role is as important as the allegory.[39] What gives these works the little passion that they do possess derives from the vitality of the language of the pastoral conventions they so frequently depend on, and which provides at least a basis for the attachments of these generalized characterizations.

With Bartolommei as with the others the language is the same in the secular as in the sacred works, and in the Ovidian poetry and the love poems there are the same intensities and extravagances as in the religious productions. Francesco Rovai writes a poem, 'Loosed from the bonds of love the poet turns to His Lord', and the language of one and the other love is the same. And often there are the same deficiencies as well as the same extravagances. His 'Roses in the bosom of a pale lady' promises more of passion and of wit than it effects— perhaps it means to use the words hollowly, to eschew intensity. It is the same with Coltellini when he takes up the worn classical figures to describe the coming of night and the invitation to love—apparently he cares more to provide an ornate frame than to honour or communicate passion—

D'auree fiammelle il negro manto adorna,
Dalle Cimmerie grotte

Placidissima sorge amica notte,
Con l'ombre a tranquillar l'opre del giorno. . . .[40]

But however much the aspiration for grandeur may be thought to characterize the deepest interests of these writers, almost to a man the very ones who were celebrating the rich and the grand equally in their love poetry and in their religious works, the men who in the academies were maintaining a tone as close to an idea of the heroic as opportunity and taste permitted, were also writing verse of the most extreme plainness. It was a sophisticated simplicity, of course, and in many respects it appears to have been the reverse of the coin, an inversion of the heroic and the magnificent. Literary men throughout Italy were constantly drawn to try their skill in these ways, and in Florence it gave scope to the realism that is at the heart of *fiorentinità*. But more significantly still, I think, it bore a profound relationship to their pastoralism and their piety.

To modern taste some of the efforts in this vein are most attractive—Alessandro Adimari's poem on the Adoration of the Magi, for example, and Buonmattei's charming idyll on the *Befana*, the legendary old woman who brings gifts to children at the time of the Epiphany. In the midst of the florid and the spectacular here were chances for the familiar that the Florentine humour makes so much of. Perhaps with Gaddi in his *De cane matre, & cane filio Cameratæ Gaddiæ* the effort put too much strain upon his habitual disposition for the grand, but no more perhaps than Milton's own *Ad Joannem Rousium* put him to the test. Where the simplicity rang truest —as it would have also in the famous conversations after dinner at Dati's house—is evident in such a collection as his *Lepidezze di spiriti bizzarri*; or better still, in Antonio Malatesti's longish poem about himself, where a certain sad humour gives off an unforgettable charm—

E il lume va mancando a poco a poco,
Tal che, s' io non do d'olio alla lucerna,
Ell' è per farmi qualche brutto gioco.[41]

But an even more extensive effort along these lines was

made in bizarre and enigmatic and fantastic verse. Something
of the spirit of this is obvious in the names of so many of the
academies, and not only in Florence—the Thoughtless Ones,
the Will-less, the Buried, the Passionless. Coltellini sent a poem
to Chimentelli, *Gyneroticomania seu Muliebramorosedelira-
mento*, and he apostrophized Malatesti as 'Poeta lepidissimo,
epico, lirico, enigmatico, faceto, etc.'[42] There is a great delight
in such sport, as well as in pursuing simple-mindedness to the
point where it makes a new sense. Sometimes in this spirit a
great many of these writers took to the mock heroic and the
mock tragic, but more often they turned to burlesque and the
bizarre for their own sake. Italian poetry had for years given
play to mockery and obscenity, and Berni and Aretino were
the acknowledged models, but whatever the desire for emulation, as the very reverse of the baroque and of the grand, it
seems that almost everyone took up with it.

In part this must have represented a criticism of the taste
for the lushness of Ovid and Tasso and Guarini and also of the
elaborate sensuality of the religious writing. The richness of
Marino and Adimari—at once inflated and decorous—is being
translated into a certain factuality. Andreini alternates between
the piety of *L'Adamo* and *Maddalena lasciva e penitente* and
the explicit obscenity of his *Spensierati*. The poet of *The
Slaughter of the Innocents* is also the poet of the enigmatic
obscenities of *L'Adone*. The point has been made that this
kind of writing is rapid in pace and spirited, and that in its
edge as in its conciseness it provided a valued relief from the
strain, the swollen vocabulary, and the torturing of conceits
that the academic tradition, and orthodoxy, were imposing
upon expression.[43]

Galileo himself had taken to burlesque verse in his satire on
academic pompousness, and he had written in the manner of
Berni on the *Befana*. As for indecency, while Coltellini argued
that those who wished to make ill use of a thing had only
themselves to blame, the more serious argument he proposed
was that the indecent and the obscene were as proper to
language as they were to thought, and if such writing was
vivacious and happy it could make the most miserable of
human conditions not only endurable but interesting. For

himself, he valued the opportunities it afforded him for the most malicious satire and the most pointed wit.[44]

The wry, the absurd, the humourously lascivious, the dry, make for a style that it is hard for readers who are strange to Mediterranean ways to distinguish from the immoral and the cynical. It certainly aims to keep a balance between clear-sightedness and voluptuousness, and it is often sustained by a respect for morality and religion that are obviously genuine. It is almost with the perfection of assurance that it avoids impiety at the moment of the most extreme outrageousness. There were many precedents for such daring in the medieval traditions and in Ariosto, and *il seicentismo* was no doubt confined more narrowly in its preoccupations. But when one compares its writing in this kind with the sensuality of twentieth century fiction, for example, the point is clear enough—the plain and the simple are having their day, and they are taking the form they do because the attractions of conceits and the spectacular and the ornate have been as absorbing as they have.

Milton, too, was devoted to the most ambitious uses to which secular as well as religious poetry could be put, and from the beginning his words expressed a most wonderful sense of beauty. But in him the celebration of smell and sound and touch never led to anything like a blinding sensuality nor, of course, to wildness or sustained humour. The pastoral and the masque might celebrate love, but never voluptuousness—he communicates the sense of it, but it remains hidden or subdued. As for expressing love for God, not even in the Nativity Ode did the elaborate and the imaginative and the sensitive impose themselves upon the marvellous gravity of his thought.

Elsewhere in English poetry, in Crashaw most strikingly, we see something of the combination of religious intensity with the most vividly luxurious displays of sensuality, and this is indeed an important phase of the religious development of many countries in the seventeenth century. But Milton holds himself apart from this. He might have meant to express as deeply and movingly as any ever had the very body of the senses, in the delights proposed by Comus and Echo and in the love of Adam and Eve. It is certain that in presenting such matters he cared profoundly to inform them with his religiousness. But whatever limited or constrained him in exploiting sensuality in the language of love as in that of devotion it is also clear that he was not concerned to let humour and sensuality lead him into the bizarre or the grotesque or the obscene. He was like his Italian friends in being cut off from such humour as Chaucer's and Boccaccio's, but he was also alienated from the passion as well as the refinement of Tasso and Guarini. And also he is not much drawn to the poetry of wit. It is this, and a certain frailty of mind, the lack of intellectual power, that make obscene poetry attractive to such a gentle person as Antonio Malatesti, just as it is the mere force of Milton's intellectuality that cuts him off from the pathetic, the charming, and the obscene.

As for the collection of sonnets Malatesti presented in manuscript to Milton, and that he brought back to England with him, it may be that Malatesti did not intend to print them. They are, as the title says, equivocal,[45] and no doubt the cleverness of the word play is an important part of their interest—a sustained series of allusions only partly masked. But in one sense the masking is not Malatesti's—he is using colloquial and dialect and slang words that are themselves masked. Whether the poems in his time would have been thought evil is hard to say, for although restraints were sometimes placed upon publishing obscenities, versification and wit seem to have justified much. Malatesti's notebooks, however, were burned after his death because they were judged to be 'contro i buoni costumi'.

The obscene and the bizarre do loom rather large in Malatesti's production, but what is most important in the poems is the character of the humour. It lies only partly in the enigma, in confusions of meaning, and in the unexpected moving back and forth between one part and the other of a double meaning. The humour is finally and most memorably in the vividness of the contrast of the poet and the country girl, partly in contrasting the skill of the smart person taking advantage of—or is it aiding?—the stupid one, and fooling nobody, and partly in the use of language that is so clear and unambiguous about what is gross and incongruous in sexuality. The poems are anything but stupid, and far from being enigmatic, they are comically clear.[46]

As it turned out, among the Svogliati and the Apatisti there were very few to aspire to epics or even to musical drama in the grand style. Bartolommei Smeducci had these ambitions and his achievements were considerable, but he was unique, and although he wrote many plays on Old Testament stories there is nothing in his writing that brings Milton's poems to mind as directly as Andreini's *L'Adamo*. That work—printed first in 1613—was still being produced, although I believe there are no records of its presentation in Florence in the 1630s. This *sacra rappresentazione* embodies so many of the interests of the time that in its substance as well as in its methods I think one may say it undertakes what many of Milton's friends would have aspired to if their ambitions had not been more modest. In his time Andreini had been active here and some years before one of the Florentine academies had produced a work of his. Although somewhat dated by 1638, I think a view of his most famous work can help fill out our understanding of what the life in Florence presented to Milton to contemplate and weigh and enjoy.

Andreini was caught up in the vogue for combining pastoral imaginings with the opportunities for spectacle that the musical drama was opening up. Music, drama, religion, and the contemplation of idyllic love, all these he brought to the stage to serve a public as eager to enjoy every opportunity for spectacle that the stage could provide as it was to accept the claims of orthodox religion through music and poetry. In all his work, and in *L'Adamo* in particular, in its scope and grandiosity as well as in its particular material, Andreini helps us as much as anyone can to see what the Counter-Reformation was continuing to inspire.

A visitor from beyond the Alps with that perspective would certainly appraise it as coming from the very heart of contemporary Catholicism in Italy, and if he were at all sensitive to style he would see how much Andreini's ideas about the fall and redemption of man were rooted in the particularities of Italian culture. Milton certainly would have seen how in his imaginings and in his phrasing Andreini was drawing upon a state of mind and sensibility that was all but the very projection of Tasso's. And he would have perceived instantly how by that very fact the story of the Fall of Man must differ if it were to be reconstructed by an imagination not born to that language and that temper. His own love for Tasso was deep, he admired and it even seems that he was sympathetic to Marino and Chiabrera, and one may be certain that he learned much from them, but no more than one could who was by birth alien to their ideas of luxury, to their as it were native orientation to the very springs of classicism, and to their wit. And when one considers that Milton was to put to use much of what he learned from the Italians into works forwarding the Christianity of Protestantism, one may understand how shrewdly he would have judged the manner as well as the content of the writing of men like Andreini and Bartolommei as they addressed themselves to great spectacular productions honouring their religion.

L'Adamo was composed to be sung by individuals and choruses, and it made use of elaborate choreography as well as theatrical machines for spectacular effects. In the first three acts the play proceeds through representations of the Creation, the Temptation, and the Fall. In the last two the character of the production changes—here there are many allegorical personages—the World, the Flesh, the Devil, the Seven Deadly Sins—all portraying the temptations to which man will be subject. Choruses of angels and devils alternate, and in the end the Archangel Michael drives all the evil creatures into the Abyss. The work concludes, as has been said, with 'baroque sumptuosity', but the style and initial conception owe to the somewhat simpler inspiration of the *sacra rappresentazione*,[47] a form of drama composed for music that owed considerably to the conversations of the Camerata.

In his preface to *L'Adamo* again and again, as in the work itself, Andreini showed his fascination with the theatrical—the universe is a theatre, the inner life of man is theatrical, poetry aspires to drama. In the course of the essay Andreini offered observations that bring to mind much that has been said about *Paradise Lost*, about the use of the story of Adam and Eve as a means of presenting the story of mankind, and about the use of the experience of these two as the image of all human experience, a fable of what is always taking place in the soul of every man:

Let [my work] be surveyed, therefore, with an eye of indulgence, and blame not the poverty of style, the want of
dignity in the conduct of the circumstances, sterility of conceits, weakness of spirit, insipid jokes, and extravagant
episodes, to mention (without speaking of an infinitude of
other things,) that the world, the flesh, and the devil, present themselves in human shapes to tempt Adam, since there
was then in the universe no other man or woman, and the
serpent discovered himself to Eve with a human similitude;
moreover this is done, that the subject may be comprehended
by the understanding through the medium of the senses:
since the great temptations that Adam and Eve at once sustained, were indeed in the interior of their own mind, but
could not be so comprehended by the spectator; nor is it to
be believed that the serpent held a long dispute with Eve,
since he tempted her rather by a suggestion to her mind
than by the conference, saying these words, 'nequaquam
moriemini, et eritis sicut Dii scientes bonum et malum,'—[you
shall by no means die, but you will be like gods, knowing
good and evil]—and yet it will be necessary, in order to
express those internal contentions, to find some expedient to
give them an outward representation. But, if it is permitted
to the painter, who is a dumb poet, to express by colours God
the Father under the person of a man silvered by age, and to
describe under the image of a white dove the purity of the
Spirit, and to figure the divine messengers or Angels, in the
shape of winged youths; why is it not permitted to the poet,
who is a speaking painter, to represent in his theatrical
production another man and woman besides Adam and Eve,
and to represent their internal conflicts through the medium
of images and voices entirely human? [Here, of course, one
notices the special problem for Andreini, who is thinking
of a theatrical production even while he is also speaking of
the conflicts within the minds of the Adam and Eve of
history as an internal one.] not to mention that it appears
more allowable to introduce in this work the Devil under a
human shape, than it is to introduce into it the Eternal
Father and even an Angel; and if this is permitted, and seen
every day exhibited in sacred representations, why should it

not be allowed in the present, where, if the greater evil is allowable, surely the lesser should be allowed? Attend therefore, gentle reader, more to the substance than to the accident, considering in the work the great end of introducing into the theatre of the soul the misery and lamentation of Adam, to make your heart a spectator of them, in order to raise it from these dregs of earth, to the magnificence of heaven, through the medium of virtue and the assistance of God.[48]

So Andreini pursues the idea that the stage provides us with a means of representing the drama in the universe. There seems to be no limit to the vast assemblies of demons and angels entering the scene from the regions beyond the immediate stage. The very profligacy of the production itself signifies the infinite variety of the powers abetting and defying God. While the errors and the repentance of Adam and Eve are brought to our attention often and tellingly enough to remind us of their central importance to the story, in the effect of the whole work there is relatively little emphasis upon the idea that in Adam and Eve one views the struggles in Everyman. The main effect is in emphasizing the magnitude of the energies both for good and evil at work everywhere— the great engagements of power, the grand alliances, the endless treating and negotiating. And yet it is precisely here, however, that Andreini fails most—in the reading at least— for this adds up too often to hardly more than wars of words, and the urgencies of drama as well as of thought fail to make themselves felt. And only occasionally is the poetry moving and then in the matter least important to the spectacle, in the expression and representation of physical desire. The rest is seldom moving or affecting although now and then there may be an effect of pity. But generally I imagine that a performance would give most enjoyment as a spectacle and only slightly for the religiousness.

Andreini lacks the power to bring before us vividly the sense of tragedy, or of the awfulness of God, and he does not feel the need that so exercises Milton, to communicate the power and depth of the human understanding in these matters.

He is apparently pleased to accept and to stage the received accounts, always in the light of the one contribution he insists on, that life is a stage, and a play, but he is not interested in suspense because he is not interested in tragedy, or in the idea that the theatre of the universe is providing a tragedy for mankind to watch. Instead he is satisfied to embody the assurances of doctrine, to affirm the divine structure of things and the Church's solace.

On the other hand, the plan of the whole is interesting not only in retrospect but because one is led on by the anticipation of novelty. One cannot know as the scenes proceed what is to come next—and indeed there is almost never, perhaps never, any causal connection between scenes, there are only the sequences justified by chronology and by the filling out of the themes, and by the possibility of new variations of the spectacular. And all proceeds as it were confidently, as if it were in its conception as sustained and complete as it is elaborate.

Within this proliferation of spectacles—crowds of devils, cyclops, angels, personifications—and in the midst of a mixture and concentration of the teachings of theology and sacred history, the language of the choruses as of the *recitatif* sometimes proceeds in sustained and complex images, at other times in a procession of images so concrete they seem to be repeating the very forms the baroque sculptors were devising in order to call attention to stone as such, to gilt as such, to motion as motion. At times it seems that Andreini is using words to represent pictures and carvings more for themselves than for what they are supposed to stand. So it seems, for example, in the speech of *Carne* that begins the fifth act:

If in a bosom form'd in lonely woods,
An amorous lure, the engine of deceit,
May wake a blazing spark,
And raise an inextinguishable fire;
This day to me shall shine a day of triumph,
When in desire's fierce flames
I shall behold that heart,
Which love's devouring flame yet has not touch'd.
And now if aught of potency resides

In golden tresses, or a breast of snow,
A radiant eye, a cheek of rose and lily,
And teeth of pearl, and lips that vie with coral,
In beauty, grace, allurements, arts, and gestures,
To make a wretched mortal heart their captive,
Such tresses, such a breast,
A cheek, and teeth, and lips,
And my intelligent engaging manners,
Will hold thee fetter'd in a thousand snares.[49]

In this passage to some degree, but more elsewhere, the language can go beyond the simply physical into the more evocatively sensual, and quite richly. The overlay—if it is that —of sensuality upon the baroque whorls becomes itself so impressive that the pleasure it gives becomes an end in itself, very much as Eve herself has come to think:

How I rejoice in viewing not alone
These flowers, these herbs, these high and graceful plants.
But Adam, thou, my lover,
Thou, thou art he, by whom the meadows seem
More beautiful to me,
The fruit more blooming, and the streams more clear.

And Adam replies to her in kind even more impressively:

The decorated fields
With all their flowery tribute cannot equal
Those lovelier flowers, that with delight I view
In the fair garden of your beauteous face.
Be pacified, you flowers,
My words are not untrue;
You shine besprinkled with ethereal dew,
You give the humble earth to glow with joy
At one bright sparkle of the blazing sun;
But with the falling sun ye also fall:
But these more living flowers
Of my dear beauteous Eve
Seem freshen'd every hour

By soft devotion's dew,
That she with pleasure sheds
Praising her mighty Maker:
And by the rays of two terrestrial suns
In that pure heaven, her face,
They rise, and not to fall,
Decking the Paradise
Of an enchanting visage.[50]

As so often in the poetry of Tasso and Guarini themselves, the sense of the pastoral enjoyments transforms even the most damnable temptations into a magically beautiful infatuation. The Serpent's words to Eve would, in short, seduce duller senses than hers:

If 'tis forbidden thee
To taste a fruit so fair,
Heaven does not choose that man should be a God.
But thou with courtesy, to my kind voice
Lend an attentive ear: say, if your Maker
Required such strict obedience, that you might
Depend but on his word to move and guard you;
Was there not power sufficient in the laws
Sublime of hope, of faith, and charity?
Why then, fair creature, why, without occasion
Thus should he multiply his laws for man,
For ever outraging with such a yoke
Your precious liberty, and of great lords
Making you slaves, nay, in one point inferior
Even to the savage beasts,
Whom he would not reduce to any law? . . .
Oh hadst thou tasted this, how wouldst thou gain
Advantage of the Lord, how then with him
Would thy conversing tongue,
Accuse the latent mysteries of heaven!
Far other flowers and other plants, and fields,
And elements, and spheres,
Far different suns, and different moons, and stars
There are above, from those thou viewest here

Buried below these; all to thee are near,
Observe how near! but at the very distance
This apple is from thee.[51]

For Adam himself Paradise has been a place of luxury,
with much of the pastoral character, it is true, the concupiscent
restrained, or at least left latent, but the beauty of everything
is rich and intoxicating:

Look thou, my gentle bride, towards that path,
Of this so intricate and verdant grove,
Where sit the birds embowered;
Just there, where now, with soft and snowy plumes,
Two social doves have spread their wings for flight,
Just there, thou shalt behold, (oh pleasing wonder,)
Springing amid the flowers,
A living stream, that with a winding course
Flies rapidly away;
And as it flies, allures
And tempts you to explain , sweet river, stay![52]

When the time comes for God to punish the transgressors,
the language is strong, and yet it lacks the sense of the depth
and complexity of the pride that has brought on such awful
effects, nor for that matter does it communicate any just idea
of the weight of concupiscence that will give Milton's words
their authority. The sources are the same, the terms of the
condemnation and of the curse are the same, but Milton's
words are to the point as Andreini's are not. Andreini's are relatively unfeeling, as if he had no idea that he, too, was
caught in the disaster:

Thee, cruel Serpent, I pronounce accursed;
Be it henceforth thy destiny to creep
Prone on the ground, and on the dust to feed.
Eternal strife between thee and the woman,
Strife barbarous and deadly,
This day do I denounce;
If one has fallen, the other, yet victorious,

Shall live to bruise thy formidable head.
Now, midst the starry spheres,
Myself I will seclude from human sight.[53]

And Milton:

Because thou hast done this, thou art accurst
Above all Cattel, each Beast of the Field;
Upon thy Belly groveling thou shalt goe,
And dust shalt eat all the days of thy Life.
Between Thee and the Woman I will put
Enmity, and between thine and her Seed;
Her Seed shall bruise thy head, thou bruise his heel.[54]

The preface to Andreini's *L'Adamo* begins with a praise of
Adam that recalls Galileo and Pico della Mirandola and
Milton himself when they speak of mankind at his best: 'I
seemed to behold the first man Adam, a creature dear to God,
the friend of Angels, the heir of heaven, familiar with the
stars, a compendium of all created things, the ornament of
all, the miracle of nature, the lord of the animals, the only
inhabitant of the universe, and enjoyer of a scene so wonderfully grand.'[55] So many authors using the same illustrious
words, and seeming thereby to be sharing in the cardinal
humanism of the Renaissance, but if one looks further,
to see just what such affirmations meant to the ultimate conclusions of their thinking, the differences are very great
indeed.

When, for example, one asks how far the meaning and the
effect of *L'Adamo* depend upon the idea of man as paragon, one
must say that mostly it carries a very different burden. The
main conception unquestionably is of a universe in which man
seems to be but one among myriads of figures and powers, and
if any one personage is at the centre of it is God, or Christ
Triumphant, but not Adam surely, and not mankind. The
last words of *Paradise Lost*, in which Milton tells us of Adam

and Eve beginning the long journey of their expulsion, would seem to say that the activity of the entire work and indeed God's creation itself centred upon that moment and that sight, the picture of those two, hand in hand, the emblem that embraced what still remained of the grandeur and refulgence of human dignity even in its sorrow.

And when one considers the conclusions Galileo drew from his contemplations of the power of reason in humans, when one considers his admiration at the magnitude of the human understanding, one sees how he was turning the words that were all but sanctified by Pico's humanism into something very much like the vocabulary of Titans. It is by contrast with Galileo's confidence that Milton's seems humble, and for reasons that continue to puzzle us. For that very faculty of reason which Milton values as the key to what is God-like in man is finally abased: when the chips are down the issue between Copernicus and Ptolemy is left unresolved and the wisdom of antiquity is scorned. As he sees it, the love of God and the pursuit of virtue undermine the pride that alone can maintain a confidence such as Galileo's in pursuing the prospects of thought that Galileo at least could hardly be brought to confine.[56]

Milton's friends in Florence may have judged it otherwise, but substantially he was to take a position more like theirs than Galileo's. The assurances of religion that sustained their imaginings and their writings excluded many of the invitations of doubt, much as it was with him, and yet none of them, not even Dati, could have sustained in him as Galileo did what he still cherished at the heart of his religion, a holy love of liberty. In any event, he would sound the dilemma.

In Andreini any reliance upon the grandeur of mankind ultimately failed as finally as it did for Milton, but the reasons are very different. With him as with Monteverdi, and very likely as with Milton's friends, it was because, quite apart from the character of their Catholicism, they were wholly in accord with one of the fundamental convictions of classical culture—whatever they may have believed about the dignity of humans, they were more powerfully held by the idea of the might of the universe and of its laws and of the powers at work in it.

It is in this respect that Andreini's classicism supports his Catholicism, even while it may be working against his efforts to exploit passion and pathos. And however much Milton was drawn to admire the great baroque theatricalities and even to imitate and absorb their style and their use, in this respect he was no more classical than he was Catholic; and if not so much the individualist as Galileo, he was too deeply rooted in that love of freedom—perhaps if Dr. Johnson is right, in wilfulness even—ever to subordinate the actor to the play in any such way as Andreini did, to stand so rapt in contemplating the theatre of the universe he would all but lose sight of mankind. More sympathetically, one would say that in the end all his imaginings would come to rest in the idea of life as a solitary walk with God, as Andreini and Bernini and Monteverdi and Gaddi could never have conceived it to be.

And so as one thinks of Milton in Florence, enjoying his days there, and going on to Rome and Naples to take up with whatever might serve him out of this loved and alien civilization, in the years to come in his greatest work paying Galileo a compliment he paid to no other contemporary, and in a variety of other ways giving testimony to his appreciation of Italian art and style, one comes to judge the fixedness and firmness of his initial Puritanism, and the success it led to that his Catholic friends fell short of.

For after Tasso there is no Italian epic of great stature, although energy and intellectual power and great gifts were put to the composition of the most ambitious kinds of work; there was to be nothing to compare with *Paradise Lost*, for truth and life and magnitude. However one characterizes the Italian civilization of the major part of the seventeenth century, *il seicentismo*, it was taking directions in which the poets at least were coming to no more satisfying effects than Chapelain and Dryden, say, as they laboured for the heroic and the grand and the religious. And yet I think that the depth of the Italian admiration for Milton—manifested so early by the translations of his work and by praise that has continued eloquently until this day—testifies not only to the individual character of his achievements but to something general as well, an achievement that was being denied them by the very nature of the kinds of classicism in vogue as well as by the restraints and formings they derived from the doctrines of the Counter-Reformation.

For a man like Dati there must have been at least a hope that piety and the love of truth would always be one and the same. Like the others the very basis of all that he served rested on the acceptance of authority, and in particular on the authority of the Church. How far that dependence would endanger the desire to know it would take more than the labour of his century to discover. Galileo had said, 'Doubt is the father of invention, opening the way to the discovery of truth.' But in the academies this was not yet a doctrine to be held in just that way. Nor would it be a doctrine Milton for all his love of liberty could ever have sustained. Like the others in Florence, he, too, caught in the same cross-fire, would ultimately take his stand on the side of authority.

But instead of glorifying God in the manner of Tasso and Marino and Andreini, instead of dealing with the resources of the *ratio studiorum*, of the doctrines of the Council of Trent, and of the resources of sensuality in the idea of a pastoral innocence, he would establish a balance in which the Holy Spirit rather than the Church would be understood to establish its hegemony in the reasoning of men; in which a classicism, however sympathetic to Euripides, would take the place of the theatricality and splendour and grandiosity of baroque culture, quickened into life and beauty as if grace itself were at work; and a concept of things in which the state of man in his innocence would be known as a state in which temperance and chastity are seen to inhere in nature, in love, and in delight.

What seems to have been lost to the Italians was the idea of serving the inborn temperance—the idea that in man, in his passions as well as in his thought, and as in the universe and its orderings, a single principle allied God's love to the governing of nature, a 'temperance in the very whirlwind of passion'. The long efforts of the Florentine Platonists to establish the authority of reason conceived as the principle of even the life of the individual soul had been overwhelmed by the imagining of the pastoral innocence of the passions and by all the beauty and wretchedness with which that idea could present literature and the other arts for their subject. The image of man was lost in the spectacle of the divine finger-paintings.

Charles V had said that Florence was so beautiful it deserved to be shown only on holy-days, and in looking on the country-side John Raymond made the other remark that seems as true now as then: 'For eight mile round about the City there seemes another *Florence,* so full are the fields speckled with Country seats. Neither are those delights to private men alone, but there are likewise publike walkes, witness that of Pines two miles long: that of *Cypresses* leading to *Poggio Imperiale,* and many more.'[57]

One and the other city welcomed the visitor. It is perhaps not possible to know for certain why Milton spoke of Galileo studying the heavens from Fiesole, although it is known that the philosopher did delight in visiting his friends in the country and even sometimes working there. The Duke of Salviati—not Filippo, the particular friend of Galileo—owned several villas to the north of the city, one of the most beautiful of all near San Domenico and overlooking Fiesole. Here he kept several telescopes for the entertainment of his guests, and very likely for serious uses as well.[58] But whether at Fiesole or along the Mugnone or in the palaces and gardens within the city Milton was welcomed warmly.

As one reads here and there in the records, it is one of the pleasantest of experiences to observe in this small city, so many aspiring to an eminence that they at least still thought would be world-wide, how like a family they all were. The remembrances of growing up together, the common undertakings, the going back and forth, all point to a sense of community and a pervasively social spirit.

There is the charming reminiscence of Dati's:

In going over in my mind my past life there is no remembrance that comes to me that goes farther back, or from all

my childhood is any happier than, in those early years
before good and evil are distinguished, having known
Galileo Galilei. Afterwards, in my more adult state, I
admired him as the prime ornament of my own country
which was also his, and the prime ornament of the age in
which he lived, accomplishing so many and such excellent
things. He used to frequent the house in which I had been
brought up from my infancy, and delighting in the happy
welcome I gave him he would caress me lovingly and often
bring me candies. In my youth I always found him easily
approachable, and a splendid opportunity was mine to
draw abundantly from that inexhaustible sea the waters of
the noblest of sciences. . . .[59]

There are many records of the early, happy intimacy of
Galileo and Maffeo Barberini, the one who as Pope would be
finally responsible for his condemnation. Giovanni Baptista
Doni taught the child Dati languages, and Dati was later to
say, 'If ever I accomplished anything worthy in literature, I
owe it to him';[60] and, dying, Doni would give his own children
over to Dati for their education. And when one looks at the
volumes one or another of the literary sort prepared in honour
of a friend's latest work, or as a memorial volume, one is
impressed by how widespread the gifts were, not merely for
civility, but for friendship. And everything goes to show that
Milton was freely accepted in their easy and warm companionship. Years later, writing to Dati, he recalled his sorrow at
leaving his friends:

> Very sad to me also, I will not conceal from you, was that
> departure, and it planted stings in my heart which now
> rankle there deeper, as often as I think with myself of my
> reluctant parting, my separation as by a wrench, from so
> many companions at once, such good friends as they were,
> and living so pleasantly with each other in one city, far off
> indeed, but to me most dear.[61]

Along with its hospitality Florence was famous in those
days for what has been called 'the theatrical sense of life'. It

seems that every occasion was taken to offer elaborate entertainments, to glorify feast-days, to provide spectacles. For this
or that occasion stages were set up in the *cortile* of the Pitti
Palace, in the Piazza della Signoria or in the square before the
Cathedral.

The spirit and the quality that so took the city we may see
in the arrangements made about this time for an important
wedding. The procession to the Duomo was to enter the city at
the Porta del Prato, which was festooned 'capricciosamente',
and other temporary arches were erected along the way, they,
too, as the buildings fronting the street, decked out with
ornaments and flowers. The long procession, magnificently
dressed, passed as from one triumph to another into the church.

During the Mass, and while the Princess was still kneeling,
from the great ceiling there descended a gilded cloud which
opened slowly to the accompaniment of the organ and the
choir, and within it one could see circles of seated saints and
hear them urging the faithful to pray. Then there descended
from the heavens all the protecting angels of the city with
their banners. When the ceremony came to an end they returned above, and the cloud closed as the singing ended.[62]

And all the while the city was becoming more itself. The
new façade of Ognissanti was completed in 1638. Santo
Stefano was being rebuilt, and in it were incorporated some of
the most exquisite of architectural inventions, and most
especially the marvellous altar railing. The most elaborate of
the baroque additions were yet to be made, but already the
Buontalenti façade of Santa Trinità presented to the view that
half-theatrical, half-pastoral idealization of holiness that is at
the heart of the baroque inspiration. And always the Florentine
character dominated the innovations, and continued to add a
beauty and serenity to the baroque style it seldom achieved
elsewhere.

And while so much appeared warm and assured yet beneath
the surface there was much that was far from serene—the
remembrances of the terrible plague of 1630, the continuous
tension as the forces of the Vatican and of Venice confronted
each other, the imprisonment of Galileo and the vigilant enforcement of orthodoxy everywhere.

NOTES

1 This particular comment was relayed to Galileo himself by Benedetto Castelli in a vivid note: 'Il Padre Scheiner, ritrovandosi in una libraria dove un tal Padre Olivetano venuto di Siena a' giorni passati, si ritrovava, e sentendo che il Padre Olivetano dava le meritate lodi a i Dialoghi, celebrandoli per il maggiore libro che fusse mai uscito in luce, si commosse tutto con mutazione di colore in viso e con un tremore grandissimo nella vita e nelle mani, in modo che il libraio, quale mi ha raccontata l'istoria, restò maravigliato; e mi disse di più che il detto Padre Scheiner aveva detto, che avrebbe pagato un di questi libri dieci scudi d'oro per poter rispondere subbito subbito.' (*Dal Carteggio e dai Documenti, Pagine di Vita di Galileo*, edd. Isidoro del Lungo and Antonio Favaro, Florence, 1915, pp. 284–5.)

2 The precise nature of Galileo's accomplishment has been very judiciously weighed in recent years by Ludovico Geymonat, who again and again makes the point that Galileo was not so anxious to offer new perspectives in metaphysics as he was to render impossible an attachment to the Aristotelian system. The Copernican theory gave him the opportunity of pressing for the most perfect rigour in relating observation to theory. (*Galileo Galilei*, Turin, 1962—pp. 76 and 167 contain particularly discriminating statements on this matter.)

3 Shortly after the trial the Pope himself allowed Galileo to move from Siena to Arcetri, 'per starvi con ritiratezza e senza ammettervi molte persone insieme a discorsi nè a magnare, per levar ogn' ombra che ella faccia, per cosi dire, accademia o tratti di quelle cose che le posson tornare in pregiudizio, come io son sicuro che la farà per conseguire tra qualche tempo la grazia intera'. (From a letter of Francesco Niccolini to Galileo, December 3, 1633—*Dal Carteggio e dai Documenti*, p. 373.)

When in March of 1638 Galileo was permitted to dwell briefly on the Costa di San Giorgio he was not permitted to leave the house in order to go into the city, nor to receive in his house, in either public or private conversations, 'uomini tali che gli possano dar campo di far discorsi della sua dannata opinione del moto della terra'. (From a letter of the Cardinal Francesco Barberini to Giovanni Muzzarelli, March 6, 1638—*Dal Carteggio e dai Documenti*, p. 442.) The Cardinal's correspondent communicated these cautions to Galileo, and in replying to the Cardinal he assured him that Galileo's son would scrupulously oversee his father's conduct.

4 Translated from the beginning of a manuscript in the Biblioteca Nazionale in Florence (Cod. Bald. 253[1]), entitled *Veglie di Carlo Dati cioe Occhiali Geometria Numeri*, etc.

Dati tells of another visit to Galileo in Arcetri when a friend was reading Ariosto to him by the fire, and Dati and a friend of his, Braccio Manetti, came to visit him. Galileo greeted them courteously, inquired into Manetti's studies, and especially encouraged him to apply himself to geometry. The incident is summarized from the *veglia* by Guidi Andreini, *La Vita e l'Opera di Carlo Roberto Dati*, Milan, 1936, p. 127, and is based on a reprint of Dati's *veglia* by Giovanni Targioni-Tozzetti, *Notizie degli Aggrandimenti delle Scienze Fisiche Accaduti in Toscana*, Florence, 1780, II (*parte prima*), 314–27.

[5] Professor Giorgio De Santillana has assembled several statements of this character in *The Crime of Galileo*, Chicago, 1955, pp. 328–30.

[6] Francesco Orestano, *Leonardo, Galileo, Tasso*, Milan, 1943, pp. 232–4.

[7] *Areopagitica*, in *Complete Prose Works of John Milton*, Vol. II, ed. Ernest Sirluck, New Haven, 1959, pp. 537–8.

In 1647, writing to Dati, apologizing for not having sooner presented him with his volume of poems, Milton recalled not only his own frankness in speaking of controversial matters but the tolerance of his friends in Florence: 'I should have sent it of my own accord long since, had I not suspected that they would be unpleasing to your ears because of those words spoken rather sharply on some pages against the Roman Pope. Now I beg you to obtain from my other friends (for of you I am certain) that same indulgence to freedom of speech which, as you know, you have been used to granting in the past with singular kindness—I do not mean to your Dante and Petrarch in this case, but to me; I crave it now whenever mention be made of your religion according to our custom.' (Translated by Lawrence A. Wilson, in *Complete Prose Works*, II, 764.)

[8] '. . . una amabilissima Civiltà . . . lo rendeva il desiderio primario della curiosità de' Forestieri, che da Paesi lontani passavano per Firenze.' (P. Giulio Negri, *Istoria degli Scrittori Fiorentini*, Ferrara, 1722, pp. 326–7.)

[9] The first academies in Italy established with the particular purpose of furthering the sciences were in Naples and Rome. It was not until after Galileo's death that any sustained efforts were made to form such an institution in Florence, and finally, under the active encouragement of the Grand Duke Ferdinand II and his son Leopold, the Accademia del Cimento commenced its distinguished career.

[10] Almost all the documentary evidence relating to the circumstances of Milton's visit to Florence is reproduced in *The Life Records of John Milton*, by J. M. French, Vols. I, II, and V, New Brunswick, 1949–58.

Milton at one place or another spoke of his friendship for Jacopo Gaddi, Carlo Dati, Piero Frescobaldi, Agostino Coltellini, Benedetto Buonmattei, Valerio Chimentelli, and Antonio Francini. He mentions Giovanni Baptista Doni, whom I think it very likely he met in Rome, but Miss Edith Hubbard has shown that the Doni who read part of his tragedy at a meeting of the Svogliati that Milton attended was Niccolo Doni. (*Notes & Queries*, N. S., VIII [1961], 171–2.)

Milton brought back to England a manuscript of sonnets that
Antonio Malatesti dedicated to him, and Dati some years after his
return to England wrote to ask Milton to contribute to a volume
honouring the remembrance of Francesco Rovai, whom Dati seems
to remember that Milton knew.

Milton's own remark is the only record of the visit to Galileo to
survive, and the fact of the visit has been questioned most especially
by S. B. Liljegren in his *Studies in Milton*, Lund, 1918, pp. 3–36,
and with somewhat less firmness by Piero Rebora, in 'Milton a
Firenze', *Nuova Antologia*, LXXXVIII (1953), 159–62, and elsewhere. The most telling defence of the accuracy of Milton's reminiscences is B. A. Wright's 'The Alleged Falsehoods in Milton's Account
of his Continental Tour', *Modern Language Review*, XXVIII (1933),
308–14. On the visit to Galileo in particular the authority of Antonio
Favaro carries the most weight—he was of the opinion that it was
hopeless to expect other confirming documents to turn up, but even
in the lack of such and with what other information was at hand he
saw no reason to doubt that the visit took place. ('Galileo, Milton,
e il "Lauro d'Arcetri",' *Serie Ventesimiprima di Scampoli Galileiani*,
Padua, 1912.)

The most recent survey of Milton's visit to Italy is Professor J. H.
Hanford's, 'Milton in Italy', *Annuale Medievale*, V (1964), 49–63.
Over the years there have been several extended studies of the subject,
but the most lively and suggestive is still Masson's account in his
Life of Milton.

[11] Several years before he became Pope, Galileo's friend, the Cardinal
Maffeo Barberini, warned him to stay within the bounds of his
subject. Piero Dini, writing to Galileo, repeated the warning: 'Ho
ben di poi trattato con l'Illmo Barberino, il quali mi disse l'istesse
cose che si ricordava haver detto a V.S., cioè del parlar cauto e come
professore di matematica.' (In a letter of March 14, 1615, in *Dal
Carteggio e dai Documenti*, p. 162.)

[12] *Paradise Lost*, I, 288.

Galileo himself used the words *arte* and *artista* according to the
scholastic distinction between artists and jurists—philosophers, and
himself, too, in this sense, being reckoned among the artists. He used
the phrase 'artisti scientifici', which his editors gloss as 'professori
delle scienze'. (In a letter to Antonio de Ville, March 1635—*Dal
Carteggio e dai Documenti*, p. 394.) Galileo is using the term in
thinking of a professor in a university, and in referring to the professor's use of a telescope. (See La *Prosa di Galileo*, edd. I. del Lungo
and A. Favaro, Florence, 1911, pp. 73 and 418.)

[13] *Dialogue on the Great World Systems, In the Salusbury Translation*, ed. Giorgio De Santillana, Chicago, 1953, pp. 116–17.

Raffaele Spongano's characterization of Galileo's own manner of
writing can hardly be bettered: 'Questo riempie di un potente
respiro di vita le sue opere e il suo epistolario, che ve lo mostrano

instancabilmente operoso, inesauribile di energie: dopo Leonardo, forse l'uomo che più vegliò sopra la terra e la cui mente indugiò meno in riposi, in ozi e in godimenti contemplativi. Per questo lo stile suo è tanto diverso da quello tutto aria e serenità dell'Alberti o tutto magica ed evocatrice fascinazione dei migliori frammenti di Leonardo, e distende maestosamente la forza sua nelle più vaste pagine che noi abbiamo. Dico pagine, non periodi, la cui palma, per ampiezza di giro e complessità di pensiero, suole darsi al Guicciardini storico d'Italia. Ma il complesso di un pensiero di Galileo abbraccia solitamente più periodi e richiede a volte il campo d'intere pagine per chiudersi: come la giornata di un grande ed operoso lavoratore, fatta di mille respiri, e che pur nondimeno si misura come un solo ampio respiro.' ('Galileo Scrittore', in *Il Sei-Settecento*, ed. *Libera Cattedra di Storia della Civiltà Fiorentina*, Florence, 1956, p. 121.)

[14] From a letter to the Grand Duchess Cristina di Lorena, 1615, in *La Prosa di Galileo*, p. 192.

[15] *Ibid.*, p. 191.

[16] In a letter to Benedetto Castelli, December 3, 1639, in *Dal Carteggio e dai Documenti*, p. 452.

[17] From the letter to Cristina di Lorena, in *La Prosa di Galileo*, p. 192.

[18] From a letter to Benedetto Castelli, 1613, in *La Prosa di Galileo*, p. 166.

[19] *Dialogue on the Great World Systems*, p. 63.

[20] Carlo Roberto Dati, *Prose*, ed. Ettore Allodoli, Lanciano, 1913, p. 7.

[21] *Cod. Magl.*, VI, 163, in the Biblioteca Nazionale in Florence.

Articles X of the statutes specifies that only visitors of distinction are to be admitted into the Academy: ' . . . non però s'accetti in Accademia, fuora, ò di qua dall' Alpi suggetto si sangue, o virtù, o scienza chiarissima, non sia notabile'.

[22] The phrase was part of his official permission for the printing of G. B. Doni's *De Restituenda Salubritate Agri Romani, Opus Posthumum*, Florence, 1667, p. 192.

[23] *In Morte di Raffaello Gherardo Orazione*, Florence, 1638, p. 9. This same volume contains poems by Adimari, Malatesti, Rovai, and Francini, among others.

[24] *Ibid.*, p. 22.

[25] 'Era in Firenze la sua Casa la magione de' Letterati, particolarmente Oltramontani, da lui ricevuti in essa, e trattati di ogni sorta di gentilezza.' (Salvino Salvini, *Fasti Consolari dell' Accademia Fiorentina*, Florence, 1717, p. 548.)

[26] Francesco Fontani, *Elogio di Carlo Roberto Dati*, Florence, 1794, p.19.

[27] Translating a poem printed by Edoardo Benvenuti, *Agostino Coltellini e l'Accademia degli Apatisti a Firenze nel secolo XVII*, Pistoia, 1910, p. 135.

[28] *Ibid.*, p. 72.

[29] *Ibid.*, p. 54.

[30] *Ibid.*, p. 19.

31 *De Scriptoribus Non Ecclesiasticis, Græcis, Latinis, Italicis, Jacobi Gaddi Academici Svogliati*, Florence, 1648, p. iii.

32 He expatiates on this in his *Elogi Storici in Versi, e 'n Prosa*, Florence, 1639, p. 335.

In the letter to Dati it was to 'the whole Gaddian academy' that Milton asked to be remembered, and indeed it was also Gaddi's hospitality that he like so many others had cause to remember. There is indeed a tradition that Milton stayed at his house in Florence. A biographical sketch of Gaddi that appeared in a volume honouring the members of an academy in Venice to which he belonged praised him in the characteristic style of contemporary courtesy, and other evidence supports its truth: 'tutti i Virtuosi Italiani, Francesi, Inglesi, Tedeschi, e d'ogni altra natione Oltramontana; che per godere delle bellezze di quella augusta Città concorrono in Firenze; ricorrono parimente alla sua Casa, per riportare dalla sublimità del suo ingegno gli Oracoli della Sapienza'. (*Le Glorie de gli Incogniti O vero Gli Huomini Illustri dell' Accademia de' Signori Incogniti di Venetia*, Venice, 1647, p. 182.) At one time or another Gaddi entertained the Duke of Guise, the Arch-Duke of Austria, and many others of highest rank.

33 Gaddi himself provides us with a certain amount of information about his houses and galleries and his leadership in the social and literary life of Florence, and some of his friends add to this in passages and poems they contributed to volumes he printed. (See especially his *Corollarium Poeticum scil. Poemata*, Florence, 1936, p. 53; and *Eliographus, Scilicet Elogia Omnigena Iacobi Gaddii Accademici Suogliati*, Florence, 1638, pp. 256, 260–1, and 263–5. The Villa Camerata is described in the anonymous *Trattato Istorico della Famiglia de' Gaddi dedicato all' Eminentissimo Sig. Cardinal. Monti*, Padua, 1642, p. xxix.) One of these poems is entitled, 'De pulcherrima Venere marmorea Iac. Sansovini in Gaddio cubiculo, ubi nunc habetur Academia.' (*Corona E selectis Poematiis, Notis, Allegoriis contexta*, Bonona, 1637.)

34 The title of one of the *Due Veglie Inedite di Carlo Roberto Dati*, Florence, 1814.

35 Writing to Peiresc in 1636—*Lucæ Holstenii Epistolæ ad Diversos*, ed. J. F. Boissonade, Paris, 1817, p. 279.

36 Written in Florence, September 10, 1638. Translated by Masson, *Life of Milton*, I, 625.

37 'Di alcuni aspetti del Classicismo nella Letteratura Italiana del Seicento', in *II Mito del Classicismo nel Seicento*, ed. Stefano Bottari, Florence, 1964, p. 255.

38 In his dedication of *Maddalena al Sepolcro*, in *Drammi Musicali Sacri*, Florence, 1656, p. 211.

39 It is in part a consideration of this that supported Henri Hauvette's speculation on an obligation of Corneille to Bartolommei. (*Un Précurseur Italien de Corneille*, Grenoble, 1897.)

[40] From a madrigal in part transcribed by Benvenuti, *Agostino Coltellini*, p. 138.

[41] *Lettera Familiare di Antonio Malatesi a Lorenzo Lippi Descrivendogli la sua vita*, ed. Giulio Piccini, Florence, 1867, p. 15. 'The light fails ,little by little, and if I don't bring a little oil to the lantern, it will play an ugly joke on me.'

[42] *Endecasyllabi Fidentiani del Signor Ostilio Contalgeni Accademico Apatista*, Parte Seconda, Florence, 1652, pp. 16 and 26.

[43] Benvenuto, *Agostino Coltellini*, p. 151.

[44] At certain places in the argument Coltellini makes his points quite subtly:

'Se gli Alchimisti per similitudine chiamano una lor materia sperma metallicum che ò da far io se altri lo voglia applicare a quello dell'uomo? Io l'ò usato per quello dei metalli, e se essi lo vogliono in quel senso piglinlo anche per quello della Donna, che a me poco importa; se noi avessimo a guardare a questo non si potrebbe più nè leggere nè scrivere cosa alcuna, perchè dalle persone maligne et empie anco alle cose per lor natura buone e sante, si posson dar sinistre interpretazioni benchè pazzamente e senze fondamento alcuno.' (Quoted from the volume, *Rime piacevoli d'Ostilio Contalgeni, Accademico Apatista*, Florence, 1652, p. 17, by Benvenuti, *Agostino Coltellini*, p. 149.)

[45] *La Tina, Equivoci Rusticali in Cinquanta Sonnetti di Antonio Malatesti, Fiorentino, Composti nella sua Villa di Tajano il Settembre dell' Anno 1637 e da lei Regalati al Grande Poeta Inghilese Giovanni Milton*, Londra, A Spese dell' Editore.

The volume bears no sign of the date of printing, which was probably in the first quarter of the nineteenth century. The introductory, and well-informed, notice is by Giovanni Lami.

The manuscript is not known to survive.

[46] A typical enough sonnet is number VII, 'On climbing a Fig Tree':

Tina, questo tuo fico castagnuolo
    È così liscio, e i rami ha così alti,
    Che l'adoprar le mani e i piè non valti
    Per andar com' uccello in vetta a volo.

Tu se' per starci tutto il dì a piuolo
    Or con lanci provandoti or con salti,
    E non far altro al fin di tanti assalti
    Che sudar senz' alzarti un piè dal suolo.

Ma stà, che farti un tal servizio io posso:
    So ben il modo, e come vi si sale;
    Sta allegra, Tina, or or te lo do scosso.

Abbassa il capo e appoggialo al pedale,
    Che se fai ponte e ch'io ti salga addosso
    Vi monterò ben su senz' altre scale.

Carducci judged Malatesti highly as a baroque poet, and Antonio
Belloni spoke of 'the innocent wordplay' of his humorous poetry.
(*II Seicento*, Milan, n.d., p. 207.)

47 The most famous production of this character is the first one,
La Rappresentazione di Anima et di Corpo, with the verse of Laura
Guidiccioni and the music of Emilio Del Cavalieri, presented in
Florence in 1600.

48 Cowper's translation (*The Life and Works of William Cowper*,
edited by Robert Southey, Vol. X, London, 1837, pp. 242–3).

49 Act V, scene 1, in Cowper, *Works*, X, 343; *L'Adamo*, edited by
Ettore Allodoli, Lanciano, 1913, ll. 2936–58.

Cowper's translation is good and the language poetic, and for the
most part I judge it adequate to the points I wish to make, but in
this instance the reader may appreciate a sample of the original also:

Se forza avrà da un cor di selce alpestra
Amoroso focil seca d'inganno
Di trar favilla ardente
Onde s'accenda inestinguibil foco,
Oggi per me lampeggerà quel giorno
Che tra le fiamme ardenti
Arder verdò quel core
Che non l'accese mai fiamma d'Amore.
E s'anco in sè riverberà valore
Chioma d'or, sen di neve, occhio lucente,
Guancia di giglio e di vermiglia rosa,
Denti di perla e labra di corallo,
Beltà, grazia, valor, vezzi, arti e gesti
Da far prigione un miser cor mortale,
Ben questa chioma e 'l seno,
La guancia, i denti, il labro,
E le maniere mie sagaci e scaltre
L'avvolgeran fra mille lacci e reti.
Ecco, che appunto il semplice augelletto
Non molto lunge i' scorgo
Ch' al mio dolce richiamo
Abbandona l'albergo, e la compagna
Per traboccar ne l'amoroso inganno.

50 Act III, scene 1 (Cowper, *Works*, X, 302–3; *L'Adamo*, ll.
1733–59).

The response of Adam to Eve in *Paradise Lost* at the same point
in the relation may serve to point up what so dominates Andreini's
way of looking at things:

Sole *Eve*, Associate sole, to me beyond
Compare above all living Creatures deare.

Well hast thou motion'd, well thy thoughts imployd
How we might best fulfill the work which here
God hath assign'd us, nor of me shalt pass
Unprais'd: for nothing lovelier can be found
In woman, then to study household good,
And good workes in her Husband to promote.
Yet not so strictly hath our Lord impos'd
Labour, as to deter us when we need
Refreshment, whether food, or talk between,
Food of the mind, or this sweet intercourse
Of looks and smiles, for smiles from Reason flow,
To brute deni'd, and are of Love the food,
Love not the lowest end of human life.
For not to irksom toil, but to delight
He made us, and delight to Reason joyn'd.

(IX, 227–43)

[51] Act II, scene vi, in Cowper, *Works*, X, 292–3; *L'Adamo*, ll. 1410–50.
[52] Act III, scene 1, in Cowper, *Works*, X, 300; *L'Adamo*, ll. 1664–74.
[53] Act III, scene vi, in Cowper, *Works*, X, 316.

Serpe crudel, ti maledico, e sempre
N'andrai col ventre il nudo suol strisciando,
La tua fame di terra ogn' or saziando.
Fra la donna, e fra te guerra fatale,
Guerra cruda, e mortale
Oggi formo, oggi fondo:
E s'una cadde, ben vittrice l'altra
Dovrà spezzarti il formadibil capo.
Or fra stellanti giri
Mi chiudo, e celo da l'umano sguardo.

(Lines 2146–55)

[54] *Paradise Lost*, X, 175–80.
[55] Cowper, *Works*, X, 240.
[56] One of the most inflexible and even prejudiced judgements on this matter is A. O. Lovejoy's in his essay 'Milton's Dialogue on Astronomy', in *Reason and Imagination*, edited by J. A. Mazzeo, New York, 1962, pp. 129–42. Another kind of judgement, summarized by Kester Svendsen, draws the issues better: 'If, in a poem based on the Christian humanist assumptions, it is anti-intellectualism to subordinate all learning to man's prime duty to God, then the case is proved. But it is not proved to those, like Bush, who see the disparagement of astronomical controversy in *Paradise Lost* and of classical culture in *Paradise Regained* as perfectly consistent with the

acceptance of an ordered universe in which learning and art have their hierarchies too. The poems "believe" in science the way they believe in classical mythology; the real truth is not in it except as it is analogue.' (*Milton and Science*, Cambridge, 1956, p. 241.)

57 *An Itinerary Contayning a Voyage, Made through Italy, In the yeare* 1646, *and* 1647, London, 1648, pp. 45–46.

58 Guido Fanfani, *Voci e Volte delle Ville Fiorentine*, Florence, 1939, p. 115.

Dati seems to be referring to the use of the garden of this villa when he related an anecdote about showing a visitor the mountains on the moon and phases of Venus with a telescope. (*Cod. Baldi.* 253[1] in the Biblioteca Nazionale in Florence.)

59 This remembrance is the beginning of a veglia of Dati's, *Esortazione allo Studio della Geometria*, printed in Florence in 1814.

60 From a letter to Nicholas Heinsius, printed in Francesco Fontani, *Elogio di Carlo Roberto Dati*, Florence, 1794, p. 38.

61 The letter is dated April 21, 1647. Translated by W. A. Turner and A. T. Turner, in *Complete Prose Works of John Milton*, II, 763.

62 Valerio Mariani, *Storia della Scenografia Italiana*, Florence, 1930, p. 54.

Rome

The Barberini portraits show them to have been men of intelligence, self-willed, almost shockingly vulnerable to anger, and with a control over their expression that is not meant to be taken for composure. The faces are no more intense perhaps than Bernini's own, or more passionate and intelligent than the character they were helping Rome establish. There that way of creating a city where everything worked to the glorification of the public life, the progressive unfolding of noble dimensions from hill to hill and in the valley; the very idea of a multiplicity of views—in short, in the city as in what one sees in those marked faces one is beholding stages in the transformation of classical ideals.

The manifestations of Christian piety in this phase of the Counter-Reformation were everywhere to be defined in forms developing the idea of display. In 1633 Pietro da Cortona accommodated the interior of a church to the idea of a theatre—a semicircular colonnade, niches holding statues looking towards an altar upon which a great gold sun poured down its rays, the altar itself upheld by two great angels for all to look on. The inner life, even the mysteries, were brought into the open, and brought there because the energies of existence were understood to be performers in 'the theatre of the universe', and the actors of the occasional plays, the men and women governing the time, were to make their very faces into spectacles. A poet of the time wrote of a splendid stage production sponsored by Cardinal Antonio Barberini:

> Tam benè noster Atlas aurata palatia versat,
>   Aurea quàm magnus sydera vertit Atlas.
>   Quis verò hoc aperit tibi fœlix Roma Theatrum?
>   Qui laudum in sese viva Theatrum refert.[1]

In one of the most famous of Bernini's stage productions the scene opened to reveal two theatres facing each other. In one

actors were acting out a play, in the other mirrors were so
arranged that the same actors seemed to be acting in that
theatre. Bernini meant to astound the audience when it saw
the same persons performing at the same time in different
places—the accounts say he succeeded wonderfully—and he
also wanted to make something of his constant interest in
illusion. And so with the planning of the city—it was anything
but a stage-piece, but it was meant at times to seem so, and
scenes were being devised to set off its life in such a way that
the public might marvel at itself and might become absorbed
in the spectacle of itself.

Because there seems to be something incongruous in the
thought of Milton enjoying Rome we have been inclined to
take his remark about the Jesuits' surveillance as a proof of the
awkwardness of his presence. This has helped confirm us in
emphasizing what he also did, his attention to the remains of
antiquity. And when all has been said one has known how to
about the charm of Leonora Baroni, about the friendship
with Holstein and Doni, and the hospitality of the Cardinal
Francesco Barberini, we have neglected to imagine seriously
what held him there those three or four months, on those
separate visits. Even when we weigh the appropriateness of
the terms baroque and mannerist in characterizing the style
of the epics, and when we speculate on the likeness of the conceptions of Poussin and the sweep of the imagination in
Paradise Lost, we turn back and hardly allow ourselves to
make anything more of the stay in Rome than the most rudi-
mentary suppositions, that he would have been contemplating
ruins and oppressed by the thought of being in a city whose
rulers were still keeping Galileo prisoner. But surely there
was more to it than that.

In the last stages of his journey, when he had returned to
Florence, he wrote to Lucas Holstein in Rome, thanking him
for his courtesies, and in a certain indirect way characterizing
something of his experience there:

> . . . when I went up to the Vatican for the purpose of meeting
> you, you received me, a total stranger to you (unless per-
> chance anything had been previously said about me to you

by Alexander Cherubini), with the utmost courtesy. Immediately admitted with politeness into the Museum, I was allowed to behold both the superb collection of books, and also very many manuscript Greek authors set forth with your explanations. . . . Then I could not but believe that it was in consequence of the mention you made of me to the most excellent Cardinal Francesco Barberini, that, when he, a few days after, gave that public musical entertainment with truly Roman magnificence [ἀκρόαμα illud Musicum], he himself, waiting at the doors, and seeking me out in so great a crowd, nay, almost laying hold of me by the hand, admitted me within in a truly most honourable manner. And when, on this account, I went to pay my respects to him next day, you again were yourself the person who both made access for me, and obtained for me an opportunity of conversing with him at leisure, such as, with so great a man (than whom, on the topmost summit of dignity, nothing more kind, nothing more courteous), was truly, considering the place and the time, too ample rather than too sparing.

He is even effusive in his compliments:

For the rest, you will have bound me by a new obligation, if you salute the most eminent Cardinal with all possible observance, in my name; whose great virtues and anxiety to do right, singularly ready also for the promotion of all the liberal arts, are always present before my eyes, as well as that meek, and, if I may so say, submissive loftiness of mind, which alone has taught him to raise by humbling himself; concerning which it may truly be said, as is said of Ceres in Callimachus, though with a turn of the sense: '*Feet to the earth still cling, while the head is touching Olympus.*' Herein might be a proof to other princes how far asunder and alien from true magnanimity, is that sad superciliousness of theirs, and that courtly haughtiness. Nor do I think that, while he is alive, men will have to miss any more the Este, the Farnesi, or the Medici, formerly the favourers of learned men.[2]

The words are warm, and apart from the mannered flattery

they speak of appreciation and enjoyment. Indeed, if we know anything of what was going on in Rome that autumn and winter we would be sure that for a poet and musician this would have been much more than a suspicion-ridden experience or a time for undistracted study of the past. That same winter in Naples in an interval between his stays in Rome Milton would be turning over in his mind subjects for a great poem. For years he had been considering how he was to dedicate his life, and he had looked forward to travelling in Italy and Greece as a continuing exploration of his purpose. So far, in Florence, he had evidently enjoyed much and been stirred deeply. It must have been the same in Rome. There more than any other place in the world the mere sight of ancient things brings to the present an energy and charm that adds as much delight as it does understanding to every turn of the head. And when, as at this time, artists were moving the great humanist undertakings in the direction of the baroque; when classical ideals were being translated into still another ideal in which Christian piety and imperial ambition and the authority of ancient thought were to be shown capable of balancing the demands of body and soul—in such an environment the mind of a man intent on continuing the work of the Reformation would be challenged to measure the strength and quality of what was to take on new life and new form in his own imagination.

Milton was to speak more than once of the love he bore Florence, but the fact that after two months in Rome he returned there for two more also speaks plainly of its appeal. In what survives of his writing he does not refer to his stay there with the sort of detail he brought up in speaking of Florence, and he mentions the names of fewer persons, but from several indications we gather that he was drawn into the musical life of the city and that it made deep and wonderful impressions upon him—the three Latin poems to Leonora Baroni point to an enthusiasm that must have been absorbing.

Nam tua præsentem vox sonat ipsa Deum.[3]

And Rome was full of music. It lacked a genius of the quality of Monteverdi or even of Cavalli to crown all that was going on there, but that is all it lacked. The musical dramas of Cardinal Rospigliosi year in and year out in the 1630s were passing from one success to another. Individual churches established reputations for excellence in many kinds of choral music for the various seasons of the liturgical year. Cantatas were developing into new forms and the oratorio was coming into being. Concerts of every variety were being offered, some informally, some sumptuously set in the midst of magnificent entertainments. Encouragement and patronage came from all sides, and in the quality of its singers and instrumentalists Rome was competing with Mantua and Parma and Venice. For this decade at least its achievements were at the pinnacle.

It was a time also when music and the theatre were coming into a new relationship with each other, and the rage for music must sometimes have been identified with the love of the spectacular. And it is this coming together of music and drama that would have meant the most to Milton, not only because of his perpetual enthrallment to 'the sphere-born sisters', poetry and music, but because for him, in the deepest part of his termperament, and in whatever cast of his mind that set the terms in which he would form his style, poetic expression again and again took the form of argument, and most especially the argument of voices.

One thing stands out from the time of Milton's earliest writing in verse—almost everything tends towards dialogue, The opposing of *L'Allegro* and *Il'Penseroso* is characteristic, and perhaps, most tellingly of all, Saint Peter's speech in *Lycidas* introduces into the poem a dramatic factor that threatens to dominate the poem. And the rest of the poem is as much as anything a recording of questions and answers. Something of the same thing is true of several of the Latin poems, and it seems indeed a rooted disposition of Milton's for his dialogue is a habit that is almost identified with thought.

But a certain formality in the speech is clearly not so much a matter of disposition and nature as it is of training, and here the style of the prolusions of his early education seems to me to justify the idea that Milton thought of speech and of the interchange of dialogue in writing more as declaration than as drama.[4] Again and again the dialogues are more plainly directed towards argument and persuasion than towards the less aggressive exchanges of conversation; they take the tone and manner of the performance that belongs to public roles. And indeed the controversial prose is also something he took to not only out of the pressures of controversy and political and religious commitment but out of this primary disposition of his—the self-opposing and self-dramatizing, the idea of reaching a resolution through the exchange of utterances.

In the epics dialogue is peculiarly important, and there is no doubt that the form it takes sometimes endangers the epic power of the poem. On the other hand, the deficiency of dramatic intensity in the masque of *Comus* as well as in the acknowledgement that *Samson Agonistes* was not meant for production point to the equally obvious fact that Milton's way of composing dialogue is not that of one who is born to write for the stage. There is almost never in any of the speeches he gives his characters the quickness and excitement and suspense that belong to the kind of representation that brings an audience to a theatre. Much deeper in him than the need for that kind of re-creation is the need to sound the depths he wants to imitate by means of argument, or to present the situations in which the resolution of the argument is embodied. One observes this in even the most tender talk of Adam and Eve—argument for him is as dear and perhaps even as lovely as the desire to re-create the momentary urgencies of souls and bodies. Even when as in *Samson Agonistes* he succeeds so marvellously in imitating the passions by the means of persons imagined to be speaking to each other, they speak more in the manner of declamation than in the speech 'which soul to soul affordeth', and less in the manner of private exchange than of public song.

This way of making poetry in which the resolutions of thought take shape as it were publicly he adapted to many forms. As over the years he turned from pastorals and sonnets and masques to the most sustained narrative and dramatic poems, he adapted the different forms to this same key as it were. The speech always owed more to the formality he made his own, the formality of one whose greatest need is to treat with the divine, than it would ever owe to an interest in portraying individuality or idiosyncrasy. He was to stamp his greatness on all his verse, and the language was to create the most memorable effects again and again, but there was very rarely to be that marriage of form with matter in which even lesser artists achieve effects of such simplicity that one hardly knows whether to regard the perfection of their work as the products of nature or of art. Even when the music of his words is so articulated that they do indeed seem inspired from Oreb or from Sinai, we feel his own presence presiding over them, he has imposed himself upon our attention over and beyond our delight and wonder in the beauty and truth of what he says, imposing his manner upon us like another Bernini.

In part the elevation of Milton's style is a way he came upon in making terms with the kinds of expression his age encouraged and to some extent allowed. Rome would have put a fresh light on many of these considerations, too, for in his earliest writing he was evidently responsive to what the times themselves were bringing forth, and most plainly to mannerist and baroque methods. To be in Rome, where the baroque was flourishing, would surely have revealed even more to him. That the achievements of architecture and painting might have meant something to Milton in the imaginings of *Paradise Lost* is one thing, which one may follow up in various ways.[5] But there is also the other possibility, that the developments in music and in musical entertainment would have contributed to Milton's idea of a dramatic poem. If Bernini could find in the production of plays further conceits with which to extend the working of his imagination, Milton's cultivation of the idea of tragedy may similarly have extended the idea of the progression of a poetical conception as he worked that out in the *Nativity Ode* and in *Lycidas*, ways that have justifiably been spoken of as baroque.[6]

One will never be able to say what Rome as Rome meant to Milton's art as the years passed, but in characterizing a little of the quality of its life when Milton was visiting it, one may come to a somewhat more feeling understanding of what there was in it that was congruent with the life of Europe and of

England and of the movements in which he was to play so
fervent a part.

The city would hardly have permitted anyone to ignore it.
Then as now there was the saffron and gold-coloured stucco
on the buildings to make the sunlight into a Roman welcome,
walls covered with the *tufo litoide*—reddish-brown with
orange spots (the *saxum rubrum* of the ancients), or the
puzzolano stucco, volcanic ash, a mixture of red-brown and
yellow; and everywhere 'the stone of Tivoli', travertine.
Rome nearly as much as Venice was enamoured of stone and
colour, and the warmth and depth of the Roman colours over-
laid every day.

At many points even in the crowded quarters there would
have been the sense of the perennial and the opulent, the
great buildings in the midst of 'the medieval squalor', the vast
ruins, and time and again the spectacular religiousness. The
calendar as an ordering of feast-days was part of the very
nature of the city. What happened every year on the first of
September would have been but one of the markers Milton
would have observed in its specially Roman manner. That day,
for the feast of San Egidio, a procession passed from one
part of the city to the other between the two churches named
for the saint. In the late afternoon a great line of pilgrims,
led by clergy with banners, passed through the streets,
many in carriages and on horseback, some in farm-carts many
more on foot, and as the procession extended into the night
from the hills the file of torches could be seen outlining the
parade.

On other days there would be greater celebrations, on some
days no doubt none of note, but the idea of celebration was
constant. At many of the churches there would be music the
whole city would be talking about, for there were singers here
now and instrumentalists that were examples for all Europe.
Frescobaldi performed at the church of San Marcello where
the Friars of the Holy Cross were reputed to be the best
musicians in the city. They were particularly famous for the
recitatif, accompanied by an organ, a large clavecin, a lyre,
violins, and archiluttes. At particular churches elaborate productions accompanied feasts of special significance. At Santa

Maria sopra Minerva in August 1638, at the feast of Saint Dominic there was a remarkable celebration. In the musical part the two organs on either side of the main altar both played. On platforms eight or nine feet high, set up at selected points, there were eight choirs each with its own portative organ. A master conductor in the first choir led his singers with gestures in such a way that the leaders in the other choruses could follow him and lead their singers with the proper timing. The singing in counterpoint, André Maugars said, was 'ravishing.'[7]

If a visitor might have attended any number of such performances, there were perhaps as many occasions in which he might have enjoyed concerts that were put on informally. It is Maugars who reported a small affair Leonora Baroni arranged for him: 'Il faut que je vous dise qu'un jour elle me fit une grâce particulière de chanter avec sa mère et sa sœur, sa mère touchant la Lyre, sa sœur la Harpe, et elle le Thorube. Ce concert composé de trois belles voix et de trois instrumens différens, me surprit si fort les sens et me porta dans un tel ravissement, que j'oubliay ma condition mortelle, et creuz estre desia parmy les anges, jouyssant des contentemens des bienheureux: Aussi pour vous parler Chrestennement, le propre de la musique est, en touchant nos cœurs, de les élever à Dieu; puisque c'est un eschantillon en ce monde de la joye éternelle, et non pas les porter aux vices par des gestes lascifs, où nous ne sommes que trop enclins naturellement.'[8]

As for Leonora Baroni herself—' . . . elle l'entend [la musique] parfaitement bien, voire mesme qu'elle y compose: ce qui fait qu'elle possède absolument ce qu'elle chante, et qu'elle prononce et exprime parfaitement bien le sens des paroles. Elle ne se picque pas d'estre belle, mais elle n'est pas désagréable ny coquette. Elle chante avec une pudeur asseurée, avec une généreuse modestie, et avec une douce gravité. Sa voix est d'une haute estendüe, juste, sonore, harmonieuse, l'adoucissant et la renforçant sans peine et sans faire aucunes grimaces. Ses eslans et soupirs ne sont point lascifs, ses regards n'ont rien d'impudique, et ses gestes sont de la bien-séance d'une honneste fille.'[9]

Besides music there were other events to attract a visitor

that year. There was a remarkable exhibit of painting in the
Pantheon, and some important buildings were under way,
although there was nothing to match the excitement attending
the completion of the Bernini baldachino a few years before.
But mostly there would have been the plays and musical
entertainment put on at the time of Carneval—in the theatres
at the Barberini and Corsini and Pamphili palaces, at the
French Embassy, at the English and German Colleges, at the
theatre Bernini built for himself in the Fondiaria room of the
Vatican, and even in the open places of the city. Lady Sydney
Morgan has given a somewhat florid but well-attested account
of one of the most famous affairs in the Carneval Milton would
have seen:

> Towards the close of the Carnival of 1639, when the spirits
> of the revellers (as is always the case in Rome) were making
> a brilliant rally for the representations of the last week, a
> car, or stage, highly ornamented, drawn by oxen, and
> occupied by a masked troop, attracted universal attention by
> its novelty and singular representations. The principal per-
> sonage announced himself as a certain Signor Formica, a
> Neapolitan actor, who, in the character of Coviello, as a
> charlatan, displayed so much genuine wit, such bitter satire,
> and exquisite humour, rendered doubly effective by a Nea-
> politan accent, and 'i motivi dei lazzi nazionali', or national
> gesticulations, that other representations were abandoned;
> and gipsies told fortunes, and Jews hung, in vain. The whole
> population of Rome gradually assembled round the novel,
> the inimitable Formica. The people relished his flashes of
> splenetic humour, aimed at the great: the higher orders
> were delighted with an improvvisatore, who, in the inter-
> vals of his dialogues, sung to the lute, of which he was a
> perfect master, the Neapolitan ballads, then so much in
> vogue. The attempts made by his fellow-revellers to obtain
> some share of the plaudits he so abundantly received,
> whether he spoke or sung, asked or answered questions,
> were all abortive; while he (says Baldinucci) 'come capo di
> tutti, e pur spiritoso, e ben parlante, con bei ghiribizzi e lazzi
> spiritosi teneva a se mezza Roma', at the head of everything

by his wit, eloquence, and brilliant humour, drew half Rome to himself. The contrast between his beautiful musical and poetical compositions, and those Neapolitan gesticulations in which he indulged, when, laying aside his lute, he presented his vials and salves to the delighted audience, exhibited a versatility of genius, which it was difficult to attribute to any individual then known in Rome. Guesses and suppositions were still vainly circulating among all classes, when, on the close of the Carnival, Formica, ere he drove his triumphal car from the Piazza Navona, which, with one of the streets in the Trastevere, had been the principal scene of his triumph, ordered his troop to raise their masks, and, removing his own, discovered that Coviello was the sublime author of the Prometheus, and his little troop the '*Partigieni*' of Salvator Rosa.[10]

The life of the arts permeated the city and all this was favoured by the rivalries of politics and in particular by the competition among the great families. There was not merely the usual effort to match wealth and power, there was most especially the politics of the Church, and always the ambition that the next Pope should be from this or that family. As in any society that respected the past as much as the future, most of the time the competing families made terms with each other and maintained the forms of peace, but there were also times of crisis and open war.

It has been said that with the Barberinis papal nepotism reached its high-point, and in part it must have been that such an extreme was a response to the fierceness of the rivalry. How ruthless that was the event shows—on Urban's death the enemy struck, and within a short time his nephews were forced to flee the city. Now for a while it was the turn of the Pamphili. Soon it was to be the Rospigliosi. By the next century the Barberini family in the male line had been extinguished, and the vast fortune passed to the Colonnas.

In one way or another a visitor staying in Rome for any length of time would guess something of all this. Ordinarily he would not be acquainted with the intimacies of intrigue, but he would know clearly enough where authority and responsibility were, and he would be seeing with his own eyes what it was doing—strengthening the fortifications, building new palaces, establishing museums, advancing the study of science, entertaining princes, and controlling a passionate populace.

Towards the end of the sixteenth century Sixtus V began the changes that were to transform Rome, and after an interval, when Urban took up the Papacy, he continued the work vigorously and imaginatively. Rome was still, and much of it was to remain, a medieval town, clusters of small buildings crowding the great ones. But there were also open spaces— grassy river banks, great private gardens, orchards and vineyards on the hills, grazing land near some of the ancient monuments. The sense of the Latian countryside intruded frequently. But it was a city of more than a hundred thousand persons and it lacked paths for the processions that belonged to its most characteristic life, some of the most-used churches needed better approaches, and the business of the city needed more room. The hills and the valleys determined much of what was needed and what was possible, but the ways of the past were also to maintain their controls. Rome was to remain as it had been in antiquity, a city of many centres.

As the centuries passed some of the most illustrious churches were established at these very places, and the plan of Sixtus was to clear avenues between some of them. There were a half-dozen chief routes, several leading to Santa Maria Maggiore—one from the Lateran, another from the Pincian. Others were to lead to Santa Maria dei Popoli and to the Column of Trajan. Sixtus set up seven obelisks in the central piazzas as markers and focuses for the city's life. He set up the statues of the Dioscuri at the Piazza del Quirinale and he raised the first of the monumental fountains, the Acqua Felice. The plans were partly to serve the needs of the people for moving and gathering, but they were also, of course, meant to enhance and glorify.

When Urban became Pope in 1623 the work went on with the help of some of the greatest names the city had ever known—Maderno, Borromini, and Bernini. Still other routes were cleared—the most significant one leading from the Vatican to Saint John of the Lateran. The rebuilding of Saint

Peter's which had been long in process, continued with the marvellous addition of the Bernini baldachino. Plans were prepared for the colonnade in the piazza before the church. The Borromini masterpiece, the church of San Carlino, was built at the Quattro Fontane. The Barberini Palace came as a climax to the construction of the great private houses of the last century. The city's fortifications were vastly improved. And so by means of every kind Urban worked to make the city look like what in the minds of many it was, 'the Capitol of the Universe'.

The nature of baroque theory made the aim possible—particulary the taste for staging perspectives, the emphasis upon the spectacular and the picturesque, and the sense of the universe and the city as theatres. The resources not only of wealth but of energy were there to create and to justify the *grandiosità monumentale*.

Yet it is interesting to notice how many of the works that we now think of as the very hall-marks of the city were not to be seen when Milton was there. The Treves Fountain and the Fountain of the Triton in the Piazza Barberini were constructed in 1640. The Fountain of the Four Rivers in the Piazza Navona was not placed there until 1647. The construction of the Colonnade of Saint Peter's took place in the 1650s and 60s. The Barcaccia had been set up in the Piazza di Spagna by Bernini's father, but the stairs—'the grandest staircase in the world'—would not be rising to Santa Trinità dei Monti till the next century. Many plans had been discussed but there were still winding paths ascending the slopes, and in contemporary prints one sees olive groves and shepherds here and there.

Pilgrims, emissaries, petitioners were coming and going all the time. The strains of politics and religious controversy, even of war, led from time to time to the expulsion of suspected enemies, but generally hospitality prevailed. The defeats of the Vatican in the past century were not to be made up for, but there were all the same continuing and vigorous efforts to re-establish the political as well as the ecclesiastic authority of the Church. There were constant negotiations and quarrels with the Italian cities and their rulers. The Thirty Years War continued to magnify confusion. The French Cardinals were aggressive and brilliant, and the Pope came to rely much upon them in trying to hold his ground against the Germans and Spanish. The Turks were threatening again. The uprisings in Scotland were reported on and studied. In short, the Vatican was listening-post and magnet and vortex, and in Urban's view it also needed to be a fortress, so he built up stores of arms and strengthened the city's fortifications.

And all the while the pilgrims, the scholars, and the curious came every day. Painters famous elsewhere came here to learn more. Foreigners came to commission portraits. Kings sent ambassadors to get the advice of architects. There was a great going back and forward of musicians—Parma and Ferrara and Venice luring Rome's singers away from her while she continued to draw talent from everywhere. It was as cosmopolitan a city as it had ever been, as much as ever setting its own style, asserting its own tropic lavishness and ferocity and humour, its own grandeur.

It is difficult in a few words to catch the tone of a city's life, but perhaps the best way is to listen to its humour. The Romans themselves were pleased to think that the *pasquinate*—brief satiric sayings, often versified, and with a special savour of libel—were true to the inmost spirit of their city, and there is one of these that was circulating in the 1630s that is as brilliant as it is scurrilous. Many thousands of pounds of bronze were needed to make the baldachino in Saint Peter's and the rumour was that the Pope had finally pillaged the bronze ornaments of the Pantheon to complete the work. And the wonderful epigram went everywhere—*Quod non facerunt barbari, fecerunt Barbarini*.

For the authorities this was too much to take, and it was said that it cost two men their heads. And here, too, there is a significance an outsider might miss, for this was no mere matter of a punishment fitting a crime—the crime was of a particular sort, as the diarist reveals: 'On the fourteenth of July Monsig. Amodei had his head cut off, for a homicide he had committed, and other crimes, and particularly—*particolarmente*—for the *pasquinate* that were found upon his person.'[11]

The winter of 1638 passed much as the others of Urban's reign. He had become Pope in 1623, some of his great works were completed, some were still in progress. There was prosperity, there had been no plague for some time, and there were the usual splendours. Next autumn the Jesuits were to celebrate their centenary and the preparations for this were already under way.

Gigli's diary records many of the matters that people were talking about. This was the second year in succession when the grape harvest was so rich large quantities of wine were wasted for the lack of containers. It was a season of miracles, and on one day, in December, in Santa Maria sopra Minerva the image of Saint Dominic effected astonishing recoveries—a blind man regained his sight, spirits were driven from two others, and several persons were cured of diseases.

Almost every month there were festivities in honour of distinguished visitors. In October they were for the Prince of Coblenz, who had made his entrance into the city in a characteristic way, heralded by gold trumpets, attended by couriers and horsemen and a train of gilt carriages. The next month the ambassador of Ferdinand III of Etruria, newly elected King of the Romans, made an even more splendid entrance. He was attended by Germans clothed in scarlet, sixty mules covered with red velvet embroidered with gold, the mules shod with silver and adorned with plumes.

But outside the Carneval the greatest festivities that winter were in late November, celebrating the birth of the Dauphin of France, who was to become Louis XIV. There were pageants, fireworks, boat-races, and at many palaces there were plays. The Secretary of the French Embassy, a close associate of Bernini's, put on several plays there.

Ordinarily in Rome comedies and *melodrammi* were restricted to the time of Carneval, although the most elaborate musical performances were being offered in the churches at all times and especially in Lent. In the colleges and seminaries the custom was well established of producing comedies and tragedies in Latin, often for purposes of instruction, throughout the year, and since 1636 *melodrammi* had been permitted in the convents,[12] but the time of Carneval saw more elaborate productions that were a long time in preparation.

The Carneval of 1639 followed the example of previous
years, although that of 1634 was to appear to historians to
have been the most elaborate of the century. Carneval was
restricted to the eleven days before Ash Wednesday, and with
Sundays and Friday excluded that meant eight days for the
entertainments. It was, of course, a time for masking, for
zanies in their traditional costumes of white striped with red,
or black striped with yellow, masks with sharp-pointed noses,
clowns dressed as doctors carrying urinals and syringes. It
was a time of egg-throwing in the streets, or from carriages—
as the Barberini Cardinals themselves enjoyed doing—of the
races of naked Jews in the Corso, of fireworks. And it was a
time for plays—in wagons at the street corners day and night,
in the seminaries and palaces. A single play could be performed
more than once, sometimes moving from one theatre to
another. At some of the performances there might be only a
couple of hundred in the audience—in the Barberini Palace
more than three thousand. I think one may get a just idea of
the intensity of the celebration by recalling the remark of a
French traveller who was in Rome during the 1632 Carneval—
returning from a 'spectacle' at the Seminario Romano at four
in the morning he came to a street-corner where comedians
where still performing upon a cart.[13]

A private person coming to the city—like Milton, with his
man-servant—would easily find accommodations, and there
were many who could help him get into the life of things. A
traveller from the north would normally enter by the Via
Flaminia and the Porta del Popolo, and in that quarter, near
the Vatican, there were many lodgings. The Five Moons, The
Pilgrims, The Sword, and, most famous of all, The Bear, had
good reputations and provided guides. Boats on the river were
much used for getting about and coaches could be hired. A
few years later John Evelyn found a place for himself near the
Piazza di Spagna, and his behaviour reveals the desire everyone knows to begin the discoveries immediately:

I came to ROME on the 4th of November 1644 about 5 at
night, and being greately perlex't for a convenient lodging,

wandered up and downe on horse back, till one conducted us
to one Monsieur Petits, a French mans, who entertaind
strangers, being the very utmost house on the left hand as
one ascends Monte Trinità, formerly Mons Pincius, neere
the Piazza Spagnola. Here I alighted, delivered my horse to
the Veturino, and having bargain'd with mine host for 20
crownes a moneth, I causd a good fire to be made in my
Chamber, and so went to bed being very wet.

The very next morning (for resolv'd I was to spend no
moment idly here) I got acquaintance with several persons
that had long lived in Rome: being especially recommended
to Father John a Benedictine Monke . . . and some others:
from whom I receiv'd instructions, how to behave our selves
in Towne, what directions, Masters, and bookes to take in
search and view of the Antiquities, Churches, Collections
&c: and accordingly, the next day, being November 6t, I
began to be very pragmatical.

And in the first place (as our Sights-man, for so they name
certaine Persons in Rome, who get their living onely by
leading strangers about to see the City) we first went to
see . . .[14]

A wealthier visitor, like Lord John Somerset, planning a
longer stay, might take apartments in the Cancelleria, one of
the great palaces in which apartments were put to all sorts of
uses. Whether Catholic or not, some visitors would be entertained, as Milton was, at the English College, or even put up
at a college or seminary.

A quite wonderful courtesy derived from an office in the
Vatican held by the Cardinal Francesco Barberini. He had been
designated 'Protector' of the Kings of Spain, Portugal, Scotland, and England, and their nationals, and he made a point of
looking after the people of those countries when they were in
Rome. The courtesy he showed Milton was of a kind with the
rest. Masson quotes from a letter of a young Englishman in
Rome in 1636, 'I have been to visit the Cardinal Barberino,
who, having notice of my arrival here, sent to visit me first.
He is so obliging and courteous to all our nation, that I have
less wonder at the honor he doth me.'[15] It was Cardinal

Francesco who showed special courtesy to young Patrick Cary
when he came to live in Rome,[16] but indeed this was his habitual manner and it was not restricted to those for whom he had
this special charge. A French visitor to Rome in 1632 remarked
on the courtesy done him at a musical entertainment at the
new Barberini palace—he is speaking of himself in his diary in
the third person, by the name of Orestes: 'The Cardinal himself led Orestes in through the entry beneath the scaffolding,
and taking him by the hand had him sit at his feet on a small
bench, and he ordered Lucas Holstein to stay near him and explain what was going on.' (Bouchard goes on to say interest-
ingly that after the performance he went with Holstein
to take supper with some gentlemen of the city, one of
whom was Stefano Landi, the composer of the famous *Sant'
Alessio*.)[17]

There is almost unlimited evidence of the hospitality of
the Barberinis, and of the various ranges to that familiarity
that so impressed Milton. An emissary of the Duke of Modena
told of a striking example of both the graciousness and the
plainness that he had observed at a performance of *Chi Soffre
Speri* at the theatre in the Barberini Palace during the 1639
Carneval:

> While many of us were standing in a small court where the
> Cardinal Antonio had asked us to remain until he had taken
> care of some persons of less account, in order that he might
> obtain a better place for our company, after a little bit we
> saw him enter the salon and almost immediately come out
> again pushing someone before him, threatening him harshly
> and in particular I heard him say, 'I'll teach you to be
> insolent!' Then he struck him quite fiercely five or six
> times with a stick he was carrying. The fellow he struck
> was a young chap about twenty-five years old, well dressed
> with a long silk robe.
>
> A little later I saw the Cardinal Francesco enter the salon
> and he passed from tier to tier, and with the most gentle
> manners and the perfection of courtesy had the guests press
> more closely together with the result that it was possible to
> find places for six hundred more persons.[18]

But it was not only the Barberinis; this must have been in the character of the people of Rome, for on one occasion, when the castrato Loreto Vittori was to sing in a certain church, the crowds were so great that cardinals and bishops were pushed out of the way and some of the most important never succeeded in getting within the church at all.

Urban VIII was not so dominating a personality as Sixtus V, of whom Queen Elizabeth had said that he was the single man she knew who as a man was worthy of her hand. Urban was more ingratiating, full of nerves, although in his depths he was as strong and inflexible as any ruler needed to be. And he made his own policies.

If it is true that the dominant element in him was the will to rise, it is also true that all his activities were subordinated to the political ministry. He evidently understood the complexity of his position, and in his ambitions as in his governing he demonstrated how rich a sense he had of the varieties of power. It may also be true that as he consolidated his position his morality declined and that on occasion he allowed himself the pleasures of tyranny. But all such judgements must not be permitted to leave out of sight the society in which he moved, and a city in which Mazarin was applying the most supple of intelligences to his particular ends, where Bernini must have brought Alcibiades to mind, where in-fighting continued to rage over the problem of Galileo. For a man of Urban's ambitions and intelligence it was necessary to rule in order to survive.

His energies were inexhaustible. He worked almost feverishly to increase the wealth of the family. He fortified Rome in the conviction that as a fortress it must be impregnable. And all the while he worked to enhance the city's beauty and distinction, supporting countless artistic and scholarly works with unfailing sensitivity and intelligence. It was perhaps justly said that he was the greatest Maecenas of all the Popes.

He worked as hard, although certainly less effectively, to extend the political power of the Church. In the previous century much of its influence had been lost and the power of its enemies had grown. Although there were the most vigorous and restless political and diplomatic manoeuvrings in the affairs of the Continent as well as of the peninsula, open conflicts were presently more restricted.

Urban was equally energetic in increasing the intellectual authority of the Church and in this he was more effective. He strengthened the Propaganda Fide, he supported the Jesuits in their efforts to strengthen orthodoxy, he established schools and colleges. How zealous he was in this is evident in the rigour with which he enforced the confinement of his old friend Galileo, but at the same time he was showing an extraordinary independence in helping Campanella escape from the Spaniards.

Urban regarded the welfare of Rome itself as a matter of prime concern to Christendom, and in labouring to provide the form it deserved as the centre of power and pilgrimage he drew on the learning and the talents of the finest minds he could recruit. And this, too, was for him as much a work of piety as it was of pride.[19] The age was with him, and he succeeded as he did not only because the talent was to be found, but because more vitally and brilliantly than anyone in Florence he knew how to direct the energies of humanism and the arts into the practices of devotion and the sustaining of orthodoxy. One sees this now above all in the buildings and in the plan of the city; but it is also evident in the libraries and the academies he supported, in the fostering of music, and in the development of the oratorio. One sees it in the career of Cardinal Rospigliosi, later to be Clement IX, whose very successful operas brought saints' lives to the stage, and in the support the Pope gave Bernini in every direction in which his genius and his piety led him. 'You are made for Rome,' Urban is reported to have said to him, 'as Rome is made for you.'

Urban himself had some reputation for both his Latin and Italian verse, and there is an early poem of his that tells something of the quality of his interest in allying the arts with religion, and that tells also of his consistency. It is a poem praising the countryside near the Castel Gandolfo, where later he was to establish a summer palace, a scene that in the very year of Milton's visit Claude Lorrain was to paint at the Pope's request. Coming from anyone else the poem might seem to express the kind of deistic piety that was in fashion throughout Europe. From a man in his position, however, and with his character it indeed signified the genuineness of his love of the arts and of his belief in the service they provided for religion. And incidentally it almost explains why under his patronage this could be called 'the golden age of landscape painting', and why Poussin himself had settled in Rome.

Dalla vaghezza della Villa di Castel Gandolfo
s'inalza la mente a contemplare l'eterne bellezze

Qui dove il lago Alban le limpide onde
   In vago giro accoglie, e 'l mar Tirreno
   Lo sguardo alletta col ceruleo seno,
   Il Sol per l'aria i raggi d'or diffonde.
S'ammantan gli arboscei di verdi fronde,
   Di fiori il prato, e 'l Ciel di bel sereno,
   Dolce mormora l'aura, à cui non meno
   In dolci note il russignuol risponde.
Chi non rinuigorisce? e al cor non sente
   Gioia stillar? O s'erga pronta, e ascenda
   Per questi gradi al Gran Fattor la mente.
Deh squarci homai del van desio la benda,
   Drizzando al vero ben le voglie intente,
   E nel bel ch'è lassù d'amor s'accenda.[20]

Urban was the absolute monarch but he needed the help of his nephews. He delegated much, to Francesco and Taddeo especially, but again and again he took decisions out of their hands.[21] It is characteristic of his assurance that he was able to speak of his relatives so freely. He delighted to complain of their 'worthlessness'—Francesco, he said, was a friar who had no patience; Antonio, an orator who did not know how to give a speech; and Taddeo, a general who did not know how to carry a sword. Francesco, the eldest of the three, he made Cardinal in 1623, and Antonio, the youngest, might have been made one at the same time had not Francesco protested. He wanted to be sure of his own dominance before Antonio was

elevated. Taddeo married—the Colonna dowry was immense—
and he was to be the means of passing on the family's posses-
sions.

He seems to have been the least intelligent and the least
sympathetic of the three. His love of power and his arrogance
were the simplest. Given the office of *Praefectus Urbis* in
1631—a title that for a long time had been an empty one—
he, and his uncle, thought to return to it something of the
power and splendour it had under the emperors. On his elevation he therefore arranged for himself a triumphal entry into
the city, assembling one of the most glorious processions seen
in years. He established a court, made knights, he went everywhere attended by twelve pages, and, most significantly of all,
he insisted that all foreign ambassadors defer to him. The last
was hard to effect, and the great conflict rose when the
Venetian ambassador—partly because of all the cities Venice
remained the most steadily hostile to the Barberinis—refused
to have his coachmen stop and give precedence to the Prefect's
men whenever they should meet in passing through the city.
At one point Taddeo threatened to execute one of the coachmen, and as a result he gained a kind of temporary advantage.[22]
Indeed, it seems that more than one man was unlucky enough
to suffer death because the Pope's family was inclined so
often to identify civic interests with issues of personal honour.

Antonio, born the same year as Milton, and made Cardinal
in 1627, in his younger days was somewhat wild. He kept a
household of musicians, singers, poets, clowns—one of these
a Negro, one a dwarf—and evidently permitted his pensioners a
certain licence and even protection from the enforcers of the
law, in one scandalous case protecting the castrato Loreto
Vittori from a proper punishment. He seems himself to have
been arrogant and spoiled rather than vicious, and this, I
think, is what the early characterization of him signifies, when
he was called 'virginal, learned, modest, but very critical'.[23]
His learning and his taste in music were of a high order. He
was the patron of Giovanni Baptista Doni, as was his brother,
and both of them supported Doni in his work in the Greek
Academy that met in the refectory of the monks of Saint
Basil in San Giovanni de Mercato.[24] But it was in his patronage

of musicians that Antonio left his mark most profoundly. Then as now many men of talent required financial support and Antonio provided this in various ways, especially for a 'stable' of those he judged to be among the best instrumentalists and singers and composers in the city. (His special preference was for music, Francesco's was for poetry and drama.) It was from his household that the opera came that Romain Rolland called one of the glories of the age—the *Galatea* of Loreto Vittori, presumably produced during the Carnival of 1639 and therefore one that Milton might have seen. In praising it Rolland is also characterizing the standards set by Antonio: 'C'est surtout par l'émotion d'un cœur amoureux et malheureux d'amour, qu'elle se distingue de Hændel et garde son caractère propre de grandeur dramatique. Le musicien retrouve le sentiment antique, moins dans la joie que dans la douleur. Certains chœurs lamentos ont une hauteur de calme tristesse, digne du sujet. Le style est toujours simple et fort; et deux pages sont pénetrées d'un souffle dramatique qui émeut encore, comme une œuvre de Racine.'[25] It has been said that Antonio and Mazarin worked together day and night over such productions as this to see that they came off perfectly.

Both Francesco and Antonio seemed to possess taste and judgement in literary and musical matters equal to Urban's in architecture and painting. Although Antonio had the greater reputation for learning, the library that Holstein presided over in the Barberini Palace was Francesco's—ultimately judged as one of the nine finest in Rome. And Taddeo for that matter established in the family palace on the Via Giubbonari collections of books and works of art of the highest quality.

But just as it has been said that the Papacy learned to use the developing opera to distract attention from matters troubling the State, so the Barberinis were willing to spend their collections to serve their larger purposes. It was Franceso who had sent many paintings and sculptures and sacred mementoes to King Charles and Queen Henrietta Maria in England, and as he wrote to Mazarin, 'The statues go on prosperously, nor shall I hesitate to rob Rome of her most valuable ornaments if in exchange we might be so happy as to have the King of England's name amongst the princes who submit to the Apostolic See.'[26]

The great palace at the Quattro Fontane was meant as a headquarters for Taddeo, and he did live there for several years, but after that he returned to the original family home on the Via Giubbonari (the 'Casa Grande') which he continued to enlarge year after year until it must have been one of the greatest in the city. Francesco stayed mostly at the Quattro Fontane, although he too, after an interval, seems to have maintained apartments in the Cancelleria, and Antonio alone seems to have been content to keep to the new palace at the Quattro Fontane.

It is, of course, one of the masterpieces of the city, and in its making it represented the most concentrated use of talent and energy that the world could supply. It was meant to represent the family at the height of its aspirations, and it was to be equally the seat of power and of culture. Superlative in its own design, vast in extent, the galleries were to include the most excellent works obtainable, it was to house one of the world's richest libraries, the gardens were to be a model for botanists, the collections of antiquities were to challenge any, and finally there was a theatre for musical entertainments that was to rival the greatest in the world.

The beauty of the façade—beginning with the conception of Maderno, and on his death turned over to Bernini and possibly others—is above all a testimony to a new kind of civic style, with something more of the assurance of a stabilized society than the great fortress-palaces of even the recent past. But the ornament of the interior tells even more about the spirit of the dwelling.

In the left wing there were wall paintings of the creation of the world, of the Earthly Paradise, of the creation of Adam and Eve, and their expulsion. In the summer apartments were paintings relating episodes in the lives of Ulysses and Orpheus. The building contained individual works of Leonardo, Raphael, Tintoretto, Caravaggio, indeed of almost every great painter of the Renaissance. There were sculptures at many parts, and, most famous for a while, an ancient Faun unearthed during the recent fortification of the Castel Sant' Angelo.

But the great showpiece was the ceilings in the central salon that Pietro da Cortona had just completed in 1639. The painting illustrated subjects that had been outlined by the poet Francesco Bracciolini, who was one of those the Barberini family maintained, and the allegorical scheme was meant in part to glorify the family. But the central figure is of God upon a throne and the magnificence and beauty of the work, the light, the colour, the grandeur made this one of the great works of the century, and a model for the ceiling painting of Europe.

Indeed, the whole palace was meant to be not merely a kind of assembly of the best the world had to offer. It was to be alive in the best sense, to offer not merely beauty but a direction for it. Urban delegated much to Taddeo and Francesco in the years it took to make, but it seems that at every point Urban's eyes and hands were at work in it—in short, his sense of the life in art was as true as it was intense.[27]

The new theatre at the Quattro Fontane was completed in 1632. It seated more than three thousand persons—it was to rival the Farnese theatre in Parma. For the great opening there was a production of Stefano Landi's *Sant' Alessio*, with the libretto of Cardinal Rospigliosi. The Barberinis had already sponsored one production of this work, in 1631, at their palace on the Via Giubbonari, in succeeding years it was to be repeated several times, and there was a remarkable production of Bernini's in 1634.

The play begins with Alexis's desire to conscerate himself to God and to flee the world. While still in his own palace he disguises himself in a monk's habit and observes his parents and his wife as they mourn over his disappearance. Their grief so touches him that he is on the point of unmasking himself and returning to his life with them, but before that happens God in His grace calls him back to Himself.

In the central situation there is no story—it is hardly more than a situation, but it is obviously full of significance and the potentiality for suspense is there. And it is this that is developed through the introduction of matters in which the significance of it all is made plain. There are panoramas of Heaven and Hell, the Devil appears in various forms. There are many spectacular scenes in which we are permitted to see the workings of other worlds.

Rospigliosi's taste harmonized with Bernini's in introducing into a pious work not only the spectacular but the facetious, the *buffonesco*—the Devil appeared once in the form of a bear—and Bernini apparently was delighted to amplify in the most spectacular ways the opportunities for the hurly-burly in what had begun as a drama of a conflict in a man's soul. It is this very development that substantially set the character for musical productions in Rome in the rest of the decade. [28]

And it was beautiful. A French visitor said that the production at the Quattro Fontane was in the general opinion one of the most beautiful works Rome had ever seen. As for himself, he had never seen anything so sumptuous. The *stilo recitativo*, the clarity of the voices, a cast of extraordinary excellence—the *élite* of the *élite*, the perfection of the instrumentalists—he could hardly limit his praise.[29]

Sant' Alessio is not strictly a *melodramma*, or even an oratorio, although it is sometimes called one or the other. It portrayed the life of a saint, but it had gone beyond the form of the *sacra rappresentazione*, in which a series of episodes are presented upon a stage to music, but without an interweaving of them into a plot. On the other hand, the narrative interest of the *oratorio* is not dominant. Yet as a form for presenting a saint's life it is asserting one of the cardinal purposes of earlier musical drama, for however much these forms were eventually to prepare for works with secular subjects, the religious impetus in the origins remained at the centre of the work's spirit.

The Barberinis were to sponsor other musical entertainments in the coming years that also related the lives of saints —Rospigliosi's *Santa Teodora* in 1635 and his *San Bonifazio* in 1637. The latter was to be a great success, being repeated in 1638 and 1639 at the theatres at the Quattro Fontane and the Cancelleria, and probably elsewhere as well. But Rospigliosi himself came to be increasingly attracted to secular subjects, and his taste for mingling the dramatic and the *buffonesco* led him to collaborate with Mazzochi and Marazzoli in *Il Falcone* of 1637, which in a somewhat altered form seems to have become the *Chi Soffre Speri* of 1639 that so many have thought Milton saw. How fast the taste of Rome was changing in this most productive period may be estimated from a summary of its action.

Egisto, an impoverished gentleman, is in love with a young widow, Alvida, who does not believe in men's love. But by many sacrifices he convinces her of his affection, and finally he overcomes her reluctance and gains her consent to be his bride. There are many intertwined episodes, and several *intermezzi*, one including the famous *fiera*—with street vendors, merchants, singers, charlatans, men on horseback, knights, and ladies. The effect was evidently delightful:

'There was never the equal of this for the spaciousness of the scene in which it was presented, for the beauty of the setting, for the variety of the rich and exotic costumes, for the exquisite performance of the musicians and those who recited. There were two sets. In one there was a fair—everything was true and life-like. There was a cart drawn by oxen, a carriage drawn by mules and a person within it, and this followed by a horse and rider. In the other set there was represented part of the palace of Cardinal Antonio with himself looking out upon the garden where it is the custom to play pilotta. In both scenes there was a great crowd of people of all kinds and of carriages and horses and litter-chairs and pilotta players and spectators.' And in one of the most telling phrases the reporter speaks of hucksters 'parlando in musica vanno procurando de vendere le merci'.[30]

Not all musical dramas, and certainly not all comedies, were being put on in such a splendid manner—a manner that was in part possible because a great lord like the Cardinal Antonio maintained in his household a permanent staff, so to speak. In the academies, where the plays were so often in Latin, they were sometimes produced without costumes, or with anything but the most generalized stage-setting. There are no records to tell just what the production was like of a *Theodobertus* by a certain Lomellini that Francesco Barberini sponsored in the Seminario Romano in 1634, nor of the *David* of 1637 that was partly in Italian, partly in Latin. But some of these productions may also have been quite elaborate—one visitor to Rome sought out a performance at a Jesuit college because he heard that the performance was distinguished by the singing of forty working-class women.[31]

The Jesuits developed a practice of mingling diverse matters in a single work, and whether it is in this respect their influence upon the baroque, or of the baroque upon them, the mingling was very ingeniously put to the service of religion. There seems to be some oversimplification in the nevertheless meaningful observation that the typical Jesuit play alternated mythological and allegorical scenes—the first presenting the drama proper, the second offering an explanation significant to Christians.[32] For example, in the prologue to the *Abraham sacrificans*, at the command of the Nereids Cepheus binds Andromeda to a rock and leaves her to be devoured by a whale. The play proper then begins with Abraham, who has just received the order to kill Isaac. The two stories then proceed alternately, in a succession of acts and intermezzi. In the last act the angel prevents the sacrifice of Isaac, and in the epilogue Perseus rescues Andromeda and marries her.[33]

But this is not merely a confrontation of stories, or of the mythical Greek past and the world of revelation, it is also a contrasting and mingling of the fantastic and the real that exploits the drama of the contrast. Father Simon, who was putting on plays at the English College about this time, also spoke of this mingling as a device for making the mythological and the fantastic intelligible to an audience that did not know Latin, 'al grosso publico',[34] and therefore of bringing the resources of humanism to the diffusion of piety.

But in all this wonderful history of the mingling of music and drama, of invention and spectacle, one idea is constant, the idea of the life of the universe as a play in a theatre, and of the theatre as the image of all—the two are interchangeable. At this time the idea is fresh and alive and delightful; it has not yet fallen upon the threshold of sterility when Dryden, involved as he, too, is in the attraction of the device, will allow his spokesman to say that love is

A meer Metaphor, a painted Fire.[35]
At this time the idea has the spontaneity of the newest life.
And how true this is one may easily see in the account of a
famous improvisation of Bernini's.

During the Carneval of 1635 Bernini had put on a play with
a setting in Naples where the story had to do with two academies, one of painters, one of sculptors, and it made no
great impression, but something in the way of contrast and
reflection in treating the parallel incidents evidently stuck in
Bernini's mind. And one day, when Donna Anna, the wife of
Taddeo Barberini, came unexpectedly to call upon the Cardinal
Antonio when he was at dinner with Bernini, bringing with her
twenty-five ladies in attendance, the Cardinal generously set
about enlarging the dinner and providing a banquet for all.
Presumably during the delay of providing more accommodations a group of gentlemen who were also present were placed
at one end of the hall and a curtain was drawn before them.
When it was drawn back they were discovered as in a play, in
their usual dress, some playing at dice, some feasting, some in
small groups talking. It was a picture of their ordinary activity.
Then the talk began to take a certain direction, someone
brought up something about the Carneval, one thing led to
another, and so then and there the men thought up an idea for a
play. Immediately they set to work on it, and it turned out to be
something about the way gallants go about entertaining ladies.

A play within a play, a picture within a picture. The success
of the entertainment, one of the guests reported, was 'miraculous'.[36] As it was with Andreini, and later with Milton, the
drama to be seen in the world outside the soul was parallel to
the drama within. And always in Bernini there was not merely
the analogue, there was the irony of contrast, not unlike that
in the plays of the Jesuits.

The point is often made that Bernini laboured to confuse
the boundary between artifice and reality, between the stage
and life, but this was also the labour of the age. And it requires
but little humorousness to see the *buffonesco* in Fortune's own
plans for the Barberini. On the death of the uncle the family's
enemies moved in, and almost immediately Francesco, Taddeo,
and the latter's three sons and daughters took flight:

'they departed about 8 ith' night all afoot and disguis'd in poore men's habits till they were gott out of towne where they mett with coaches and men to guard them'.[37] Taken to the coast they were picked up by a Genoese fishing vessel.

NOTES

[1] Lælio Guidiccioni, in Hieronymus Tetius, *Aedes Barberinæ ad Quirinalem . . . Descriptæ*, Rome, 1642, p. 124. 'Our Atlas moves the gilded palaces every bit as well as great Atlas himself moves the constellations. O fortunate Rome, who is it that opens up this theater to thee? Why, he who in his very existence presents a theater of praiseworthy deeds!'
[2] David Masson, *The Life of John Milton*, London, 1859, I, 633–4, 650–1.

Masson was translating a version of the letter that had been printed in 1674 by Brabazon Aylmer. This is apparently a revision of the letter in Milton's own hand that survives in the Barberini collection, and there are one or two changes that should be noted here. The manuscript speaks of the musical entertainment 'populo' instead of 'publico'—perhaps 'populo' signified an impossibly large audience. The manuscript merely speaks of 'Cardinalem Barberinum' and the printed text names him as Francesco. (See J. McG. Bottkol, 'The Holograph of Milton's letter to Holstenius', *Publications of the Modern Language Association*, LXVIII [1953], 625.)

Liddell and Scott define ἀκρόαμα as anything heard with pleasure —read, or recited, or sung; and also as a play or musical piece.

Milton's letter is dated March 30, 1639.

It has been supposed that Milton attended a performance of *Chi Soffre Speri* at the theatre of the Barberini Palace at the Quattro Fontane in March 1639. (Alessandro Ademollo has been the most circumstantial in proposing this, in several articles, and quite fully in his *I Teatri di Roma nel Decimosettimo Secolo*, Rome, 1888, pp. 25–34.) The argument rests on Milton's quite general statement, the supposition that he had not yet left Rome, and the fact that in writing of the hospitality of Cardinal Francesco Barberini he seems to be referring to the same performance in which another visitor referred similarly to the Cardinal's hospitality in the theatre (Raimondo Montecuccoli, writing to the Duke of Modena: see above, p. 69).

Apart from the indecisiveness of such evidence a reason for doubting that it was this performance that Milton is referring to centres on the impression Milton gives in writing to Holstein that it was

only a few days before this that he had first met the librarian. Considering their common interests and Holstein's well-known acces-
sibility to foreigners, considering Milton's interest in books and the
possibility, which I happen to believe, that he had previously known
Hostein's work, it would seem that, unless Holstein had been out of
town, in the normal course of events Milton would have sought him
out during his first visit to Rome, in the early autumn. And indeed
in the *Defensio Secunda* Milton as much as says that he had met
Holstein before going to Naples (in late November or December):
'inde Romam profectus, postquam illius urbis antiquitas & prisca
fama me ad bimestre ferè spatium tenuisset (ubi & Luca Holstenio,
aliisque viris cum doctis tum ingeniosis, sim usus humanissimis.)
Neapolim perrexi. . . .' (1654, pp. 84–85, quoted from *The Life
Records of John Milton*, ed, J. M. French, Vol. I, New Brunswick,
1949, pp. 389 and 394.) Milton's memory of the sequence of events
by 1654 may have become less clear and may therefore be inaccurate,
but the letter to Holstein—written so shortly after his departure
from Rome—also gives no indication that the meeting with Holstein
took place in the very last days of Milton's stay, which would have
been so had the performance he attended been that of March 1st.

There is evidence, however, that there were other musical
entertainments that year, both at the palace at the Quattro Fontane
and elsewhere, at which the Barberinis were hosts, and the few
facts in Milton's account could as well refer to one of these productions. There only remained the uncertainty about the interpretation
of Milton's own statement to cause us to wish to fix the event so late
in Milton's stay together with the known rule of generally limiting
public musical entertainments in Rome in this period to the time of
Carneval, the eleven days before Ash Wednesday—which, in 1639,
fell on March 6th (Old Style).

As far as I can tell, the records make it plain that by far the greater
number of public musical entertainments were confined to this period
—by 'public' I simply mean formal productions with large numbers of
invited guests, The point is that Carneval was looked forward to as a
period of sustained entertainment, and theatrical productions played
a large part in the anticipations of the season. They had become one
of its chief features. And it is quite plain also that there was a concentration of theatrical activity at this time and that only at this time
was it possible to see certain kinds of performance. It is also evident
that many kinds of entertainment permitted at Carneval were forbidden at other times and that the prohibition was generally observed.

On the other hand, from the number of references to performances
of elaborate productions in January in various years as well as the
indication of performances in the autumn and early winter in connection with special occasions—the entertainment of illustrious
visitors, for example—one may suppose that this would not have been

An academy in session

(An unsigned acquarello portraying a meeting of the Accademia dei Concordi in Milan in the eighteenth century. Raccolta delle Stampe Achille Bertarelli, Castello Sforzesco, Milan.)

A synoptic scene from *L'Adamo*

(The frontispiece of *L'Adamo, Sacra Rapresentatione di Gio. Battista Andreini Fiorentino*, Milan, 1613. Bibliothèque Nationale, Paris.)

the single possible occasion for Milton to have attended an entertainment at the Barberinis.

To substantiate this possibility it is probably wisest to recapitulate a little of the history of relevant matters.

The theatre of the palace at the Quattro Fontane was ready for use in 1634. The palace standing on this site had been purchased by the Cardinal Francesco Barberini in 1625. A year later he transferred it to his brother Taddeo, but it was their uncle, the Pope, who commissioned Maderno to redesign the palace. The rebuilding was underway in 1628. On Maderno's death in 1629 Borromini and Bernini took up the work. The palace was substantially completed in 1633, but some work was being done on it as late as 1638.

The tradition is that the theatre was meant to rival the Farnese theatre in Parma, holding at least three thousand persons. (David Silvagni, *La Corte e la Società Romana nei Secoli XVIII e XIX*, Rome, 1883–5, II, 126.) The entrance into the theatre survives, designed by Pietro da Cortona, who may have designed the whole theatre, but the nature of the structure is not known. Part at least seems to have been incorporated into the main building, the rest extending into one of the gardens. The accounts of performances there do indicate that there were tiers of seats, and a spacious stage at one end allowed for the most spectacular effects. The building plans for the palace and grounds that survive in the Barberini collection do not go beyond 1632 and do not include a plan of the theatre.

Plays had been produced at the palace before the theatre was built, presumably in one or another of the great rooms, or even in temporary structures in the court or in the gardens, perhaps of the kind that was constructed for an entertainment in honour of Christine of Sweden in 1656. (A painting of this amazing structure and the entertainment is in the Barberini Collection and is reproduced in colour in the volume, *A History of Rome and the Romans*, ed. Jean Neuvecelle, New York, 1962, p. 208.) There are very few references to the use of the theatre after the exile of the Barberinis in 1642, and before many more years it was apparently dismantled.

It was in 1632 that J.-J. Bouchard was received by the Cardinal Francesco Barberini, and seated by him for a performance of the *Sant' Alessio*, the occasion at which Lucas Holstein commented on the production for him. (See above, p. 69.) The same opera inaugurated the new theatre on February 3rd, 1634, in a production honouring a visiting Prince of Poland. (Silvagni, II, 126.) There is, however, a certain confusion about this production since the famous Collignon engraving of scenes from the opera are from a production that same year not at this theatre but at the palace of the Cancelleria, where the Cardinal Francesco Barberini, who had been appointed Vice-Chancellor in 1632, maintained apartments. This palace, formerly the Palazzo Riario, one of the most magnificent of Bramante's works, contained great rooms and a famous *cortile*, but at this time, I believe, no theatre as such. Whatever the facilities, they evidently were sufficient for splendid stagings.

The Barberinis had also produced the *Sant' Alessio* at their palace on the Via Giubbonari—their first grand establishment in Rome—in 1631. (*Enciclopedia dello Spettacolo*, VIII, 1113.)

The references to particular theatrical performances in Rome in this decade are sparse. The usual sources—the *Avvisi di Roma*, the journal of Governor Spada, the Gigli diary—give certain indications, and historians piece out the information they provide however they can. (Romain Rolland and Henri Prunières are still among the best authorities. The most useful recent work is the *Enciclopedia dello Spettacolo*. Other valuable ones are A. G. Bragaglia, *Storia del Teatro Popolare Romano*, Rome, 1958, and Arnaldo Rava, *I Teatri di Roma*, Rome, 1953.) But from what little that has been presented here—and there will be more to this effect—it appears that a single work might be performed more than once in a season, that it might be presented in different years, and in different places. And while in the nature of things the audience in the theatre at the Quattro Fontane palace would normally have been the largest, yet many other splendid productions must have taken place in large halls or theatres, although some also were surely meant for 'intimate' audiences in an earlier 'piccola La Scala'.

On the Friday and the two Sundays of Carneval in Rome 'masquing' was forbidden, and sometimes, but not always, this included acting.

During the Carneval of 1632 J.-J. Bouchard attended a comedy on February 14th at the palace of the Ambassador of France. (*Journal*, MS. 502 [formerly 401], in the *École Nationale Supérieure des Beaux-Arts*, Paris, p. 275r.) On the two Sundays he attended different comedies, one performed by children (p. 276r), the other a comedy performed at the College of Capranica that the students themselves had composed (p. 279r). At the Seminario Romano, Bouchard saw a play with music and dancing about David and Goliath, with a marvellous variety of sumptuous scenes, and in one scene, in Hell, there was a 'ballet à la moresque' (p. 281r). A couple of days later he attended the 'representation' that Cardinal Francesco Barberini offered in 'his new palace' (p. 284r)—this was a production of *Sant' Alessio*, 'Toute la salle estoit tendue de satin rouge bleue et jaune, avec une dais de mesme qui courroit toute la Sale' (p. 284r).

For the Carneval of 1639 I have not found so complete an account as Bouchard's but the season seems to have begun actively on February 26 with 'Commedie in diversi palazzi.' (*Cod. Urbano* 1107, fol. 34r.) Two musical entertainments of Ottaviano Castelli were offered at the Palazzo Acquavivi by the Ambassador of the King of France—*Il Favorito del Principe* and *La Sincerità Trionfante*. (*Enciclopedia dello Spettacolo*, VIII, 1114.) Castelli and Bernini collaborated in theatrical work, and the productions at the French Embassy were certainly encouraged by Mazarin, who was in Rome at this time. Mazarin and the Cardinal Antonio Barberini had been sympathetically and closely associated for years, and it is supposed that Mazarin took a close interest in the Barberini productions as well, which this year, of course, included *Chi Soffre Speri.*

On March 2nd in the Seminary of San Pietro that one of the Barberini Cardinals had had built there was performed a Latin comedy with musical *intermezzi. (Cod. Urb.* 1107, entry of March 5.)

But in the winter of 1638–9 there are indications of other productions also.

In February 1638, the Carneval previous to Milton's visit, the Barberinis had put on a production of the Rospigliosi opera, *San Bonifazio,* at the Cancelleria, and the next November, beginning on the 21st, there were celebrations for the birth of the Dauphin of France. These were so elaborate that the entire time has been spoken of as a kind of 'bis' of the carneval of the preceding winter, including festivals and fireworks, and 'a comedy in music' that the French ambassador gave in his palace. (Filippo Clementi, *Il Carnevale Romano nelle Cronache Contemporanee 'dalle origini al secolo XVII,* Città di Castello, p. 411.) This may not, however, have been a repeat of *San Bonifazio,* although this play is mentioned in several productions in 1638 and it was given again at the Cancelleria in January 1639 some time before the 20th. (*Cod. Urbano,* 1107, fol. 19r.) The praise of it is the strongest—'la quale è musica di tutta perfettione'.

Also, in the early part of February, under entries of February 5 and 12, the *Avvisi di Roma* record a musical representation at the palace at the Quattro Fontane 'on the loves of Tancred and Armida'. (*Cod. Ott.* Parte I, 3339, quoted by Clemente, *Il Carnevale Romano,* p. 445.)

In coming to the end of the records I have noticed of specific productions during the time of Milton's stay the most provocative reference is to the possible production of *La Galatea* of Loreto Vittori. The music was printed in that year in Rome (the libretto not until 1655), its performance would seem to be certain, and although Alfred Loewenberg, a modern scholar, says that it was presented at the Palazzo Barberini during the Carneval (*Annals of Opera, 1597–1940,* Cambridge, 1943, p. 16), I believe that no record of its performance has been found. As a protégé of the Cardinal Antonio, to whom it was dedicated, Vittori's work might be expected to be offered in the palace at the Quattro Fontane, but it could also have been performed at other of the family's palaces. It is reputed to be a work of superlative quality.

Another production of Vittori's is known to have been presented in that year—*La Fiera di Palestrina,* a series of scenes with music intermixed, characterized as a 'vaudeville,' but nothing is known of the circumstances of the production. (*Enciclopedia dello Spettacolo*, IX, 1737.)

So, one may infer that strangers to Rome might have been invited to a number of productions earlier than that of March 1st, that the performance might have been at some other theatre than that at the palace at the Quattro Fontane, and, in view of the close relations existing between the Barberini and the French, that the Barberini Cardinals might even have served as hosts at the productions at the French embassy. There are records that testify to other than the Barberinis sponsoring productions at the Quattro Fontane theatre as well as to the Barberinis sponsoring productions in seminaries.

The main and perhaps only point that this review certifies is that in this year theatrical productions were offered outside the time of Carneval and one at least even before the supposed time of Milton's departure for Naples.

[3] *Ad Leonoram Romæ Canentem*, 1. 4: 'For your voice itself bespeaks the presence of God.'

[4] See E. M. W. Tillyard, *Milton*, London, 1930, pp. 13–16.

Mr. Lowry Nelson, Jr., has developed the idea that Milton depended on a process of questioning and answering as an important element in the structure of his poetry (*Baroque Lyric Poetry*, New Haven, 1961, pp. 92–94), but he also says of *Lycidas* that 'The speaker characterizes himself as a performer, or, better, the celebrant of a public ritual' (pp. 156–7).

[5] One of the most sustained arguments to this effect has been constructed by Mr. Roy Daniells, who, speaking generally at one point, remarks that 'Poetry . . . because it is a verbal art, can be used to call up in the imagination the effects of architectural and pictorial splendour in an ideal or spiritual world. Milton's Baroque structures and compositions in chiaroscuro are vaster, more overwhelming, more sumptuous than anything the dealers in stone or paint or plaster could produce, and they subsist, immune from decay, in the regions of the mind.

'By the oddest of paradoxes, therefore, it is in a society torn by civil strife, under a monarchy too harried, an aristocracy too poor, and a church too constricted to practise the expansive sumptuousness of the Baroque assertion of power, in a congeries of Puritans shot through with iconoclasm and deep suspicion of contrived aesthetic effects, that the supreme verbal embodiment of Baroque is achieved.' (*Milton, Mannerism and Baroque*, Toronto, 1963, p. 146.)

[6] By Lowry Nelson, Jr., for example, in *Baroque Lyric Poetry*, pp. 41–52, 64–76, 138–52.

Mr. Daniells compares *Samson Agonistes* to Bernini's Sant' Andrea al Quirinale, taking into account the conception of the entire church, both exterior and interior, together with the sculptures and lighting: 'The theme of the saint triumphant engrosses them both. Both see the moment of dissolution and reconstitution as an outburst of enormous energy. Milton, an Englishman, a Puritan, and a poet, emphasizes the moral struggle of *Samson*. Bernini, an Italian (with a Neapolitan mother), a Roman Catholic, and an architect, conveys the passionate suffering of St. Andrew and his apotheosis.' (*Milton, Mannerism and Baroque*, p. 219.)

Of all those in Italy with whom Milton would have been familiar, Giovanni Baptista Doni was the man of most distinction and whose interests in many matters would have responded most deeply to Milton's, his classical scholarship in general and in particular his interest in ancient tragedy and in the relation of tragedy to music upon the stage. In retrospect it seems that *Samson Agonistes* must testify to speculation of the same order that engaged Doni, and very likely others that Milton met. For one of the most striking aspects of Doni's concern was that he shared with the Camerata an interest in the reconstruction, and not merely the understanding, of classical drama, and it is in part in the light of such interests that he corresponded with Monteverdi and criticized his work.

And here and there, particularly in his treatise on music, I have found some observations that whether or not they were known to Milton do indeed suggest Milton—the common concerns of the two and even, perhaps, common conclusions. Milton's 'linked sweetness long drawn out', for example, has much in common with this: 'Portano dunque opinione i moderni Compositori, che le poesie, che si cantano, debbano essere facili, corte, semplici di concetti, e frase, e piùttosto co' sensi interrotti, e spezzati, che attaccati, sublimi, e maestosi, e con la favella allegorica, e sollevata, e in somma vogliono, che i versi siano soavi, e pieni di fioretti, e rime, e come si dice, tutto mele, e zucchero.' (*De' Trattati di Musica . . . Tomo Secondo*, Florence, 1763, p. 16.) Or again: 'Espressione non è altro, che la spiegatura de concetti mediante la favella' (p. 19). He said that in general rhyme gets in the way in drama, and while in choruses it is more to be allowed it should be used 'confusamenta, e senza ordine, come in quella sorte di poesie, che dicono oggi *Idilli*' (p. 21). But in other places as well as in dramas composed for music he advocates the most extensive use of short rather than long lines—'versetti piccoli, massime settenari, che molti chiamano mezzi versi' (p. 17). And just as there is to be great variety in the verses, so there is to be no set stanza or rhyme scheme (p. 21).

When it comes time to carry out his work in tragedy Milton will put aside the idea of stage production as well as the composition for music, and yet, as I shall be saying in the last chapter, I think *Samson Agonistes* is close in spirit as well as in many detailed matters to Italian *melodramma*, and most particularly as that was conceived to be an extension if not an imitation of the ancient compositions. And if this is so, if one were able to establish any details of Milton's acquaintanceship with Doni, I should expect that one would discover some substantial concurrence in their reasonings.

[7] *Response faite à un curieux sur le sentiment de la Musique d'Italie, Escrite à Rome le premier octobre* 1639, ed. E. Thonain, Paris, 1865, p. 28.

[8] *Ibid.*, pp. 37–38.

[9] *Ibid.*, pp. 36–37.

[10] *The Life and Times of Salvator Rosa*, London, 1824, I, 249–52. The reference to the hanging of Jews is to a Carneval custom mocking Jews in various ways.

The 'Prometheus' was a famous painting of Rosa's that had just been shown in the Pantheon.

[11] Giacinto Gigli, *Diario Romano (1608–1670)*, ed. Giuseppe Ricciotti, Rome, 1958, p. 156.

[12] In slashing at the bishops, and their supporters who had attacked him, Milton took up one of the slurs that had been made against him as a visitor of theatres. Writing early in 1642, apparently, he deflects the point towards plays generally, and in speaking of plays performed in 'Colleges' one would normally suppose he was speaking of performances in England, although what he has to say applies to similar affairs anywhere. In this reference to play-acting by future clergymen Milton wants to have it both ways, and he succeeds—he accuses the clergy of undignified behaviour, but puts so much emphasis upon the outrageousness of their performances that one is left to conclude he would have approved good acting, even by them: 'But since there is such necessity to the hearsay of a Tire, a Periwig, or a Vizard, that Playes must have bin seene, what difficulty was there in that? when in the Colleges so many young Divines, and those in next aptitude to Divinity have bin seene so oft upon the Stage writhing and unboning their Clergie limmes to all the antick and dishonest gestures of Trinculo's, Buffons, and Bawds; prostituting the shame of that ministery which either they had, or were nigh to having, to the eyes of Courtiers and Court-Ladies, with their Groomes and *Madamoisellaes*. There while they acted, and overacted, among other young scholars, I was a spectator; they thought themselves gallant men, and I thought them fools, they made sport, and I laught, they mispronounc't and I mislik't, and to make up the *atticisme*, they were out, and I hist. Judge now whether so many good text men were not sufficient to instruct me of false beards and vizards without more expositors; and how can this Confuter take the face to object to me the seeing of that which his reverent Prelats allow, and incite their young disciples to act. For if it be unlawful to sit and behold a mercenary Comedian personating that which is least unseemely for a hireling to doe, how much more blamefull is it to indure the sight of as vile things acted by persons either enter'd, or presently to enter into the ministery, and how much more foule and ignominious for them to be the actors.' ('An Apology for Smectymnuus'. in *Complete Prose Works of John Milton*, ed. D. M. Wolfe, Vol. I, New Haven, 1953 pp. 887–8).

13 Bouchard, *Journal*, p. 281v.
14 *The Diary of John Evelyn*, ed. E. S. de Beer, Vol. II, Oxford, 1955, pp. 212–14.
15 *Life of Milton*, I, 632–3.
16 Kurt Weber, *Lucius Cary, Second Viscount Falkland*, New York, 1940, p. 304.
17 Bouchard, *Journal*, p. 284r.
18 Transcribed from a report of Raimondo Montecuccoli in the Modena Archives by Alessandro Ademollo, *I Teatri di Roma nel Secolo Decimosettimo*, Rome, 1888, pp. 30–31.

If we were looking over Evelyn's journal rather than a letter of Milton's we might almost safely suppose that the repetition of incidents in the two accounts of a Barberini entertainment signified that Milton, as Evelyn so often did, was simply copying the earlier account. Evelyn assimilated quantities of others' material in his own writing as it suited him. In this instance, however, it is most unlikely that Milton had seen Bouchard's account, and what we must infer from the similarity in the events recorded at such an interval of time is that both Cardinal Francesco and Lucas Holstein were commonly at the service of foreign visitors on such occasions. Assuming this, we could not be certain that Milton is referring to the performance of *Chi Soffre Speri* that the emissary of Modena reported on—an assumption made because that account also agrees with Milton's. This reference is strengthened, of course, by the suppositions that there would hardly be more than one incident of this kind during the Carneval of 1639, and that Milton is referring to a performance at that season. There is the distinct possibility, however, that Milton was referring to a performance he had seen during his earlier stay in Rome, and if one were to suppose that one would be regarding the report of *Chi Soffre Speri* by Montecuccoli as one regards Bouchard's earlier account, as not telling anything about the particular performance Milton saw.

19 For a general discussion see Oskar Pollak, *Die Kunstätigkeit unter Urban VIII, Band I: Kirchliche Bauten (Mit Ausnahme St. Peter) und Paläste*, ed. Dagobert Frey, Vienna, 1928.
20 *In viewing the loveliness of the Villa di Castel Gandolfo the mind is raised to contemplate the eternal beauties.*

'Here where the Alban lake gathers its gentle waves in a graceful bend, and the Tyrrhenian Sea allures the eye with its azure breast, the sun diffuses its golden rays through the air. The small trees are vested with green leaves, the meadows with flowers, and the sky with a beautiful stillness. The air murmurs sweetly, and the nightingale answers it in notes no less sweet. Who would not take on new vigor here? or not feel joy distil within his heart? Let the mind quickly raise itself and ascend by these steps to the Great Maker! O, may the ties of empty desire be loosened, now turning our intent desires upon the true good, and may there be kindled in us the love

90 MILTON AND THE ITALIAN CITIES

of the true beauty that is above.' (*Poesie Toscane del Card. Maffeo Barberino Hoggi Papa Urbano Ottavo*, Rome, 1637, p. 47.)

21 The accounts of the Barberinis by Ranke and Pastor in their histories of the Papacy remain invaluable, but a more recent volume is also important, and not least for the incisiveness of the judgements —Pio Pecchiai's *I Barberini*, Rome, 1959.

22 'Minacciandolo di farlo ammazzare se non lo faceva'—Gigli, *Diario Romano*, p. 123.

The seriousness of the incident could hardly be exaggerated. In 1634 there was an appalling consequence to a misadventure between carriages belonging to the Colonna and Caetani families. As the incident was reported to the households that were concerned, forces were assembled, there was an armed quarrel in the streets, and killing. (Pio Pecchiai, *L'Ultimo Scontro fru Due Case Principesche Romane (Colonna e Caetani) 1634*, Rome, 1957, pp. 24–27.)

23 Ludwig Freiherrn von Pastor, *Geschichte der Päbste im Zeitalter katholischen Restauration und des Dreissig-jahrigen Krieges*, XIII, Freiburg, 1928, p. 254, n. 9. Quoting from a report of a certain Possevino in the Gonzaga Archives in Mantua.

24 A. M. Bandini, *Commentariorum De Vita et Scriptis Ioannis Bapt. Doni*, Florence, 1755, p. lxxxii, n.2.

In the natural course of things Milton would have been drawn to the academies of Rome, although he has left no precise indication of this. He exchanged short poems with Giovanni Salzilli, who was a member of the Fantastici that met in the Convento de' Santi Apostoli. His poems to Leonora Baroni would seem to have been appropriate to the collection printed in her honour in 1639 by others who did participate in the Roman academic life, but they were not, in fact, included there.

The leading academy in Roman was the Umoristi—it thought of itself as the leading academy in the world—and it entertained foreigners. Evelyn was received there in 1645 and Richard Symonds in 1651, and both left interesting accounts of the proceedings of the academy as it met in the house of Paolo Mancini on the Corso. (Evelyn's account may be seen in the *Diary*, II, 364–5, and Richard Symonds's is to be found in the British Museum, *Egerton MS.* 1635, ff. 47v–49. Symonds describes the rooms, the order of the proceedings —sometimes in Latin, sometimes in Italian—and he remarks that the Academy met late every Sunday afternoon). Doni, whom Milton mentions when he was writing from Florence to Lucas Holstein, had read some of his important works there.

25 *Histoire de l'Opéra en Europe avant Lully et Scarlatti*, new edition, Paris, 1931, p. 146.

26 Carola Oman, *Henrietta Maria*, London, 1936, p. 92.

27 The small monograph of Vincenzo Golzio remains one of the best surveys of the early days of the palace. (*Il Palazzo Barberini e la sua Galleria di Pittura*, Rome, n.d.)

The library was on the top floor, reached by one of the splendid staircases that rose from the vast entrance hall. The books were excellently arranged in alphabetical order, there was an accurate and conveniently systematized catalogue, and the books themselves were marked so plainly on the spine they were easy to find. In some instances particularly rich indices had been made. (Tetius, *Aedes Barberinæ ad Quirinalem . . . Descriptæ*, pp. 22–23.)

28 Henri Prunières, *L'Opéra Italien en France avant Lulli*, Paris, 1913, p. 12.

29 Bouchard, *Journal*, p. 284v.

30 Ademollo, *I Teatri di Roma*, p. 29.

31 From a letter of Zongo Hondedei, February 24, 1635, transcribed by Alfred Saviotti, 'Feste e Spettacoli nel Seicento', *Giornale Storico della Letteratura Italiana*, XLI (1903), 73–74.

32 Jakob Zeidler, *Studien und Beiträge zur Geschichte der Jesuiten komödie und des Klosterdramas*, Hamburg, 1891, p. 17.

33 Francesco Colagrosso, *Saverio Bettinelli e il Teatro Gesuitico*, 2nd ed., Florence, 1901, p. 29.

34 Gualtiero Gnerghi, *Il teatro gesuitico ne' suoi primordi a Roma*, Rome, 1907, p. 90.

35 From the Epilogue to *Mithridates, King of Pontus* (1678), line 9.

36 Colagrosso, *Saverio Bettinelli*, p. 29.

37 From a letter signed, 'John Patrick Carey', Sloane MS. 3299, fol. 177, in the British Museum, as quoted by Weber, *Lucius Cary*. p. 305.

Naples

In December Milton was in Naples. The phrases people used of the city then are pretty much what they are still saying— *Ver ibi perpetuum; Fragmentum caeli delapsum in terram; Campania felix, omnium non modo in Italia, sed in toto terrarum orbe pulcherrima plaga.*[1] And equally, 'a paradise inhabited by devils'.

But the route there and the facilities for travellers were anything but celestial. Bouchard's account[2] of the actual travelling is more vivid than Evelyn's,[3] who made more notes about historical and artistic matters, and from what the French traveller said one can get an idea of the conditions under which Milton also travelled, and of the circumstances in which he met the hermit who was to be of such use to him.

Bouchard went there in 1632, but before he was allowed to enter the territory of the Neapolitan Government he was required to obtain a certificate of good health. That condition satisfied, he hired a mule and attached himself to a caravan travelling under the protection of a *procachio*. This was a certain kind of guide, or private policeman, who undertook to protect the caravan from brigands. He was an outrider and scout as well as an armed defender, and he worked in conjunction with a number of Corsican soldiers stationed at intervals along the way. (On his journey, at a certain point in the route, Evelyn's caravan hired an armed convoy of thirty men.)

Bouchard's company stopped at Velletri the first night, then it passed through Terracina and Fondi. (Evelyn remembered that it was near Formia that Cicero—'that incomparable orator'—was murdered.) Bouchard found the hostelries appalling. The travellers would eat at a single table without either plate or knife or spoon, he said—that is, with the hands from a common platter. One drinking-glass had to serve four or five persons. The beds were merely mattresses on trestles, in rooms without doors, and always too short by the length of a foot.

Evelyn took things in better humour, and his description of
the last stage of his journey in late January—from New Capua
on—tells only of delight and pleasure:

The Passage from this Towne towards Naples (which is about
10, or 12 English post miles) is as straight as a line could lay
it, & of a huge breadth, swarming with travellers more then
ever I remember any of our greatest, & most frequented
roads neere London: But what is extreamly divertissant, is
the incomparable fertility of the feilds and grounds about it,
which are planted about with fruit-trees, whose boles are
serpented with excellent Vines, and they so exuberant, that
'tis commonly reported one Vine will loade 5 mules with
its Grapes; but what much adds to the pleasure of these
rusticities, is that the Vines climbing to the summit of the
trees in festoons & fruitages from one tree to another,
planted at exact distances, which shewing like a greene
Chayne about a field, is pleasanter than any painting can
describe it: Here likewise growes Rice, Canes for Suggar,
Olives, Pomegranads, Mulberrys, Cittrons, Oranges, Figgs
and infinite sorts of rare fruits: About the middle of the
Way is the Towne Aversa, whither came 3 or 4 Coaches to
meet our Lady travellers, of whom we now took leave,
having been very merry by the way with them, and the
Capitano, who was their Gallant.[4]

Bouchard also found the inns in Naples itself intolerable.
The accommodations, as he tells of them, were at least as crude
as those on the road, and he was particularly annoyed at being
obliged to drink water from unclean earthen jars. For each
meal it was customary to give the servant of the house a sum
of money with which to purchase food for the meal, and this
seemed to him a sure way of institutionalizing robbery. Because, too, it was generally necessary to sleep three or four in a
bed, Bouchard moved to a monastery for the several months he
was to remain in Naples and he said that this was the general
practice of persons of quality. He was provided with a cell and
he was given permission to have his own food cooked in the
kitchen. Here he had the companionship of a man who had

been a servant of Lucius Holstein, and who had fled to Naples to escape punishment 'pour avoir été trop galant le jour de Noël'.

In all fairness to the accommodations the city offered, and perhaps to the lodgings Milton occupied, it ought to be said that Evelyn a few years later was thoroughly content with the inn he found—The Three Kings—'a Place of treatement to excesse, as we found by our very plentifull fare all the tyme we were in Naples, where provisions are miraculously cheape, & we seldome sat downe to fewer than 18 or 20 dishes of the most exquisite meate & fruites, enjoying the Creature'.[5]

Milton, too, would have noticed the crowds on the highway coming into the city, for this was a much greater metropolis than Rome, with perhaps eight times the population, and apparently a never-ending activity. While no city continued to suffer more terribly from the plague—that of 1656 was said to have destroyed 450,000 lives—its vitality was such that in a couple of decades it seems once more to have held more than half a million.[6] The sense of the pullulation of life must have been as pervasive as in the Nile Valley itself.

In the streets children, running in crowds, sold almonds, clergy led files of the insane, clothed in white robes, chanting through the streets, praying and asking all to remember the coming of death. At certain times there were processions of naked men beating themselves till the blood came as they moved towards some shrine. There were street musicians and there was much impromptu singing, and people gathering at the market or on corners had the habit, out of their satiric spirit apparently, of putting on little dramatic sketches of the kind Salvatore Rosa later brought to Rome.

Perhaps every day was market day—it would be hard to say now—or perhaps the more spectacular demonstrations were relatively uncommon, but travellers agree that at all times this was the noisiest of cities, offering a most striking contrast to the 'silence' and 'solitude' of Rome. Yet despite the crowding and the mixtures of nations and races it was a city that imposed itself upon visitors as very much belonging to its ruling class. Partly, no doubt, this was because of the great central avenue where the signs of power were concentrated, the magnificence

of the Viceroy's palace, and the other splendid buildings so
placed in dominant positions that to some the whole city seemed
a single palace. But it must also have been that in the great
piazzas the aristocracy kept itself on display.

The Via Tolletana with its black and white paving, the
Viceroy's palace, and several of the great churches were the
chief focuses of the public life of the rulers, and certain piazzas
were only for them—the rest of the people (*il popolo*) had
their own piazzas. There were hundreds of churches—four
hundred, it was sometimes said—and thousands of clergy, and
it was in the public religious life that the city seemed best to
display its fervour and flamboyance. Spain, Africa, Italy,
Greece, and what else was Neapolitan and Christian made for an
individuality unimaginable elsewhere. One of its finest expressions at this time was in the wax sculpture with which the
churches were being filled, wonderful works as startling in
their colour and drama as in their delicacy—and destined, of
course, to be the means of expression of the grossest deteriora-
tions of taste in the centuries to come. Elsewhere, too, the
parading of the nobles through the streets and in entering
churches was signalled by music, but here it seems to have
been particularly striking—at the fashionable hours for mass
musicians with cornets and hautboys stood before the doors to
play as for the gayest of festivities. And everywhere also, in
the spirit of religion, there were the harshest reminders being
offered of the ugliness of death.

As for the nobles, 'they cultivate their persons but are so
given to pleasure that their lives are the shortest. Affable,
courteous, although at first meeting very stiff, wholly inimical
to any baseness associated with commerce; quick to duel,
especially the young ones, lovers of music, and in this as in
their dress imitators of the Spaniards. They have no regard for
letters but when they do embrace them they succeed marvellously in every branch, for natively they are very acute.'[7]
Such as were *cavalieri* continued to maintain the highest
standards of horsemanship, and indeed pride in deserving the
name continued to accompany the rank, so much so that the
professione di cavalcare was preferred beyond the profession of
arms.

And then, apparently as flamboyant and as striking a feature
of the scene as the clergy, were the innumerable courtesans,
innumerable were it not that almost every traveller calculates
how many there were.

In the foreign population there were colonies of merchants
from everywhere, and a well-established group of Englishmen
(it was from these that Milton heard of Jesuits in Rome who
were planning to make things difficult for him should he return
there).[8] Milton's fellow countrymen had taken on something
of the style of the city, and in themselves they must have been
a sight worth seeing: 'Our English Merchants here bear a
considerable Trade, and their Factors live in better Equipage,
and in a more splendid manner than in all Italy besides, than
their Master's and Principals in London; they rustle in Silks
and Satins, and wear good spanish Leather-shoes, while their
Master's Shoes upon our Exchange in London, shine with
blacking.'[9]

At Genoa and at Venice a northerner would have also been
struck by the exaggerations of the bizzare that the life of a
great port brought to what was strange enough in Italian ways,
but Naples then as now had established the most vivid and even
repelling of characters. The lines of its individuality as well
as the sense of its quality must have been as hard or harder to
define in the seventeenth century than now, but what was
genuinely distinctive and enrichening about it we learn, I
think, from criticism as sensitive as Bouchard's when he writes
of the music the city was producing: 'cest la principalement
qu'excelle la musique Napolitaine par linvention de mille
fugues, pauses, et reprises, es sur tous par les mouuements
bizarres et allegres, chantans la plu part des motets sur des
tons gais et folastres et an air du païs, qui est une manière de
chanter tout a fait differente de celle de Rome, qui est molle
melancholique et modeste auec quelque ordre exquise, le
chanter Napolitain tout au contraire, est esclatant et . . . dure;
non trop gai a la verité, mais fantasque et esceruelé.'[10]

There was nothing of the museum piece about it, and one
must have responded to the city's life as directly as to Vesuvius
and Posilippo.

A traveller might be drawn to admire the life of the streets

indefinitely, but in general one would have been most fortunate
to have obtained such an introduction as the hermit procured
for Milton when he introduced him to the man above all others
who could put him in touch with whatever intellectual life
there was.[11] As yet the city had no theatre, there were no
great collections of antiquities such as there were in Rome,
and there were not many monuments within the city—
however many in the neighborhood—to absorb the days.
There were the churches, of course, and some fine libraries.
The intellectual life centred around the academies even though
the matters that were being discussed at this time seem to
have been painfully 'safe'. Here as elsewhere the records tell as
frequently as of anything of talk about the preservation of the
language—whether Latin or Italian was meant. There were
sometimes rather ingenious elaborations on theological points
and now and then someone harked back to the neoplatonism
of the preceding century. And again, despite the city's distinguished participation in the developing of the mathematical
sciences, noticeably absent were discussions of matters of
current interest to astronomers and natural philosophers.

The most famous academy, the *Otiosi*, Giovanni Battista
Manso himself had founded early in the century. If Milton
attended a meeting here—as he most surely would have unless
Manso's remark about not doing enough for him 'in urbe'
signified a certain reticence in introducing him to such a
gathering[12]—he would have heard discussed matters like these:
Which is the greater, Fortune or Prudence?; Christopher
Columbus, the greatest man in the world and the author not of
one world but of two; Conjugal love is blind; Angels as mini-
sters of the mystery of the Incarnation.[13]

The procedure at these discussions was strictly regulated,
the discourses and poems being submitted to the judgement of
censors in advance of the readings; responses were similarly
censored before being brought to the floor—sometimes, in the
nature of things, at subsequent meetings. The Academy had
attained a status so nearly official, the power of its officers was
so strictly defined, and the power of the *principe* so great—it was
he alone who decided what transactions were to be published[14]
—that it is no wonder a visitor might have found the meetings

dull and even intimidating. But Bouchard's criticism went beyond this—he found the air repressive, and he concluded that everything was being devised to glorify the ruling House of Austria.[15] One can be sure that Milton would have sensed such an air as keenly.

All the same, somewhere in the city there must have continued some of the scientific discussions that in the last century had centred around Telesio, and the controversies must also have continued that Campanella brought into being. Telesio had lectured in Naples where his completed work, *On the Nature of Things*, had been published. And Campanella, although the Spanish had kept him in prison in Naples for many years for his suspect ideas, even while there had continued to write and to publish much. A little while before the time of Milton's visit he had gained his freedom, and although the Spanish rulers turned again to persecute him, he managed to die free, and more famous than ever. Partly through him, no doubt, but certainly through the presence of many other knowledgeable persons, the city gained a reputation for propagating Galileo's ideas beyond that of any other in Italy.

Whatever the attraction and the use of Rome to Milton, the visit to Naples brought from him more revealing statements about his deepest concerns. The long period of study at home, the succession of novel experiences abroad, were now, he knew, bearing the fruit he had hoped for. For some time he had been pretty clear about his vocation, but now he was becoming clearer about the fulfilling of it, the particular end in view was taking form in his mind, the great poem was finding its subject, and this, he said, he began to see quite plainly in Naples in the warmth of Manso's encouragement.

In the *Defensio Secunda* Milton related that a hermit [*Eremitam*] had introduced him to Manso, who treated him in the most friendly way all the time of his stay in Naples. 'He conducted me himself over the city and the Viceregent's court, and more than once came to visit me at my lodging [*hospitium*]'.[16]

In printing the poem that he had written to Manso before leaving the city, Milton recalled that Manso had honoured [him] 'with supreme kindness during his stay in Naples and

A view of the Palazzo Barberini showing the entrance to the theatre

(Reproduced from G. B. Falda, *Il nuovo teatro delle fabriche et edificii in prospettiva di Roma moderna . . . Il quarto libro . . . disegnato et intagliato da A. Specchi con direttione . . . di D. de Rossi.* Rome, 1699. Biblioteca Nazionale, Florence.)

A private musical entertainment in Rome

(*Festa Fatta in Roma, alli 25. di Febraio MDCXXXIV. E data in luce da Vitale Mascardi, in Roma.* [1635].
Bibliothèque Nationale, Paris.)

had done many kind things for him'.[17] And in remarking on the value Manso's friendship had for Tasso, he expressed the wish that he himself might find such a friend—and he implied that he had, and in Manso himself: 'one who knows so well how to favor the sons of Phœbus'. He went on to speak of the work that this encouragement will foster: 'if perchance I shall ever call back into verse our native kings, and Arthur stirring wars even under the earth that hides him, or speak of the great-souled heroes, the knights of the unconquered Table, bound in confederate brotherhood, and—O may the spirit be present to me!—break the Saxon phalanxes under the British Mars!'[18] He is evidently thinking of some sort of national poem to rival the heroic poems of other nations, and very likely he is thinking of Tasso's hero, Godfrey of Boulogne, as he reflects upon the choice he is to make.

The earnestness with which he offers his gratitude and friendship to his distinguished host is quite moving, imagining the wise old man almost as another Lycidas, also translated, and watching over those he had been chosen to protect. This tribute, too, ends as an elegy, but this time his own—as Masson translates the lines:

Then, when, having measured out the period of a not silent life, and full of years, I shall leave the dust its due, he would stand by my bed with wet eyes; it would be enough if I said to him standing by, 'Let me be thy charge;' he would see that my limbs, slacked in livid death, were softly laid in the narrow coffin; perchance he would bring out from the marble our features, wreathing the hair either with the leaf of Paphian myrtle or with that of Parnassian laurel; but *I* should repose in secure peace. Then, too, if faith is aught, if there are assured rewards of the good, I myself, with-drawn into the ether of the heaven-housèd gods, whither labour and the pure mind and the fire of virtue carry us, shall behold these things from some part of the unseen world, as far as the fates allow, and, smiling serene, with soul entire, shall feel my face suffused with the purple light and applaud myself the while in the joy of ethereal Olym-pus.[19]

Milton is saying here that he is more certain than ever what he is to make of himself. When he returns to England, after a little while he will be acknowledging the importance of the encouragement he received abroad, and when he speaks of his reception in the Academies—which certainly signify those of Florence if no others—he is also surely including the recognition of what he had said he owed to Manso:

> . . . in the private Academies of *Italy*, whither I was favor'd to resort, perceiving that some trifles which I had in memory, compos'd at under twenty or thereabout (for the manner is that every one must give some proof of his wit and reading there) met with acceptance above what was lookt for, and other things which I had shifted in scarsity of books and conveniences to patch up amongst them, were receiv'd with written Encomiums, which the Italian is not forward to bestow on men of this side the Alps, I began thus farre to assent both to them and divers of my friends here at home, and not lesse to an inward prompting which now grew daily upon me, that by labour and intent study (which I take to be my portion in this life) joyn'd with the strong propensity of nature, I might perhaps leave something so written to aftertimes, as they should not willingly let it die.[20]

Yet for all the warmth and confidence there is a strange note in the comment Milton made about a certain reserve of Manso's—'On my leaving Naples he gravely apologized for showing me no more attention, alleging that although it was what he wished above all things, it was not in his power in that city, because I had not thought proper to be more guarded on the point of religion.'[21]

That Manso was as forthright in his disapproval of Milton's religion as Milton of his is confirmed by the gracious epigram he addressed to Milton—

> Ut Mens, Forma, Decor, Facies, Mos, si Pietas sic,
> Non Anglus, verum herclè Angelus ipse fores.[22]

His directness testifies in a telling way to the validity of Milton's appreciation of him, and yet it is necessary to notice that Manso has not always been so highly valued. Bouchard,

who owed him much, for Manso had come to his help when he
was in serious difficulty, called him a rascal and a parsimonious
fraud,[23] and one of this century's biographers has said that 'he
made the lie his custom'.[24]

Yet Manso went far beyond what could be expected for someone who had not known him before, and on the face of it he
showed much more kindness than the Cardinal Francesco
Barberini, whose courtesy in part surely was his *souplesse diplo-
matique*, for which Milton was certainly grateful enough. He
may, of course, have misconceived the nature of the graciousness of those in the great world who have their own uses for
candour. On the whole, however, one must credit Manso with
genuine goodwill—for a distinguished, old man to call upon a
young stranger several times, at his lodgings, tells of a more
than common interest. I think Milton was right—his new
friend understood his true worth.

As for the reserve Manso expressed about Milton's 'piety,'
that can be explained in several ways. His own orthodoxy was
evidently perfect, and his own, Neapolitan piety to a northerner
must have seemed so florid as to be unsympathetic. In the
reverse, Milton's independence and his rejection of so much
that was Catholic, or at least southern, would have seemed
almost inhumane. But also there were among the clergy, and
not only in Naples, men who were intent on prosecuting heresy
(even the Roman clergy must at times have been more sophisticated than tolerant in bearing with opposition). It may be
true that Jesuits in Rome were planning something unpleasant
for him if he should return there, and despite Milton's confidence in his ability to take care of himself, one must acknowledge that almost anything would have been possible. Although
Urban had forgiven Campanella and welcomed him on his
release from the Spanish prison, and went so far as to encourage
him in his final escape to France, yet it was during his reign
that certain English workmen were expelled from Leghorn
only because they were Protestants. The Pope might set the
tone, yet even if he had wished he would not have been able to
control everything.

At any rate, Manso spoke plainly, and that is to his credit.
And there is no doubt about the respect, even the reverence,

Milton felt for this seventy-eight-year-old man—*mirandus et ipse*.[25] The patriarch of letters in his city, in his earlier years the friend of Tasso and Marino and Telesio, the founder and perennial guide of the city's finest academy, and a man so valued by those who professed his religion that on the feast of San Gennaro, when a miracle took place and the dried blood of the saint became liquid, it was he who carried the blood in the procession for the world to see.

Masson's imagining of Milton in Manso's house sounds old-fashioned, and it has more than a little of that comfortable air that intrudes so much upon the quite genuine enthusiasm of so many Victorians, but he is, I believe, essentially right as, in his mind's eye, he thinks of Milton as the guest in Manso's house:

Even for the ordinary purposes of a tourist, Milton could not have had a better guide. Manso loved his native city with the enthusiasm of an artist; he was familiar with every aspect of its sky, and with every spot around it sacred either by beauty or by tradition; and I have not seen a description of Naples more succinctly charming than that which he introduces in his Life of Tasso, where he speaks of the poet's rapture with it during the visit in which their friendship had been formed. After dwelling on the fineness of the climate, the wonderful natural art of the site, and the largeness of the city seen at the first glance, he passes to the perpetual sea-view on the south, the gentle slopes of the hills behind, the amplitude of the plains on the east, and the verdure of Posilipo [*sic*] on the west. Then, widening the circuit, he stations the visitor with himself on the delightful shore of the bay, bidding him observe how the sea sweeps into it, in a cup-like curve. 'On the right side of this,' he says, 'are the shores and rocks glorious by the sepulture of Virgil and Sannazaro, by the grotto of Lucullus, the villa of Cicero, the still and the bubbling waters of Cumæ, and the fires of Pozzuoli, all protected by the mountains of Baiæ, the promontory of Miletus, and the island of Ischia,—dear no less for the fable of Typhœus than for its own fertility; on the left are the shores no less famous by the tomb of Parthenope, by

Arethusa's subterranean streams, by the gardens of Pompeii, by the fresh running waters of Sebeto, and by the smoke of burning Vesuvius, all equally shut in by the mountain of Gaurus, by the promontory of Minerva, and by the Isle of Capri, where Tiberius hid at once his luxury and his vices. . . . All this, he says, Tasso had admired and praised; and, had there been a spot in all the world where he could have been at rest, it would surely have been Naples.

With none the less pleasure would Milton behold all this, because Tasso had beheld it before him, or because he had read Manso's description of it in the very pages in which it may be read still, or because the same Manso was with him to point out the separate beauties, as he had pointed them out to Tasso fifty years before, and to tell him how here Tasso had uttered such a saying, here he had seemed suddenly moody, and here he had lifted his blue eyes to heaven, with that peculiar soaring look which he had seen in no man else. And then to enter Manso's villa, close by the hill of Posilippo, and the grotto of Pozzuoli, with the sea at its feet, and the view of the bay from its windows, to know that Tasso and Marini had been there before him; to hear further accounts of them, and to experience the courtesies which they had experienced!'[26]

The 'inward prompting', 'the strong propensity of nature', talk about Tasso with a man who had known him, and on all sides—in Florence, in Rome, now here—the approval of those whose culture possessed a power and glamour and poetry to match the ancient, and to which, these excellent beings told him, he too must aspire.

One has to go to the poem he wrote to his father to get an adequate idea of the forces that were now resolving themselves. It was not merely a pull between poetry and music, or poetry and a career in the world, it was a reconciliation of ideas, an identification of the charm and power of music, that had held such sway for his father, with the uses of meaning and eloquence. Writing of Orpheus he was speaking of himself: 'What pleasure is there in the inane modulation of the voice without words and meaning and rhythmic eloquence? Such music is good enough for the forest choir, but not for Orpheus, who by his song—not by his cithara—restrained rivers and gave ears to the oaks, and by singing stirred the ghosts of the dead to tears. That fame he owes to his song.'[27]

A few years later he will be speaking of the power of song in words that will make it clear how holy he believes the mission of a poet to be—'These abilities . . . are of power beside the office of a pulpit, to imbreed and cherish in a great people the seeds of vertu, and publick civility, to allay the perturbations of the mind, and set the affections in right tune, to celebrate in glorious and lofty Hymns the throne and equipage of Gods Almightinesse, and what he works, and what he suffers to be wrought with high providence in his Church, to sing the victorious agonies of Martyrs and Saints, the deeds and triumphs of just and pious Nations doing valiantly through faith against the enemies of Christ, to deplore the general relapses of Kingdoms and States from justice and Gods true worship.'[28]

There is through all such words of his a wonderful constancy. There may have been uncertainty about the shape his work was to take, but not about the dedication, and not about his idea of the grandeur of poetry. From the earliest time he must have had the sense of this, but Masson is pretty certainly right, too—the knowledge of Manso's association with Tasso would have stirred and fired Milton anew.[29] Nowadays, when those in English-speaking countries think of Tasso, he brings before us an image of feverish poetry, however magical, and the poet presents himself as not only at times mad but as a prey to passion, ravaged and morbid beyond even Euripides. The strain in his piety that we also feel we lay to what Anglo-Saxons at least judge to be insupportable in the Counter-Reformation, leading him to mortify his great work in order to make it more evidently orthodox. So he has become more than anything else a pathetic figure and a kind of monument to weakness. Yet it is clear that this is neither the character of the poet or of his writing as Milton saw it—for him the word that seems most to apply when he thinks of Tasso is 'heroic'. When he thinks of Tasso he thinks of Godfrey of Boulogne, the Christian warrior, and he thinks the poet as possessing that same heroism. No doubt he also at times thinks of him as the distraught lover, as a witness of the fury of passion, as well as one who took the beginning of the Book of Genesis as the subject for a poem. He must have thought of him as a man possessing just such universal interests as Spenser whom he also loved, but Tasso, it seems, kindled a particular enthusiasm. As far as I can characterize that, I would say that Milton was especially taken by his way of conceiving a hero in the perfection of decorum and in the perfection of piety[30]. I think it would be as a figure of heroic powers serving a kind of perfect Christianity—not one who stands and waits, but one who posts o'er land and ocean without rest. That, and the luminous language.

So one must suppose that in the onrush of ideas and passions in his stay in Florence—in the stimulation of the Tuscan language and the Tuscan styles; in seeing Galileo; in enjoying the beauty of Vallombrosa and Fiesole and the mists in the Arno valley, just as in the grandeur and theatrics and music of Rome, Milton's sense of his aims and of the way he will be going about them is being strengthened. What his mind in its independence has been marking out as the direction of his life and of his talents he is grasping more firmly as he settles upon the glorious idea of a work to do such honour to his nation that the world will not willingly let it die.

The records tell us little about the particular circumstances of the Naples visit, only that it lasted about a month, a much shorter time than one might have expected, seeing how much the city had to offer and remembering the fantastic wealth of the surroundings—the ruins, the countryside, Vesuvius— Evelyn was to stand looking into the crater 'for hours'— and the reminders of Virgil and Horace and Catullus and a thousand others.

As for books and academies, there was hardly greater wealth in Rome. What the city was deficient in was the new kind of musical entertainment, and while the city's genius for music was as alive as it was ever to be, it had not yet caught up with those experiments in combining music with narrative and music with drama that were leading elsewhere in Italy to the perfection of the oratorio and cantata and opera. Perhaps he wanted to hear more of this, or wanted to see more of the friends he had made in Rome and Florence, and it was such lacks that caused Milton to make his stay in Naples so brief. Or perhaps it was the main thing—the purpose of his travelling was fulfilled, the aims of his life were resolved and confirmed even beyond his hopes. Apart from the further assimilation of the riches he had come to value, a few months more of a life with its now known beauty to enjoy before returning home, there was nothing more to do. His resolution was established.

NOTES

[1] 'There Spring is everlasting; a piece of the sky fallen to the earth; blessed Campania, the most beautiful shore not only of Italy but of all the globe of earth.'

[2] J.-J. Bouchard, *Journal*, MS. 502 (formerly 401) in the École Nationale Supérieure des Beaux-Arts, Paris, pp. 12–14, 23–35, 60–64, 173.

[3] *The Diary of John Evelyn*, ed. E. S. De Beer, Vol. II, Oxford, 1955, pp. 315–25.

[4] *Ibid.*, pp. 324–5.

Earlier Evelyn remarked on the presence of 'two Cortizans in Mans Apparell, who rid astride, booted, Sworded and Spurd, & whereof one was marvelous pretty' (p. 316).

[5] *Ibid.*, p. 325.

[6] Carlo Celano, *Notitie del Bello, dell' Antico, e del Curioso della Città di Napoli*, Vol. I, Naples, 1692, p. 23.

[7] G. C. Capaccio, *Descrizione di Napoli ne' Principio del secolo XVII*, edited by the Società di Storia Patria, Naples, 1882, pp. 41–42.

[8] 'As I was about to return to Rome, the merchants gave me an intimation, that they had learnt from their letters, that, in case of my revisiting Rome, the English Jesuits had laid a plot for me, because I had spoken too freely on the subject of religion: for I had laid it down as a rule for myself, never to begin a conversation on religion in those parts; but if interrogated concerning my faith, whatever might be the consequence, to dissemble nothing.' (George Burnett's translation from the *Pro Populo Anglicano Defensio Secunda* in the *Columbia Milton*, VIII, 125.)

9 *The Familiar Letters of James Howell*, ed. Joseph Jacobs, London, 1892, I, 87.

10 *Journal*, p. 13v.

11 'Here I was introduced by a certain hermit, with whom I had travelled from Rome, to John Baptista Manso, Marquis of Villa, a man of the first rank and authority, to whom the illustrious Italian poet, Torquato Tasso, addressed his book on friendship.' (*Defensio Secunda*, in the *Columbia Milton*, VIII, 125.)

12 See Manso's remark quoted in note 22 below.

13 These and other discourses were summarized by Francesco De Patris, *I Problemi Accademici del Signor Francesco de' Pietri, L'Impedito Accademico Otioso, Ove Le più famose Quistioni proposte nell' Illustrissima Accademia de gli Otiosi di Napoli Si Spiegano*, Naples, 1642.

14 See Carlo Padiglione, *Le Leggi dell' Accademia degli Oziosi in Napoli*, Naples, 1878.

The academy had originally met in the cloister of Santa Maria delle Grazie e Sant' Agnello, but at this time it was meeting at San Domenico Maggiore. Here there was a famous library which included a manuscript of the *Celestial Hierarchy* of the Pseudo-Dionysus. (Cœlestini Guicciardini, *Mercurius Campanus*, Naples, 1667, p. 96.)

It is good to remember that these Italian academies were always spoken of in the terms Ficino had earlier used, of love and virtue, since learning was always to rise from these. The constitution of the Oziosi, whose patron was Saint Thomas Aquinas, begins: 'Conciosacosa che il fine recercato in ciascuna Academia sia la perfettione nelle virtù; et non meno nelle speculationi che nell' attioni, guindi a noi, che dopó lungo spatio di tempo habbiamo preso a ravivare le quasi spente faville dell'antiche Academie che con tanta gloria in questa Città risplenderono' (p. 9). And once again one must be struck by the affirmation that the necessary bond between men of learning is love: 'con si stretto legame di charitatevole amore esser fra noi uniti, che di noi tutti, se ne formi unico, et compite il corpo della nostra nascente Academia' (Padiglione, p. 10).

15 Journal, p. 23r.

16 *Defensio Secunda*, in the *Columbia Milton*, II, 125.

17 From Milton's remarks prefacing the poem he called *Mansus*, first printed in 1645.

18 *Mansus*, lines 78–84. (Masson's translation.)

19 *Ibid.*, lines 85–100.

20 *The Reason of Church-Government Urg'd against Prelaty*, Book II (*Complete Prose Works of John Milton*, ed. D. M. Wolfe, Vol. I, New Haven, 1953, pp. 809–10).

21 *Defensio Secunda*, in the *Columbia Milton*, II, 125.

22 'If your piety were equal to your mind, form, grace, and manners, then, by Hercules, you yourself would be, not an Englishman, but an angel.'

These verses which were first printed in the 'earliest' biography of
Milton are transcribed from *The Life Records of John Milton*, ed.
J. M. French, Vol. I, New Brunswick, 1949, p. 399.

23 *Journal*, p. 23r.

24 Angelo Borzelli, *Giovan Battista Manso, Marchese di Villa*,
Naples, 1916, p. 157.

One reason for such a judgement is not merely the inaccuracies
and misinterpretation, but in a certain respect the falsification in his
Life of Tasso. It has been shown, for example, that ninety-one of the
one hundred anecdotes Manso relates of Tasso have, in fact, literary
sources. (M. De Filippis, *Anecdotes in Manso's Life of Tasso and
their Sources*, Berkeley, 1936.)

25 *Epitaphium Damonis*, line 183.

26 *The Life of John Milton*, Boston, 1859, I, 644–5.

27 *Ad Patrem*, lines 50–55.

28 *The Reason of Church-Government*, Book II (*Complete Prose
Works*, I, 816–17).

29 As Ettore Allodoli remarked, the inspiration of Tasso may very
well have been at work even in the poem to Manso, for Tasso, as
Milton might have known, or as Manso in talking with him might
have brought out, had spoken of Arthur as a fit subject for an epic
poem in his *Discorsi dell' Arte Poetica*. (*Giovanni Milton e l'Italia*,
Prato, 1907, p. 26.)

There is also Dr. C. P. Brand's flat statement which is probably
too categorical to be accurate: 'Tasso had already done for the Italian
epic what Milton had in mind for the English.' (*Torquato Tasso, A
Study of the Poet and of his Contribution to English Literature*,
Cambridge, 1965, p. 255.)

30 For example, after referring to Tasso's deliberations upon the kind
of hero proper to the epic poem, Milton mentions his own desire 'to
present the like offer in our own ancient stories.' (*The Reason of
Church-Government*, in *Complete Prose Works*, I, 814.) And I judge
from what he had earlier written in *Of Education* that the idea of the
hero was not to be separated in his mind from the idea of the laws of
decorum. Thus, in citing the concord of Aristotle, Horace and Tasso
in distinguishing the kinds of poetry, as he sees it their thought seems
to centre on 'what *Decorum* is, which is the grand master-piece to
observe'. (*Columbia Milton*, VIII, 286.)

Venice

Englishmen had been coming to Venice on commercial and political missions for many years, and those who came to study at the University at Padua were also inevitably drawn to the wonders of this city. Many of the travellers wrote down for those at home about what they saw and what they made of it—Coryat, James Howell, Evelyn, Raymond, Lassels—one after another set down its marvels in detail, its beauty, the manners of its people, the ceremonies that were so splendid. Often, too, they wrote of their incomprehension and criticism of a kind of life they found fantastic, Catholic, pagan, superstitious, wicked, and even sometimes admirable.

The city has always dazzled, and too many have overlooked the gravity and nobility that are at its very heart although Shakespeare might have reminded anyone how deeply the city is committed to justice and honour. The Senators who permitted Othello's marriage were anything but opportunists, and Othello himself testified to the worth of the city he served.

As with Constantinople, Venice thought of itself as above all else a Christian city, and although not, like Rome, the head of the Church, it was, like Rome and like Constantinople, a leader of Christian civilization, the resting-place of the body of Saint Mark, facing the East, with ambitions to rule and convert it. Its missionaries went everywhere, following as well as advancing the empire—Crete, Cyprus, Rhodes, Alexandria, Lebanon—and the world came to it.

The records of Venice in this century give a picture of a kind of integrity and harmony. Everything seems to be part of a single life, of a single way of meeting life. Perhaps this is the truth of the matter, and perhaps the way the people had coped with the plague of 1630 is one of the reasons for this. Throughout Venetia it killed 700,000 persons, in the city itself nearly 50,000, in Murano more than 30,000. And despite the flight of thousands into the country, the way in which so many remained at their posts showed the strength and success of the resistance to demoralization. And while it was then a city in which luxury and beauty were so highly valued, it was also one in which the note of austerity was always pervasive.

It was a city in which the piety of Sarpi, a persistent quietism, and in the most significant sense an official piety— the piety of office—was felt everywhere. The promise had been made that if the plague ceased a great church would be built and each year the Doge on behalf of the city would come there to offer thanks for the final mercy. When it did, the vow was fulfilled, and the church that was built was Santa Maria della Salute.

Not too far from the time of Milton's visit[1] James Howell wrote that at his first arrival 'I was for some days ravished with the high Beauty of this Maid, with her lovely Countenance'.[2] He elaborated on the ancient characterization of the city as a virgin, never having suffered violation, and he repeated the prophecy that she should continue a maid until her husband, the sea, to whom the Pope had married her, should leave her.

I admired her magnificent Buildings, her marvellous Situation, her dainty smooth neat Streets, whereon you may walk most days in the year in a Silk Stockin and Sattin-Slippers, without soiling them; nor can the Streets of Paris be so foul as these are fair. This beauteous Maid hath been often attempted to be vitiated; some have *courted* her, some *bribed* her, some would have *forc'd* her, yet she hath still preserv'd her Chastity entire: and tho' she hath lived so many Ages, and passed so many shrewd brunts, yet she continueth fresh to this very day without the least Wrinkle of old Age, or any symptoms of Decay, whereunto political Bodies, as well as natural, use to be liable.[3]

Always, too, it communicated the air of a capital, 'From the top of the campanile of Saint Mark's'—Coryat wrote:

you see the whole model and forme of the citie sub uno intuito, a sight that doth in my opinion farre surpasse all the

shewes under the cope of heaven. There you may have a
Synopsis, that is, a general view of little Christendome (for so
doe many intitle this citie of Venice) or rather of the Jerusalem of Christendome. For so me thinks may a man not
improperly call this glorious citie of Venice: not in respect of
the religion thereof, or the situation, but of the sumptuousness of their buildings, for which we reade Jerusalem in
former times was famoused above all the Easterne cities of the
world.[4]

The splendour of religion showed everywhere in it, and whatever else was to be thought of its life and politics, the city's
hostility to Rome, its thirst for empire, its follies, it was always
at the same time 'this most beautifull Queene, this untainted
virgine, this Paradise, this Tempe, this rich Diademe and most
flourishing garland of Christendome'.[5]

As for Saint Mark's Square:

Truely such is the stupendious (to use a strange Epitheton
for so strange and rare a place as this) glory of it, that at my
first entrance thereof it did even amaze or rather ravish my
senses. For here is the greatest magnificence of architecture
to be seene, that any place under the sunne doth yeelde.
Here you may both see all manner of fashions of attire, and
heare all the languages of Christendome, besides those that
are spoken by the barbarous Ethnickes; the frequencie of
people being so great twise a day, betwixt six of the clocke
in the morning and eleven, and againe betwixt five in the
afternoon and eight, that (as an elegant writer saith of it) a
man may very properly call it rather Orbis then Urbis
forum, that is, a market place of the world, not of the citie.[6]

Some of the well-known inns—the White Lion, the Black
Eagle, the Violet—provided visitors with gondolas for the
length of their stay. But whether by water or by foot, street
after street opened up delights. Evelyn stayed here six months
and he seeemed never to tire of the wealth and wonder of it:

Hence I pass'd through the *Merceria*, which I take to be

the most delicious street in the World for the sweetenesse of
it, being all the way on both sides, continually tapissry'd as
it were, with Cloth of Gold, rich Damasks & other silks,
which the shops expose & hang before their houses from
the first floore, & with that variety, that for neere halfe
the yeare, which I spent chiefly in this citty, I hardly
remember to have seene the same piece twice exposd, to
this add the perfumers & Apothecaries shops, and the innumerable cages of Nightingals, which they keepe, that
entertaines you with their melody from shop to shop, so as
shutting your Eyes, you would imagine your selfe in the
Country, when indeede you are in the middle of the Sea:
besides there being neither rattling of Coaches nor trampling
of horses, tis almost as silent as the field.[7]

There were also glimpses of the world of the East to enhance
the glamour—'the strange variety of the severall Nations which
we every day met with in the Streets & Piazza of Jewes, Turks,
Armenians, Persians, Moores, Greekes, Sclavonians, some with
their Targets & boucklers, & all in their native fashions,
negotiating in this famous *Emporium*, which is allways crouded
with strangers'.[8]

As time passed the character of the people impressed itself
upon visitors almost equally. Everyone who speaks of the ruling
classes remarks on their dignity, on their combining of gravity
and fashion, on their nobility as much as on their pride, and,
of course, on their independence, still maintaining their resistance to the ambitions of the Papacy. 'Me thought when I
came from *France* to *Venice*', Lassels wrote,

I came from *boyes* to *men*. For here I saw the hansomest,
the most sightly, the most proper and grave men that ever
I saw anywhere else. They weare alwayes in the towne (I
speake of the *noblemen*) a long *black gown*, a *black cap knit*,
with an *edgeing of black wooll* about it, like a fringe; an
ancient and manly weare; these little caps not pressing it
downe as our hats do; and *Perywigs* are here forbid. Under
their long gownes (which fly open before) they have han-
some black sutes of rich stuffs with stockins and garters,

and Spanish leather shoes neatly made. In a word, I never
saw so many proper men together, nor so wise, as I saw
daily there walking upon the *Piazza of S. Mark*. I may
boldly say, that I saw there five hundred gentlemen walking together every day, every one of which was able to
play the *Embassador* in any *Princes Court* of *Europe*. But
the misery is, that we strangers cannot walk there with
them, and talk with them, but must keep out of their way,
and stand aloof off. This *state* (as all *Republics* are) being
hugely gealous of her liberty and preservation, forbids her
Noble men and *Senators* to converse with *Forrain Embas-
sadors*, or any man that either is an actual *servant* or
follower of an *Embassador*, or hath any the least *relation* to
any *Princes Agent*, without expresse leave; and this upon
payne of being suspected as a Traitor, and condignly
punished.[9]

The women, so carefully guarded that they were seldom
seen in public without companions, were remarkable for the
splendour and extravagance of their dress, the ladies,

on *Choppines* about 10 foote high from the ground. These
are high heeld shoes particularly affected by these proude
dames, or as some say, invented to keepe them at home, it
being so difficult to walke with them, whence one being
asked how he liked the *Venetian* Dames, replyd, they were
Mezzo Carne, Mezzo Legno; & he would have none of
them. The truth is their Garb is very odd, as seeming
allwayes in Masquerade, their other habite also totally
different from all Nations; The[y] weare very long crisped
haire of severall strakes and Colours, which they artificially
make so, by washing their heads in pisse, and dischevelling
them on the brims of a broade hat that has no head, but an
hole to put their head by, drie them in the Sunn, as one
may see them above, out of their windos.[10]

Their costumes were, of course, most elaborate at the great
celebrations, especially for the Fair at Ascension-time: 'In their
tire they set silk flowers & sparkling stones, their peticoates

coming from their very armepetts, so high as that their very breasts flub over the tying place; so as they are neere three quarters & an halfe Aporn.'[11]

It was at the Feast of the Ascension that the Venetians celebrated their Marriage with the Sea, and following this there was the great fair. Evelyn's account of the ceremony is substantially accurate:

> 'Tis reported that when the *Hunns* overran all *Italy*, some meane fishermen & others left the Maine land, & fled to these despicable & muddy Ilands for Shelter, where in processe of time, & by Industry, it is growne to the greatness of one of the most considerable states in the World, consider'd as a *Republique* & having now subsisted longer, than any of the foure antient Monarchies, & flourishing in greate State, welth & glory by their Conquests of greate Territories in Italy, Dacia, Greece, Candy, Rhodes, Slavonia, & at present challenging the Empire of all the Adriatique Sea, which they yearly espouse, by casting a gold ring into it, with greate pomp & ceremony upon Ascention day: the desire of seeing this, being one of the reasons, that hastned us from *Rome;* First the *Dodge* or Duke (having heard Masse) in his robes of State (which are very particular & after the Eastern) together with the Senat in their gownes, Imbarkd in their gloriously painted, carved & gilded *Bucentoro*, invirond & follow'd by innumerable Gallys, Gundolas, and boates filled with Spectators, some dressed in Masqu[e]rade, Trumpets, musique, & Canons, filling the whole aire with din: Thus having rowed out a league into the Gulph, the Duke at the prow casts into the Sea a Gold ring, & Cup, at which a loud acclamation is Echod by the greate Guns of the Arsenale, and at the Liddo.[12]
>
> *Desponsamus te, mare, in signum veri perpetuique dominii.*

Among the foreigners resident in Venice there were, of course, many Englishmen. Sir Henry Wotton had left some time ago, and he could have introduced Milton as few others could to anyone he would have liked to meet. He had recommended Milton to Michael Branthwaite in Paris, who was being asked to be of help to Milton when he should come to Venice.[13] But there was also here a man who shared many interests with Milton and who was also in a position to be of great use to him. Basil Feilding had been an ambassador to Venice and northern Italy for some time although in 1638 his pay had been stopped. His sympathies were with Parliament and before much longer he would be returning to England to lead troops on Parliament's side. But he enjoyed Venetian life immensely, he collected paintings, for himself and others, and he was known throughout the city for his interest in music. In 1638 Benedetto Ferrari in quite charming terms dedicated his musical drama *La Maga Fulminata* to him,[14] and there are other indications of his very active participation in musical affairs.[15]

But, in fact, there are no records that tell anything of acquaintances Milton may have made here. One may only canvas the likelihoods and survey some of the opportunities of the kind that in other places Milton did take advantage of. One must suppose he paid some attention to what the city was offering in the way of musical entertainment, and above all else one must suppose with Masson that he would have taken an interest in the leading academy of the city, the *Incogniti*, which had already established a reputation for hospitality to foreigners. Moreover, its founder and guide was a friend of many of the persons Milton had also come to know, and he was indeed a man of considerable distinction.

Gian Francesco Loredano belonged to one of the greatest Venetian families, one of whose members, as Doge, is known to all the world from the Bellini portrait. The son of Lorenzo Loredano and Leonora Boldu, he was born in 1606 and died in 1661.

Before he was twenty years old he had written a volume of verse that made an impression in the northern countries of Europe as well as in Italy, and thereafter he maintained a preeminent place in the life of letters of his own city, putting out volumes of many different kinds of writing, both prose and verse. He founded five academies, held post after post in the government of the city, and ultimately became a Senator.

Like Milton's friends, Gaddi in Florence and Manso in Naples, he was called the Maecenas and Cicero of his city. A writer in the next century said that the greatest part of the literary men of Italy and of Europe sought membership in the *Incogniti*, and whoever came to Venice presented themselves to Loredano. And the volumes of his correspondence that have been published bear this out. It was said that those who knew him loved him 'for his simplicity and plainness'.[16]

Several of Loredano's writings were translated into other languages, and even his correspondence was translated into French. In the history of Italian literature he is best known for his *novelle*. At the *Incogniti*, meetings were often given over to the reading of such pieces, the most famous of them, the *Diana*, being modelled on Barclay's *Argenis*.

The life of Marino is impressive, written out of immediate knowledge, like some of Doctor Johnson's *Lives*, and it is easy to see why Marino's family encouraged him in this work. It has a certain vivid sympathy and direct apprehension that give it as biography the best kind of authority. He wrote several saints' lives. He wrote a life of Adam. Like many of Milton's Italian friends, his piety was elaborate and rhetorical, with much of the intensity one associates with the Counter-Reformation. His paraphrases of the *Psalms* were translated into English. At the same time one of his letters, introducing a Jew, tells us something of a spirit in the city that was far from fanatical: 'To Signor Andrea Bragadino. Salomon Vita Serravale, a Hebrew, is a man who merits everyone's protection. May his claims upon you have primacy above any other, being head of his university, with the title of Rabbi.'[17]

Loredano, somewhat like Doni and like the Frenchman Bouchard, had a fine critical intelligence and a certain unsparing incisiveness—'Poetry in our time has arrived at the place where it does not please the few and it disgusts the many.' And on returning a work that has been sent to him for an opinion—'Excuse me for returning this without having read it, because time is too precious to spend unprofitably. To write a Turcheide in these days is to declare oneself an enemy to Christians. . . .'[18] His independence was not always praised, for the Inquisition had admonished him on the publication of one of his works, *The Rebellion and Death of Wallenstein.*

The *Incogniti* met every Monday evening,[19] and ladies as well as gentlemen were present. For the sake of the ladies, and also because persons of the highest rank were members— princes and cardinals—all wore masks, for modesty, and 'so that the eminence of the person would not discourage the comments of the more humble'.[20]

The Loredano palace had stood beside the Ponte San Silvestro, not far from the Grand Canal and close to the Rialto. If anything is left of the great house it is lost—the house of Bianca Capello, however, which was near by, is still pretty much as it was.

Entering the apartments of the Palace, where the academy met, one came first to a small room over whose door was the emblem of a lion bearing olives and laurels. On each side of the doorway were two small pyramids of porphyry from whose summit flames seemed to rise, symbol of the ancient greatness of the Loredano family, which had settled in Venice after it was driven from Rome by Attila. Entering the main chamber, one saw upon the walls the representations of innumerable figures with inscriptions—warriors and men of letters, and portraits of many women of the past who were famous for their contributions to literature; the first place was given to Vittoria Colonna, the friend of Michelangelo's old age. There were also ideal representations of the chief princes of the world, bearing sceptres, glorious in purple, figured with 'an art equal to Nature's'.

The walls were lined with bookcases holding a collection, one of the members wrote in a surprising comparison, equal to that of Albertus Magnus. The cases were carved walnut with cornices of ebony.

From this room one passed to the study, adorned with portraits of all the members of the Academy. On a table Loredano used for a writing-desk there were small marble statues of Pallas and Mercury, and in the centre a crucifix, to signify, a biographer explained, that whatever passed here was always to be judged by the eyes of Almighty God.[21]

The academies of Italy were not merely places devoted to lectures and conferences, as modern ones might be, or even to the advancement of knowledge as we think of that. What Loredano said of the *Incogniti* was said of all, and had been true of Ficino's original Academy in Florence: 'It is an instrument for purging the soul, making it ready and apt for the attainment of virtue and as a consequence for felicity.'[22] It is from such a formation that the members would be discussing a matter such as this—'Between a Friar and a true Academic there is this difference, that the one is chaste by election, and and the other by destiny.'[23]

There was, of course, much else that could have drawn Milton into the life of the city, and even though one passes over the wealth of painting simply because in other circumstances Milton does not offer us enough indications of his interests there. There were, of course, the wonderful libraries —Petrarch's and Bessarion's—and they were available to scholars. But whatever the appeal these might have had for a visitor the growing eminence of the city in music would certainly have imposed itself on his attention. At this time Saint Mark's had several of the most famous organists in its history, Cavalli being one of them—this would in itself certainly have drawn Milton there—and Monteverdi was Maestro di Cappella. One of the old historians remarked that 'from its very beginning Venice has always been a city of organs',[24] and it still possessed some of the finest makers of these instruments in the world. The organs in Saint Mark's with their silver pipes had just been overhauled, and there were seven pairs of remarkable organs in San Rocco. Monteverdi, Cavalli, and others were providing new music for the churches continually, and the mere mention of one of these compositions—the music Monteverdi composed to celebrate the cessation of the plague in 1631—stirs the imagination profoundly. (But like so much of his work it has since been lost.)

Monteverdi had been Maestro di Cappella since 1613. Now in his seventies he was intensely active. He had just published, in 1638, his *Eighth Book of Madrigals*, with its very important expression of some of his ideas. The *Selva Morale e Spirituale* was to be printed in 1640. In 1639 his *L'Arianna* was being newly produced, for the first time in Venice, and he was composing the *Adone* for production that same year. There was also a ballet about the same time, and perhaps most significantly of all, he was shortly to be producing the first historical opera, the remarkable *L'Incoronazione di Poppea.*

Opera had just come to Venice, and the city was indeed to take up where Rome left off, and particularly after the Barberinis lost their predominant power. The theatre of San Cassiano, which had burned down a few years before, was rebuilt to a new splendid design for the performance of Manelli's *Andromeda* in 1637. In the months just prior to Milton's visit another theatre was opened in the parish of Santi Giovanni e Paolo, and a third, in San Moise, was to open the following year with Monteverdi's *L'Arianna.*

Differently than in Rome, despite the hostility to all kinds of theatricals that was sometimes as determined in Italy and France in this period as in England itself, there were three seasons for theatrical performances. The first extended from the beginning of October until December 14th; the second, from St. Stephen's day, immediately following Christmas, through Carneval; and the third, the fortnight of the Ascension Fair,[25] which in this year commenced on May 28.

The great distinction of Venetian opera was that it was from the beginning open to the general public, and Venice then had the honour of transforming the opera, as it is so often said, from an amusement of princes to an entertainment for the multitude. The populace was perhaps no more natively musical than the Roman or the Neapolitan—it would be difficult to know how any could be—but it welcomed the opportunity to flock to the theatres.

Seats were not reserved, and tickets were sold. After the raising of the curtain the lights were extinguished, but on entering the theatre one could buy small candles to read the libretto by. Apples and cooked pears and oranges were sold during the intermissions and coffee was served in the loges.

The operas given during the Ascension Fair were from among those already produced in the preceding winter.

In January 1639 Giulio Strozzi's *La Delia, o La Sera Sposa del Sole* was given at the theatre at Santi Giovanni e Paolo, and the next month there was also given at the same place Ferrari's

Armida. At the theatre at San Cassiano about the same time,
Cavalli's first opera, *Le Nozze di Tete e di Peleo* began its long
career.[26] There is no record of specific later performances
that spring, but presumably these were the musical dramas
that were offered then and during Ascension. Monteverdi's
Adone was not to be produced until the following autumn,
repeated many times then, and all during the following
Carneval.[27]

These, then, were some of the musical productions most in
the current view. Ferrari was a man of great talent who somewhat later was to be composing an oratorio, *Sansone*, not at all
constructed in the manner of Milton's play, but extremely
interesting for the intensity of its focus upon a single incident
in Samson's state of mind. Cavalli was a still more remarkable
man, an accomplished organist, the one who 'systematized' the
orchestra's part in the production of musical dramas, a composer of enormous productivity—five of his operas were produced in one year—truly, 'the very corner stone of the musical
theatre in Venice'. And one may judge from one Englishman's
report a little later than this that the appeal of these productions was in much more than the spectacle:

> One Opera I saw represented about 16 severall times; and
> so farr from being weary of it, I would ride hundreds of
> miles to see the same over again: nay I must needs confess
> that all the pleasant things I have yet heard or seen are
> inexpressibly short of the delights I had in seeing this
> Venetian Opera; and as Venice in many things surpasses all
> places else where I have been, so are these Operas the most
> excellent of all its glorious Vanities.[28]

A world so given to splendour and ceremony—such colour,
such music, such variety to each day's progress—was equally
proud of its independence. The efforts to join the Church in
Venice to the Church of England failed, but the spirit of Sarpi
(he had stood by Galileo against the judgement of the Inquisition) and all that he represented in confronting the Council of
Trent must have strengthened Milton in his respect for the
power of thought everywhere. He could not have found in

Venice the restlessness of the Florentines, the untiring dis-
content, the indomitable rebellion almost against life itself,
but he would have found an even finer, because simpler,
nobility. And a quieter beauty.

It is all in Saint Mark's, the basilica that is above all else a
chapel. This is one of the most important observations a
traveller to Venice can make—that this is a chapel, that this
glory, this shelter away from the sky and the sea winds and
rain is only secondarily for an empire—it is first and last a
private place, as magnificent as the world could make it, for
one man to pray in, withdrawn within his empire. In Puritan
countries simplicity is associated with bareness, but there is
also simplicity in the vested world, and in this place humility
and privacy are splendid.

Venice does not recognize superfluity. Some of the churches
of the city are ornamented with every abundance, and are
nowadays even cluttered with odds and ends—old lamps and
standards, even pictures on the floor, only leaning against the
walls, red drapes covering the pillars in the midst of a thousand
candles, a crowd of shrines and prie-dieus, the magnificent
tabernacles with their gold damask dropping away in inumer-
able folds. Over the years order has been neglected, and yet the
spirit of the place is not put out, there is no sense of waste or
spoiling, only of the accumulation of time, or riches, the pro-
fusion of invention, and nothing is irrelevant.

Santa Maria della Salute, begun in 1631, massive, elaborate,
majestic, belongs to the wealth and delicacy all about it because, with all the rest, it is one further sign of the bounty of
the city's imagination. And not least here, overlooking the
great sweep of the canal, the baroque joins with the Gothic as
another child of the same parents. Faced with such variety and
wealth, foreigners often mistake it for the proof of profligacy
and worse. But this is to underestimate the city, and it is an
effort, I think, to destroy what attracts them. Like many
northerners, Thomas Mann gives Venice a corruption that is
his own. He lacks the resilience of the Venetians, who deal
with beauty as with life; they depend on it and can never be
tired of it. They would hardly know what it means to deprave
taste, not even in the grandiose. Mann misses the controlling

fineness, preferring to find the decay and death so many northerners seem to seek for here.

But if we put that kind of thing aside, together with all those accounts of travellers who expand on idolatries and vices, one sees the main thing—the city of Sarpi and Loredano and Monteverdi is one whose spirit is the noblest. Milton could not have missed that. The sight of such a city must have supported his conviction that learning and music and ceremony belong to greatness, that life may proceed in splendour and piety and in the exercise of freedom, this grave and noble city, the maiden of the sea, 'peerless and most glorious'—in Petrarch's words, 'this city that appears more quiet and tranquil than any other part of the world'.

NOTES

[1] '. . . Venetias contendi. Cui urbi lustrandæ cum mensem unum impendissem, & libros, quos per Italiam conquisiveram, in navem impondendos curâssem.' (*Pro Populo Anglicano Defensio Secunda*, in the *Columbia Milton*, VII, 126.) This information is expanded in the earliest biography: '. . . he arriv'd at *Venice*, where when he had spent a Month's time in viewing of that Stately City, and Shipp'd up a Parcel of curious and rare Books which he had pick'd up in his Travels; particularly a Chest or two of choice Musick-books of the best Masters flourishing about that time in *Italy*, namely, *Lucas Marenzo*, *Monte Verde*, *Horatio Vecchi*, *Cifa*, the Prince of *Venosa* and several others. . . .' (*The Life Records of John Milton*, ed. J. M. French, New Brunswick, Vol. I, 1949, p. 415.)

[2] *The Familiar Letters*, ed. Joseph Jacobs, London, 1892, I, 69. (From a letter to Richard Altham, June 5, 1621.)

[3] *Ibid.*, I, 69.

[4] Thomas Coryat, *Coryat's Crudities*, Glasgow, 1905, I, 326.

[5] *Ibid.*, I, 427.

[6] *Ibid.*, I, 314.

[7] *The Diary*, ed. E. S. De Beer, Oxford, Vol. II, 1955, p. 434.

[8] *Ibid.*, p. 449.

[9] Richard Lassels, *The Voyage of Italy; Or A Compleat Journey Through Italy. The Second Part*, Paris, 1670, pp. 377–9.

[10] Evelyn, *Diary*, II, 446–7.

Lassels's estimate of the height of the *choppines* is closer to the truth—'a full half yard high' (*The Voyage of Italy*, II, 380).

[11] Evelyn, *Diary*, II, 447.

[12] *Diary*, II, 431–2.

While it is not often supposed that Milton was in Venice on Ascension Day, it is possible that he was. Milton was in Geneva on June 10th as the dated entry on his inscription in Camillo Cardoyn's album shows. (*The Life Records of John Milton*, I, 419.) Ascension Thursday in 1639 fell on May 23rd, and the festivities of the period extended through the following ten days or two weeks. It is just possible that Milton was present for the beginning of this.

As I reckon it, Sebastiano Locatelli took seven days of actual travelling to pass from Geneva to Milan, but he was held up for three other days waiting for legal clearance between Switzerland and Italy. (Wilfrid Blunt, *The Adventures of an Italian Priest, Sebastiano Locatelli, during his journey from Bologna to Paris and Back, 1664–1665*, London, 1956, pp. 229–58.) His party enjoyed themselves on the way and even took small side-trips, but much of the passage of the mountains was as hazardous as could be.

Evelyn, also passing over the Simplon Pass, took, as I figure this, nine days to come within a day's journey of Geneva, where he was unable to continue—he had got smallpox, which kept him in bed for sixteen days.

Instead of crossing the Simplon, Milton might have used the St. Bernard Pass. I know of no record of journeys by this route, but I see no reason why it should have required a longer time.

The journey from Venice to Milan Evelyn had made in his usual leisurely way, dining with friends, making purchases, etc., in five days, (*Diary*, II, 478–522). Without undue haste it could have been done in three.

With good luck, then, the journey from Venice to Geneva could have been accomplished in ten days, and in that event it would have been possible for Milton to have been in Venice for the Ascension ceremonies.

[13] *The Life Records of John Milton*, I, 362.

[14] 'E da lei stata goduta, & applaudita nel Teatro; non sia per dispiacerle nel Gabinetto; Bella Dama alletta in publico, diletta in privato.' (Venice, 1638, p. 4.)

[15] Feilding kept up the custom of maintaining an Anglican chapel in the Embassy, for the need was felt, here as elsewhere, of providing this means of resisting the efforts of Catholics to insinuate the Roman religion among those who had fallen from it. (See J. W. Stoye, *English Travellers Abroad, 1604–1667*, London, 1952, p. 114.)

[16] There are at least two biographies of Loredano—Gaudentio Brunacci's in 1662 and Antonio Lupis's in 1663. A collection of his letters was edited by Henri Giblet in 1667. Apart from much information that is to be gathered from poems and inscriptions written by others as prefatory introductions to his own volumes, still more is contained in Francesco Belli, *Nella Rinovazione dell'Accademia De gl' Incogniti. Eretta in Casa dell' Illustriss. Sig. Gio. Francesco Loredano,*

Venice, 1632; Girolamo Ghilini, *Teatro degli huomini litterati*, Venice, 1647; Antonio Zanon, *Della Utilità Morale, Economica, e Politica delle Accademie di Agricultura, Arti, e Commercio*, Udine, 1771; and Michele Battagia, *Delle Accademie Veneziane*, Venice, 1826.

Jacobo Gaddi and Heinsius were members of the *Incogniti*. Coltellini and Manso were in frequent correspondence with Loredano and at this very time Manso was helping Loredano with the biography he was writing of Marino.

There were several Florentines who were members of this academy. Alessandro Adimari, a member of the Svogliati as well, and distinguished for his interest in astronomy, was one of these. Giulio Strozzi was a member of both academies. Recently he had been spending most of his time in Venice, founding an academy of his own at which concerts were given, and where he was particularly happy to provide a stage for his daughter's singing.

[17] *Lettres de Loredano, Noble Venitien . . . Traduites en François par le Sieur de Veneroni*, Brussels, 1712, p. 26.

[18] Quoted by Giovanni Getto, 'Letteratura e poesia', in *La Civiltà Veneziana nell 'Età Barocca*, Florence, n.d., pp. 148–9. (*Storia della Civiltà Veneziana: Centro di Cultura e Civiltà della Fondazione Giorgio Cini*).

[19] Girolamo Ghilini, *Teatro de' Huomini Letterati Aperto dall' Abbate Girolamo Ghilini Academico Incognito*, Venice, 1648, p. 105.

[20] Antonio Lupis, *Vita di Gio. Francesco Loredano, Senator Veneto*, Venice, 1663, p. 17.

[21] *Ibid.*, pp. 19–21.

[22] *Lettere del Signor Gio: Francesco Loredano . . .* ed. Henricus Giblet, Venice, 1660, p. 390.

[23] *Discorsi Academici De' Signori Incogniti, Hauuti in Venetia Nell' Academia dell' Illustrissimo Signor Gio: Francesco Loredano*, Venice, 1635.

[24] Francesco Caffi, *Storia della Musica Sacra nella gia Cappella Ducale di San Marco in Venezia*, Venice, 1854, II, 7.

[25] Pompeo Molmenti, *La Storia di Venezia nella Vita Privata*, 5th edition, Vol. III, Bergamo, 1912, p. 210.

[26] In his operas Cavalli followed the doctrine of Monteverdi about the primacy of the *recitatif*, but in his own right he was a figure of almost equal importance. He was a towering figure, perenially fresh in mind and manner, and the characterization of Prunières deserves noting: 'On pourrait comparer exactement Monteverdi à Titien et Cavalli à Tintoretto. L'art de Cavalli n'a pas la qualité précieuse des moindres pièces de Monteverdi, mais elle a toujours une vigueur de touche et d'accent qui frappe tout d'abord.' (Henri Prunières, *Cavalli et l'Opéra Vénitien au XVIIᵉ Siècle*, Paris, 1931, p. 28.)

Benedetto Ferrari said of him in his old age, 'Gli anni non aggravano mai una penna; et un intelletto che più invecchia più si raffina.'

(Caffi, *Storia della Musica Sacra*, I, 287.)

[27] Two of the primary sources for this information are Cristoforo Ivanovich, *Minerva al Tavolino*, Venice, 1688, and Antonio Groppa, *Catalogo di Tutti i Drammi per Musica Recitati ne' Teatri di Venezia dall' anno 1637*, Venice, 1745.

[28] From an unpublished manuscript of Robert Bargrave, about 1655, quoted by J. W. Stoye, *English Travellers Abroad*, p. 220.

Part II

Part II

Milton and Monteverdi

I

Tragedy and the imitation of the passions

I don't know when *Samson Agonistes* was written, and while it pleases me to think of it as a work of Milton's last years yet as I see it it also harks back to the visit to Italy, it has in it so much that might have been nourished by what he saw and heard there.

We are told that he shipped some books of music to England from Venice—Luca Marenzio, Horatio Vecchi, Cifa, Monteverdi—'a Chest or two of choice Musick-books of the best Masters flourishing about the time in *Italy*'.[1] In a hundred places he shows us how much music meant to him, and while many of his poems reveal this in particular ways I think in *Samson Agonistes* we see him putting into practice something he had learned from the music of Italy, and especially from the musical drama. And so, in looking once again at the form of the beautiful poem, it has seemed to me rewarding to regard it and some of the things Milton says about it in the light of the history of music and drama as he would become acquainted with that in Italy, and afterwards when he went over the books he had brought back.

In the preface to *Samson Agonistes* Milton said that in composing a tragedy of the ancient kind he intended to return the form to a dignity it had lost. He referred to Aristotle, whose authority he appeared to accept, and he indicated a considerable number of tragic writers in antiquity and in later times who had provided him with examples and who had shown him what tragedy might mean to Christian as well as pagan writers. But almost immediately it is clear that he has his own idea about things. For example, in summarizing the doctrine of catharsis—which his work also is to effect—he speaks of the 'delight, stirr'd up by reading or seeing those passions [of pity and fear, or terror] well imitated'. The debate over Aristotle's meaning never ends, but one thing is certain—he spoke of the imitation of action, and not of the passions. It is equally clear that Milton meant to put the matter in this way, for he explained that it was precisely the passions that were to be purged that the tragic writer was engaged in imitating: 'raising pity and fear, or terror, to purge the mind of those and such like passions, that is to temper and reduce them to just measure with a kind of delight, stirr'd up by reading or seeing those passions well imitated'.

The modification of Aristotle continues, for an immediate consequence of this interpretation is to lessen the importance of the plot. The preface itself makes this evident for the plot now, in Milton's words, 'is nothing indeed but such economy, or disposition of the fable as may stand best with verisimilitude and decorum'. Which is to say that catharsis is to be effected by the imitation of the passions, and the ordering of the events of the play is to be governed, not by necessity (as it is when the poet subscibes to the conception of beginning, middle, and end in necessary sequence), but by an ordering of a composition in conformance with notions of the decorous and the lifelike.

In the preface the nod to Aristotle is more a nod of respect than of deference, and the play itself makes it clear that Milton's doctrine is a revision and even a transformation of Aristotle's. For *Samson Agonistes* is much more evidently a representation of a succession of states of mind and of passions than it is the imitation of an action in any sense ordinarily accorded that word.[2]

When one looks at the Greek tragedies commonly compared with *Samson Agonistes*—*The Suppliant Women*, the *Prometheus*, the *Ajax*, the *Oedipus at Colonnus*—one is struck by the extraordinary dramatic power of these works. However extended the explanatory dialogues, however reflective and sustained an individual chorus, however our attention may be concentrated upon the sufferings of the protagonist, there is always the most live and urgent interest in what is happening or in what is about to happen in the drama as drama.

Even in a play in which the chorus figures so largely as in *The Suppliants*, we are held by the thought of discovering what the future is to bring forth, the future understood as in part determined by the present moment, the very moment of our observation of the persons in motion upon the stage. The single greatest difference of all the works one habitually places beside *Samson Agonistes* is in the power they have of holding us in suspense until the end. Our excitement and our sympathies and fears are founded upon the attention we are paying to persons performing deeds, and on the effects of the deeds. From beginning to end our concern and our reward are defined by our attention to the use and effect of force, by persons or powers upon persons. The Aristotelian criterion is central in every way—the imitation of action is precisely what drama is.

There are, of course, other views of this. There is, for example, the judgement that *Samson Agonistes* is 'much more dramatic' than *The Suppliants*.[3] There is the position of Professor Kitto that in more than one Greek tragedy—he singles out *The Suppliants* and the *Prometheus*—the drama is 'an inner drama',[4] and 'the drama lies in the lyrical plane'.[5] And most pointedly: 'What Prometheus has done for Zeus, what he has done for Man, are not only things which have led to the present situation; they *are* the present situation, part of Prometheus' present mind—for the essential drama is precisely his present mind. Milton does the same for Samson (the *Agonistes* is pure old tragedy) in those opening speeches in which Samson compares what he is with what he was; speeches which make one wonder how any critic has ever had the audacity to call Milton "undramatic".'[6] But all such criticism is juggling with the word 'dramatic', divorcing it from its root, and in so doing incidentally putting Aristotle aside. This criticism praises not only *Samson Agonistes*, but a very different kind of play as well, for their psychological interest, and then equates that with the dramatic. Dr. Johnson's distress at discovering that Milton had ignored the great principle inherent in the idea of a beginning, middle, and end is judged to be uncalled for.

I think Miss Una Ellis-Fermor puts the matter in more nearly the right light, although her reasoning, too, is confused.

In characterizing *Samson Agonistes* as a succession of stages in which Samson takes hold of himself, she is in effect describing it as more a lyrical than a dramatic composition. For one thing she uses the term 'religious drama' to signify something other than tragedy, and in doing this she argues that one may speak of the play's unity differently than one speaks of the unity of the action of tragedy.[7] This permits her to correct Dr. Johnson, or at least to offer a judgement more properly applicable to the kind of play she judges *Samson Agonistes* to be—she is proposing that the psychological coherence of the scenes in representing the state of mind of the protagonist is the same thing as the link of necessity in an action with a beginning, middle, and end. In her conclusion, however, she neglects to distinguish between the unity of religious drama and the unity of tragedy, and I think she neglects to do this because her interest has taken another turn. Milton's way of ordering his material and the attendant effect of unity she comes to characterize as not merely psychological and dramatic, but, more comprehensively, as musical: 'The play is a sustained musical composition, the parts resiliently related each to each and to the whole.'[8] This statement is perhaps deceptively inclusive, for in a certain sense she apparently wishes to speak of the play primarily as a movement of language, a movement of meaningful sound. But when she also asserts that Dr. Johnson is wrong about *Samson Agonistes*, and that the play possesses unity of action quite as certainly as 'much of the major drama of the Greeks',[9] she, too, is juggling her terms, for she is asserting that what Aristotle means by unity of action and beginning, middle, and end, is what she means when she speaks of the unity of this play as being the unity of 'a sustained musical composition'.

A lot more needs to be done, however, before one is justified in speaking of the unity of a musical composition in the same terms as one speaks of the unity of drama.[10] A musical composition may be defined as the combining of notes, melodies, phrases, or themes, creating a design, and perhaps expressing emotion. In applying the term to Milton, Miss Ellis-Fermor must have meant to emphasize the design of the work (perhaps as Milton himself did in speaking of the 'economy, or disposition of the fable'), and to play down the element of plot. Her insight, I believe, was fine, but it needed working out.

So we are left somewhat better off through her affirmation of the play's coherence and success, but we still lack an adequate way of setting off what distinguishes Milton's idea of a tragic poem from the ancient works. For the question Milton's remarks raise, as directly as his 'Dramatic Poem' itself does, is this—what models is he indeed referring to that authorize a work that is ordered so differently than the tragedies we ordinarily think of?

If neither Aristotle nor the plays of antiquity quite support Milton's statement on the nature of tragedy, neither does the practice of the Italians, in what up to this time they had generally been offering as tragedies, follow the ancient examples. In them, it seeems—again according to the preface —Milton found certain precedents for his own undertaking, although he mentioned that among their works he observed certain deviations from more approved ways of composing tragedies. The precedents that they do observe are, one supposes, in the substantial matters of the unities, the use of the chorus, and versification. The particular deviations he reproves are in the introduction of comic material and low characters. But whatever Milton found to follow in the Italians, it seems that he did not find among them anything that could be characterized as a model for his own work either in structure or tone or governing purpose. The strongly Senecan cast to most of these plays made them, if not truly dramatic in the sense of the term that the ancient Greek plays illustrate, at least works crowded with dramatic activity. Moreover, however regular in construction, these plays generally depended for their effects upon the exploitation of horror, and certainly their authors never allowed the idea of suffering to govern the succession of scenes in any such way as Milton did. *Sophonisba*, *Tamar*, and others include laments and choric songs that are grand and moving, but never, I think, is any representation of the passions allowed to subordinate the representation of events.[11]

And although the ends of catharsis are always in view, whatever the range of effects this is allowed to include, those effects are at once limited and defined by the nature of the actions that are being imitated. When Professor Herrick surveyed the history of this drama he concluded that these are primarily tragedies of blood and lust; they almost never invoke the Christian deity; and the only code of conduct they follow faithfully is that of honour.[12] It must therefore follow that any cathartic effects would be other than the effects following the presenting of action involving religious concerns, or in which religious affirmations qualify the ethical issues.

When some of these Italian plays have Biblical subjects—as, for example, Giustiniano's *Jephte* (1583)—they depend as little upon Christian religion as plays from pagan history, and the religiousness and piety are characteristically more formal and heroic than either Hebraic or Christian. In the catastrophe the playwright celebrates the values of pride and honour and patriotism, and little more.

II

Sacred tragedy

There was another kind of tragic play coming into fashion, however, and this requires special notice. Theorists as well as dramatists for many years had been weighing the possibilities of Christian tragedy. One may see in a great variety of works as well as in the speculations of Minturno, Cinthio, Heinsius, and a host of others how deep the interest was in adapting the ancient tragic forms to the expression of Christian faith. The crux would always be in the fact of catastrophe and in the nature of the effect, of catharsis or whatever, that would follow from that. It was obvious that the end must be in some sense happy, the traditional *exitus infelix* would be changed in one way or another. Once that was recognized as the matter of overriding importance, one could see that all the other fixed elements in the form had to be managed with this in view. The question was plain—could the dramatic action directed towards such an end proceed in the traditional ways of classical tragedy?

Specifically, would there be the same reasons for presenting characters of great stature, and then seeing them tested through a disaster in which the faith of Hebrews and Christians could still be known to triumph? Could the idea of simplicity inherent in the idea of the unities assimilate the values inherent in the narrative perspective of the Bible? Could the devices of discovery and denouement serve conceptions in which something other than awe at the power of fate provided the originating impetus? Could the chorus provide the resonance and the sense of universal import as provocatively as in the ancient works? Each element in this kind of composition was necessarily redirected by the idea that the notion of felicity was to be allowed to survive even after the worst had been related, and the modification of tragedy must have been understood to share in the complexity of conversion itself.

There were not only the developments of theory and the modifications in practice, there were the efforts to find other names, even the intention of defining other genres. A famous collection of dramas printed towards the end of the sixteenth century included a group of works called 'sacred comedies', and for the various modifications there were as many terms— 'sacred histories', 'sacred tragedies', 'tragical comedies', 'new tragedies', 'mixed tragedies'.[13] Stories taken from the Bible or from the lives of the saints forced the issues. When as in the story of Abraham and Isaac a happy ending results from the intervention of God, a playwright cannot rest in appealing to the example of the *deus ex machina* in Euripides; yet while so much is changed by the quality of the faith that this is the true God who has intervened, the disposition is still to call the composition tragic.

What was true of the transformation of tragedy in the use of this material was turning out be true also with dramas whose actions were taken from secular history, and even those that were invented. Christian sensibility and psychology were inevitably governing the most ambitious humanist efforts, and what under other circumstances would be an ending in misery is presented to us as glorious. *Melodramma* had commenced as an effort to reconstruct ancient tragedy, to re-create the original alliance of verse and music and dancing. In Monteverdi's

L'Incoronazione di Poppea, which belongs to the development of this effort, horrible events in the story of adulterous lovers were transmuted into a divinization of human passion, and the play ended in a foreshadowing of Heaven.

As we look back upon the history of the renewal of ancient tragedy the plays of George Buchanan seem to us as much of a beacon as they did to his own times and to the immediately succeeding generations. He inspired Grotius and Vondel, and he would have been an example to Milton, in himself and for what he meant to these others. It was he who set the style for Biblical tragedy in the ancient form, and with such authority and distinction that Corneille was to revere him. Milton, of course, had the ancient works in mind as much as Corneille did, just as he had in mind more recent developments in tragedy in Italy. I suppose that the *sacra rappresentazione*, to which Andreini's *L'Adamo* belongs, as well as the developing *melodramma*, also contributed to the conception of Milton's tragedy, but I believe that he owed his finally most important obligations to what Buchanan had established as a type of its own, the adaptation of the classical tragic form to stories taken from the Bible.

While he was in Bordeaux, between 1539 and 1544, Buchanan concentrated the only dramatic writing he was ever to do. He translated the *Medea* and the *Alcestis* of Euripides, and then composed two plays of his own, both on Biblical subjects—*Baptistes sive Calumnia* and *Jephthes sive Votum*.

Oddly, the *Baptistes* is much more Senecan than Greek, and, in what was to be the characteristic fault of the imitations of the humanists, it was to proceed more as a series of orations and complaints than as an organization of events. The speeches and the choruses are much too long for drama, and most especially if they were not to be supported by music and choreography. For the rest, the sequence of scenes is organized mostly according to the principle that insists on fidelity to the account in the Bible and that cannot accept a prior claim for a single, unified action. Nevertheless, the doctrine at the end that sums up the burden of the play is true enough to the spirit of many ancient plays—'Who needs to fear death who has lived well? Besides, death is a release from the ills of life'.

Buchanan had accomplished almost a miracle in translating this sacred material into a dramatic form radically unlike the forms the sacred stories had heretofore known when they were dramatized. And not the least astonishing feature of his work, and the testimony to the depth of his conception of it as a humanist undertaking, is that he almost completely neglected to introduce the idea that seems to Christians almost insepara- ble from any story whatever about John the Baptist, that he was the forerunner of Christ and the herald of the eternal life. However much he modified the ancient conventions or failed to assimilate them, he was not modifying the ending in disaster that is typical of ancient tragedy, and that Christian tragedy so profoundly alters.

Many years later Milton was to make notes for a tragedy he might have written on John the Baptist, and it has even been supposed that he was the author of a translation of Buchanan's play that appeared in a disguised form in the 1640s. What is more centrally significant, however, in Buchanan's example is the quality of grandeur, the elevation of style in which the Biblical material is brought over into the tragic form. In the *Baptistes* as in the much more impressive *Jephthes*, it is in a certain majesty and fineness that one sees Buchanan establish- ing the spirit and tone in which others will be fortunate if they can follow him.

In the *Jephthes*, a leader of the Israelites, warring against the nation that has kept his people in slavery, has vowed, should victory be granted him, immediately on his return from battle to make a sacrificial offering of the first living creature he meets. He cannot know that it will be his daughter running to embrace him that he must sacrifice, but at home dreams have already terrified his wife and the foreboding of disaster quickly poisons the news of the triumph when it is brought there.

The play moves grandly, and we are so carried along by its noble manner that we come to expect a catastrophe of the magnitude we know in ancient works. Yet the particular dilemma of Jephtha brings out so much in him that is less than heroic that the play finally loses its power over us. Jephtha's merely stiff-necked failure to meet the arguments

against a deed that must displease God not only demeans him,
it weakens our disposition to honour the God he persists in
worshipping so blindly. In the ancient tragedies of Iphigenia it
is this very blindness in Agamemnon and Artemis alike that
strengthens our idea of the awfulness of the powers in conflict in the world, but because Buchanan means us to attribute
perfect goodness and perfect justice to God, he is forced to
diminish the stature of his protagonist so much that he is
finally unworthy of the tragic role.

The effect of it all is also weakened by the obligation Buchanan felt to follow strictly the incidents in the order in which the
Bible presents them and as a result he lost the opportunity of
ordering the action in the most concentrated ways.

It is necessary to mention these weaknesses even while
affirming the greatness of Buchanan's achievement and in
pointing to the force of his example, for these are in part not
so much failures of talent as they are difficulties inherent in
the problem of combining the interests of ancient tragedy with
those of Christian piety. Circumstances will be changing greatly
before the dramatists of the next century will find themselves
able to resolve these same difficulties.

Buchanan's plays were soon printed and translated and
imitated. The vogue for Biblical tragedy in the classic form
took root in France, in the Low Countries, and in Italy. It was
no doubt sustained in large part by the growing vitality of
humanism itself, although it is clear enough that the writers
were continuing to exploit not only the material but some of
the devices and effects the medieval playwrights had evolved
for their presentations of stories from the Bible. The form had
changed, the language was commonly Latin, but the feeling
and the manner of the medieval drama survived even in as
profoundly oriented a humanist as Buchanan, still more so in
others. The classic form was exploited for dramas about Joseph,
about the Prodigal Son, about Susannah and the Elders, about
the Sacrifice of Isaac. As early as 1547 Jerome Ziegler had
written a tragedy on the fall of Samson. As the decades passed,
material was drawn on from the lives of the saints, and
'Christian tragedy' came to rival and sometimes supplant
'Biblical tragedy'. These were religious as well as humanist

A view of the Palazzo Barberini from the rear
(An engraving of A. Specchi in the fourth volume of Falda's *Il nuovo teatro delle fabriche et edificii in prospettiva di Roma moderna*. Biblioteca Nazionale, Florence.)

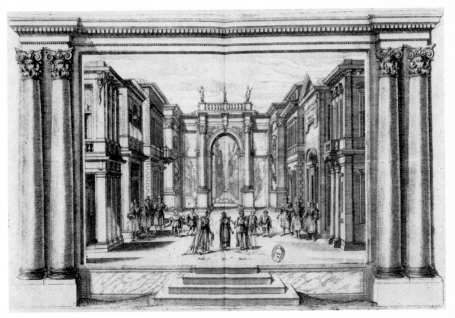

San Alessio, Act I, Scene V
(An engraving of Collignon, reproduced from Stefano Landi, *Il S. Alessio, dramma musicale*, Rome, 1634. Bibliothèque Nationale, Paris.)

Naples from the sea
(D. A. Parrino, *Napoli Città Nobilissima, Antica, e Fedelissima*, Naples, L'Anno del
Giubileo. Bibliothèque Nationale, Paris.)

The Largo San Domenico. The *Oziosi* met in a building on this square
(Parrino, *Napoli Città Nobilissima*. Bibliothèque Nationale, Paris.)

Loredano receiving a visitor
(*Lettere del Signor Gio: Francesco
Loredano*, edited by Henri Giblet,
Venice, 1660. Libreria di San Marco.)

Loredano in prayer

(The frontispiece of *The Ascent of the Soul: Or, David's Mount Towards God's House. Being Paraphrases on the Fifteen Psalms of Degrees. Written in Italian, By the Illustrious Gio. Francesco Loredano, a Noble Venetian,* 1656. *Render'd into English, Anno Dom.* 1665. [By Henry Hare, Lord Colarane.] London, 1681. Library of the University of Michigan.)

undertakings, the claims of piety were all-important, even though the adaptation of new forms signified the seriousness of the humanist ambition to create something more civilized than the medieval forms. But the matter and the piety still retain much of the medieval character. As Lanson put it so well in writing of Buchanan's *Baptistes*:

Selon nos idées, la facture antique est isolemment imposée à un sujet qui y répugne et en est mutilé. Mais il faut juger plutôt par les idées du temps: l'action directe, exposée aux yeux, on la trouvait partout, tous les mystères en étaient pleins. Ce qui manquait à notre théâtre et ce que les anciens avaient supérieurement, c'était le style, et par là il faut entendre sans doute la rhétorique, mais avec elle la morale et le pathétique, l'art délicat le relever, de dégager le sens d'un fait, d'une situation, de suggérer ou d'exprimer toutes les naunces de sentiments, de beauté de vie qui y sont contenues. Faire danser Salomé, ou faire semblant de couper la tête à Jean-Baptiste était facile: le problème auquel l'humaniste disciple des anciens s'attaquait était de rendre sensibles à tous par des mots la seduction de la danse ou l'horreur de la décollation. Ce qui pour nous est maladresse, était alors delicatesse d'art et nouveauté d'art.[14]

Sometimes in conforming to the Biblical source the plays were provided with happy endings. Sometimes the material allowed for an observance of the unities although often enough there was a series of episodes rather than a single action. Commonly there was a twofold failure—a failure to compose tragedy in the way it must be composed when it is imitation of an action and can therefore hold the stage, and a failure to reconcile the spirit of tragedy with the Christian faith. In the seventeenth century, beginning with Grotius, one sees the flowering of which Buchanan's work was the first promise. In Vondel and Milton and Corneille there is not only the perfection of the humanist temper, one sees in them both how much and how little writers needed to defer to the claims of Christian piety in writing tragedy that deserves to be called tragedy and that is also sacred and Christian. And their successes are in great part due to the transformation in the manner of piety, in the developments of faith in which the medieval temper had been transformed into the characters of faith the Reformation and the Counter-Reformation were bringing into being.

The transformation proceeded unevenly.

Grotius's first play, *Adamus Exul* (1601), observes the unities and follows most of the conventions of ancient tragedy, yet it is less in the spirit of the ancients than Buchanan's work. Grotius has a sense of the immediacy of the language of the chorus, his verse is distinguished, the stychomythia seems well contrived, and the characters strike the tragic postures, yet the play has at least as much of the medieval spirit as of the classic. For one thing, Grotius could not resist the idea of a vast panorama in which we are to imagine God overseeing all, and from time to time conversing with the angels through vast reaches. Everywhere, too, is the idea of judgement and of exile and of the Day of Judgement, an idea so much more narrowly focused and intense than any mere sense of the power of fate.

The Middle Ages has furnished much of his imagery. Several years later, in 1608, with the *Christus Patiens*, Grotius is using some of the devices of the ancients more skilfully than in the first play, but here the language brings with it so many reminiscences of medieval expression that it in itself quite dispels the possibility of a re-enactment of the Crucifixion in anything like the ancient spirit. The rhetoric, the imagery, the emotion all but annihilate the spirit of tragedy one supposes to be inherent in the ancient form, and that Buchanan had caught, and if that were not enough, there is the transformation of the catastrophe into an event which brings with it the most hopeful promise of all. Mary begins the fifth act with the words:

Sorrow is fled; Joy, a long banish'd Guest
With heavenly rapture fills my inlarged brest.

And the play's last words foretell the final joy:

In that reformed World,
Those by their sins infected, shall be hurl'd
Downe under one perpetuall Night; while they
Whom thou hast cleans'd, injoy perpetuall Day.[15]

This reminds us that Buchanan's *Baptistes* might also have ended in the promise that defies death, but the most Buchanan had chosen to offer was the consolation that those who remain may justly take in the thought of a life well lived, and a noble death.

All the same, Grotius was determined to continue to put the ancient form to the service of religion, and I suppose to bring the two to a better balance, and the ending of this play seems to have given him the hint he wanted. His last drama, *Sophompaneas* (1635), managed the happy ending more subtly, and Grotius acknowledged that this was now the key to his use of the ancient form. In dedicating the play to Vossius he justified the ending by referring to the *Danaidas* of Aeschylus and a number of plays of Euripides.

The first act is made up of a single long speech of Joseph's and a single long chorus. There follows a series of episodes in which the brothers arrange among themselves to dispose of Joseph, and then there is his fortunate rescue as the result of the dissension among them. In the last, extremely short act Pharaoh speaks words of the reconciliation that has come about not only between the brothers but between his people and the Israelites.

This can hardly be called a dramatic action, it is rather a series of situations in which there is partly enactment, partly expatiation upon a history with a significant burden. Characteristically there is not much of anything to bring that significance out. Grotius assumes that his reader accepts the story itself as sacrosanct, and he appears to think there is no need for comment, although he did introduce at least one statement to explain that God was at work benevolently in this tragic history of a suffering father and a cruelly persecuted brother: 'The mighty power of God breathes within him, and what the merely mortal mind cannot do, an ethereal spirit within him admonishes.'[16]

And so the play stands as one of those works representing what has been called 'Biblical humanism', restrained through its very humanism from the Christian elucidation that almost demands expression, the idea that the situation of Joseph is 'the symbolic situation of the destiny of Christ in the midst of his human brothers'.[17] In the fortunate ending Grotius has prepared for the Christianization of the story, but he has not elucidated it.

Vondel in translating the play the very year in which Grotius printed it saw not only how to make this into an obviously more dramatic work, he saw how to make it a representation in which the analogy with Christ would be unmistakable. He saw Joseph as the 'type' of Christ, and his story as a prefiguring. In the translation he leaves almost all this to reference, but the idea took such strong hold of him that he went on to write two other plays continuing the story of Joseph, and accentuating the typology. In one of these, *Joseph en Dothen* (1640), there is another (temporarily) happy ending—the son is restored to the father and there is a reconciliation that may be thought to be deeper and richer in promise than that which ended the first play. But here the subtlety is even more extraordinary for the play does not end in words of reconciliation but in words of complaint and misery. It is as if Vondel meant to retain in form the characteristic ending of tragedy, but by the spirit of the writing he seems to wish to have us understand that in disaster men must take heart in the thought that God is putting even suffering to good use. He seems to be asking his audience to weigh the extent of the grief God allows, and to count on its being alleviated by the promise of the relief to come (I must have recourse to the French adaptation of Jean Giono):

Ah! Seigneur! Vos desseins sont sans doute impénétrables. Peut-être marchons-nous vers la gloire avec ce vieillard qui va désormais chercher dans ses rêves déserts les membres épars de son fils bien-aimé? Ces frères sournois, cachetés de haine et de terreurs jusqu'à la gueule sont peut-être les hérauts de quelque lointain triomphe.

Avez-vous besoin de ma honte flamboyante pour allumer au fond des siècles le chandelier à sept branches d'un sanctuaire éternel? Sommes-nous dans la forge où vous continuez la création du monde? Aviez-vous besoin de l'amour de mon père, du lit de Rachel, de mes turpitudes, du viol de ma sœur, de la rage de mes frères et de la souillure d'Israel pour composer je ne sais quel paradis?

Votre volonté se fait, sans volonté seconde. Il faut que
votre volonté se fasse. Mais, où dois-je me cacher, de chagrin
et de honte pendant que votre volonté se fait? . . .[18]

It is as if he were ending the tragedy on a paraphrase of 'Why
hast thou forsaken me?'

This was only one of the ways Vondel discovered of expressing Christian meaning in tragedy. In the *Samson* of a few
years later (1660) he introduced an explicit commentary—the
typology is indentified:

                              understand
That the example of his death and life
Foretells a Saviour, of God's spirit born,
Who shall be persecuted, as was he,
And dying, deal a fatal blow to death;
But through a softer law He shall unburden
Each heart of its revenge—a law of love
That puts the highest crown on human life.[19]

Samson had died by his own hand, and Vondel evidently saw
this way as the means not only of saying that grace was at
work in Samson's pulling down the temple but in the very
ordering of his life.[20] We need to be assured that what is miserable here is but the prelude to great happiness, and so our
sorrow in the catastrophe we must accept as Christians accept
death, grievous and yet the entrance-way to Heaven. Again
the effort is to preserve the catastrophe of tragedy while lighten-
ing it.

Writers in the Low Countries were as active as those anywhere in reforming poetic theory, and the theory of tragedy
in particular. Scaliger had had a great influence upon Grotius,
and Heinsius, following after him, seems to have become the
most influential interpreter of Aristotle for the century. He
himself composed a tragedy on Herod and the Slaughter of the
Innocents, and, although it followed the classic model, it ended
in one of the happiest of conclusions, that the particular child
Herod had sought to slay was saved. But it was in his commentary on Aristotle that he chiefly provided the stay for those

who wanted to call tragedies certain works that were asserting the doctrine of the Resurrection in the midst of the tragic catastrophe.

In interpreting Aristotle, Heinsius took note of what Aristotle also had, a disposition of some writers to alter the ending most characteristic of tragedy for the sake of another order of pleasure. He spoke at some length of machines 'outside the drama', that is, devices for changing the catastrophe 'into something better'. He was referring primarily to the use of the *deus ex machina* in contriving the denouement, and while, like Aristotle, he criticized this device as likely to detract from the effects proper to tragedy, he offered at least one justification for its use. There are times, he said, when it exploits the knowledge of the future that gods possess and men do not, and there can be a certain justification for the use of this device, if this fact is well used. The *deus ex machina* may be used to conclude a dramatic action when through prior prophecy or revelation the intervention accords sufficiently with what men know of their own knowledge, or when it points to an outcome that men might regard themselves justified in foreseeing.[21]

Heinsius was not as forthright as either Grotius or Vossius in allowing for happy resolutions, and he meant to discourage the idea that tragedy might, as Vossius spoke of it, partake of comedy.[22] But there is another phase of his interpretation of Aristotle that did indeed support this radical modification, and this comes about through the way in which he interpreted the tragic catharsis. This may be particularly pertinent to the reading of Milton, for it has been supposed that Milton in the preface to *Samson Agonistes* owed his notion of catharsis as a kind of homoeopathic therapy to Heinsius—tempering and reducing the passions 'to just measure with a kind of delight . . . so in Physic things of melancholic hue and quality are us'd against melancholy, sour against sour, salt to remove salt humours'.

P. R. Sellin has brought forward the similarity of terms and ideas in Milton and Heinsius on this matter, and he has made the particularly valuable comment that on the title-page of his play, in translating catharsis by *lustratio*, Milton is using a word Heinsius also used, and in the sense in which Milton used it—as a milder purgation of the passions rather than their extirpation.

And further, that the definition of *lustratio* as a purification effected by sacrifice or rite may be particularly applicable to the action Milton's drama represents.[23]

The point may be extended. If indeed the ending of *Samson Agonistes* is believed to be effecting the tragic catharsis, it must be doing this not merely through awe but in the accompanying assurance of God's working for good through the catastrophe. And if this is so, then, indeed, the play is partaking of comedy, and the theory of *lustratio* may be another way of justifying it.

'And calm of mind, all passion spent'—this seems to mean that all conflict, all fever, has been done with, now there is to be reconciliation and content, the peace of God prevailing. The cause of the peace is God Himself, who has been at work in the very disposition of Samson as he roused himself to heroism and sacrifice, and God is at work in the very death. Grotius referred to the working of grace in the rescue of Joseph, if he did not show its workings, and more than once Vondel exploited what he thought of as a way of understanding the operation of grace in resolving the tragic conflicts of his plays, and therefore in alleviating the tragic suffering. With Milton, however, it is more as it is with Corneille:

En montrant comment Corneille a juxtaposé à l'action de la grâce divine celle de la volonté humaine et explique psychologiquement des faits religieux, en constatant qu'il a réduit le miracle à ses effets intérieurs, nous avons nettement manifesté son intention de se conformer au système de théâtre classique. Le même scrupule le conduit presque à traiter l'histoire sacrée comme une source ordinaire.[24]

In the 1640s Vondel and Corneille are in their different ways discovering how to put ideas about the working of grace to dramatic use. They are thereby learning how to assimilate the expressions to Christian religion, to the tragic form, better than Grotius or Buchanan had been able to. In their different ways, they, too, like Milton, were altering the character of the tragic catharsis. Milton's way, however, is neither Vondel's nor Corneille's and whether or not the theory of homoeopathy is to be illustrated by *Samson Agonistes* itself, he, too, aims to accomplish the effect that is proper to tragedy in the classic form through illustrating the power of divine grace, but as it happens the manner of the progression of his work is not properly dramatic.

The stories taken from the Bible are sacred simply as accounts of events in the history of a chosen people. Those taken from the lives of saints, if they are to deserve the credit of the faithful, must bear within them an explanation, or something approaching an explanation, that will satisfy doctrine as well as faith. In a sense dramas dealing with saints' lives must paradoxically stress the humanity of the saints in order to display the reason for God's use of them. In this regard it hardly matters if Joseph or Adam or Jephtha is heroic or mean, but it is most necessary that Polyeucte and Théodore and Sebastian be men and women of middle stature. This is as it is, too, with Milton's Samson—he is one of those Biblical heroes who has become a saint precisely because he had risen from a weakened state.[25] We may obtain a special help in looking at Milton's play in this light if we look at the work of a contemporary Italian writer.

Milton would have met Girolamo Bartolommei in Florence. He was the Secretary of the Accademia degli Svogliati and read from his Tuscan poems at the meeting of the academy at which Milton read some of his Latin verse.[26] Bartolommei was a Tuscan who spent most of his life in Rome, but from time to time he was in Florence. He had composed an epic on America, and he was busy writing many dramas, some of them for music. From what one may judge of the dedications he offered the members of the Barberini family he must have been deep in theatrical and musical life of Rome in the late 1630s and early 1640s when the Barberinis were lavish in their support of the theatre. He was zealous in attempting to put drama to the service of the Catholic faith, and nearly as zealous in his emulation of antiquity. The plays he wrote for music were divided into two types—'dramme morali and 'dramme sacri' —and his tragedies were either simply that or else 'tragedie sacre'.

He based several of his plays on the lives of saints, and one of these—*Polietto*—Henri Hauvette once proposed as a possible source of Corneille's *Polyeucte*.[27] There seems to be nothing to confirm Corneille's knowledge of Bartolommei's work, but there is a great deal to certify an identity of interest, even to Corneilles's calling his *Polyeucte* and *Théodore* 'tragédies chrétiennes' just as Bartolommei called his plays of the same names 'tragedie sacre'.

Bartolommei's tragedies were first printed in 1632, and then again in 1655. The volume included an extensive critical essay, and in it we see how carefully he had investigated the possibilities of Christian tragedy. I have found no one who attempted so carefully to find the terms that would allow for the distinctions that must be made, following and refining upon Heinsius.

Bartolommei began by putting aside the idea that the catharsis of tragedy was to be effected through the observance of certain rules. He firmly asserted a prior principle, that all the arts and disciplines are governed by their ends, and 'to the noblest end corresponds the noblest art'.[28] Tragedy looks towards some composing of the perturbations of men as they reflect upon incidents and episodes in which life is seen to come to an end, and in which a variety of the possibilities of felicity and misery, following upon good and evil actions, are understood to conform to the nature of things. And then he made the point he had been working for: 'sacred tragedies' treat with greater degrees of power and of compassion than other tragedies and to greater effect. This is so because on the one hand martyrs are more 'useful' vehicles than tyrants in such plays, since they are men of middle estate, not removed from the condition of the audience by reason of extraordinary eminence, and therefore they provide examples both to greater and lesser men than themselves. On the other hand, by the nature of martyrdom their stories are acquainting all men with the idea of a power greater than any human power, and in effect they are recommending all men to make themselves subject to omnipotence. When to the contemplation of such degrees of power and of submission to it there is added the promise of eternal good to follow after death, such a conclusion, and such a catharsis, are quite as truly a reduction of the excesses of the emotions of pity and terror as that effected by other tragedies.

They add a special profit also in pointing the audience to the right way of conducting what is left of its life.[29]

In the language of the definitions he is proposing Bartolommei follows Heinsius closely, but in the 1655 preface he significantly alters his terms. In both forms of the essay the primary definition of tragedy is the same:

> la Tragedia è imitazione d'azione d'illustri personaggi perfetta, hauente grandezza con favella, armonia e ballo, siche separatamente ciascuna delle spezie nelle sue parte rappresenti; non per narrazione, ma per mezzo della compassione, e dello spavento, purgazione cosi fatte terminante: ecco dunque che la commiserazione, e 'l timore sono mezzi; però l'huomo si deve intendere che si purghi, e non la commiserazione e 'l timore.[30]

In the 1632 preface the definition of 'sacred tragedy' begins in substantially the same way, but the change comes after the phrase 'non per narrazione': now the words are—'non per narrazione, ma per mezzo d'un santo timore, e d'una celeste speranza, purgazioni operante. . . .'[31] His effort, of course, was to account for a different quality in the catharsis, and as time went on he adopted terms that made the effect peculiarly Christian in nature, for in the 1655 editions the phrase now is, 'per mezzo d'un santo Timore, ed' una caritevole Compassione'.[32] This is a formula of a kind all writers of such tragedies must be looking for in seeking to answer not only those who object to a happy ending but those who ask how tragedy can be anything other than appalling if it tells that a just God permits the good to suffer. I take it that Bartolommei believes that sacred tragedy is founded upon the belief in the mercifulness of God, and he would respond to criticism of this kind as a modern scholar has spoken in defending Corneille:

> Exprimant une objection que nous retrouverons chez Voltaire et chez Vigny, Robortello, dès 1548, craignait que le spectacle des souffrances des justes ne fît douter de la Providence. Pusillanimité peu théologique! pouvaient répliquer les fidèles. Le vrai croyant sait et comprend que la vie terrestre est le purgatoire des saints et que les souffrances

d'ici-bas méritent le bonheur éternel. Rien n'était donc plus
propre à purger les passions du chrétien que le spectacle des
douleurs de Christ, des martyrs et de tous les héros de la foi.[33]

It is certain, I believe, that at the end of *Samson Agonistes* we
are meant to agree that no blame is to attach to God for Samson's
suffering.

The dramas of Bartolommei have made very little impression,
and even if one were to believe that Corneille had some knowledge of at least some of these a modern reader cannot confidently discover in their writing much of the power Bartolommei intended. For myself I find the ones I have read rather
awkwardly formed, although on occasion a scene or a speech is
admirable. It is, on the other hand, interesting to notice how
Bartolommei was trying to put his critical ideas into practice,
and that he did have a much better idea of how to obtain
dramatic effects than most of the humanists. For one thing, he
had a meaningful understanding of what it means for tragedy
to be an imitation of an action, and he governed the events of
his tragedies in ways that show that he was maintaining the
idea of an action with a beginning, a middle, and an end. He
evidently understood that the idea of causality inherent in the
dramas of antiquity embodied an idea of fate, and in the sacred
tragedies at least he worked to show that the grace of God con-
travenes fate. He will still depend upon the sequences of causality, but he will at the same time show that his protagonists
in being subdued by fate are also escaping it. In externals at
least, and sometimes, too, in a certain depth of conception, he
fulfilled his theory.

The substantial interest of *Polietto* is in the discovery of the
faith in Christ that has grown in a young pagan warrior through
knowing and admiring the religion of his friend. He is the soul
of generosity, and soon he appears before us in all his zeal—in
the proposal he makes to destroy the temple of the heathen, in
the resolution to make his profession of faith public, in his
steadfast refusal to submit to the entreaties of his wife and
children as they beg him to return to the religion of his
people. We see the strength and clarity of his faith in the bold-
ness and even royalty of manner in which he is reported to

have attacked the images of the pagan deities, and finally we gauge his quality by the passivity and humility of his martyrdom.

The various comments on the vision he has had, the continuous references to the working of divine grace, the affirmation from many sides of the peculiar excellence of the Christian faith—all these are emphases and directions that lead us to regard his steadfastness and heroism as well as his sacrifice as not only saintly but sympathetic; the play does indeed have an admirable quality in this respect, for we do get the sense of a splendid young pagan who, suffering conversion, takes the simplest and most direct of courses, as clear and untroubled in his religion as in his heroism.

Corneille's Polyeucte is perhaps also a simple person, but not so simple as this. His love for his wife, the complexity of his ties to his father-in-law, his sense of politics and society, all show forth a man who is sensitive to many interests and attractions. It is the richness of his consciousness that makes it possible for Corneille to present in him the workings of grace as indeed miraculous—bending this inclination, making use of that, implanting an idea, substantiating his various loves by a religious love—in short, that makes the working of grace seem not merely miraculous in itself but miraculous in its harmonious workings with nature. The drama is particularly moving in showing that what grace finally overcomes in Polyeucte is not his humanity or his weakness but his nobility. And this is the final contrast with Milton, where grace works to overcome ignobility.

In Bartolommei there is something in a certain sense more childlike—like something from *The Seven Champions of Christendom*—more childlike and, considering the importance of his subject, more uninteresting except at one point—in the submissiveness of the great warrior in letting his captor slay him. It is at this point that Bartolommei balances his whole idea of the catharsis of sacred tragedy—the marvel we are to feel is not only at courage in the face of death but at a submissiveness which testifies to Polietto's faith, and to the vividness of the joy he already feels in anticipating the happiness that is to be his after his death, a warrior welcoming humiliation. I think we are meant to be moved doubly—in the satisfaction of being able to affirm the faith we are supposed to share with him, and in marvelling at abnegation in so great a warrior.

The story and the circumstances of *Polietto* are very unlike those of *Samson Agonistes*, and in the substance the only significant likeness is that each protagonist is being conducted towards a growing assurance in the rule of the true God. The changes they undergo are very different—Polietto passing from strength to strength, from the exuberance of warlike valour to the ecstasy of martyrdom, and Samson moving from despair to the perfectly patient reconciliation with God's will. And one observes that in both plays, apart from the emphasis on the ways of grace, there is also the similarity of the essential device of demonstration—that is, for both protagonists the resolution of the issues that engage them occurs not as the climax to a series of events, but as a demonstration that God is intervening in affecting the very wills of the heroes. While the procession of scenes in Bartolommei's play promises more of spectacle and excitement and suspense than in Milton, and the scene with Paulina is truly pathetic, what is dominating our interest in both is our noticing the changes in the protagonist. In neither play are we being led to any great excitement over the destruction of idols nor the pulling down of a temple—what we are being led to hope for is the evidence of the peace of conviction.

In *Polietto* we are not being prepared for the drama of martyrdom, or of baptism, and when the sacrifice is made before our eyes the scene is much less dramatic than the destruction we had only heard spoken of in Polietto's dream. The scene is, in fact, an anticlimax, with much less not only of the dramatic but of the imaginative power of the speech of the messenger in Milton's play when he relates the destruction of the temple. Similarly, the series of debates towards the end—with Artabano, with the Prefect, with Paulina—they come as a series of encounters brought about as arbitrarily as in Milton's play, introduced by and commented on by a chorus. There is in their succession, however, no rising to a climax of intensity or trepidation, and there is, as far as I can tell, no correspondence to the logic of the passions and of faith of Polietto as his resolution settles and grows impregnable. There is nothing of that remarkable sense we have as of the very growth of light in

Samson. In Bartolommei's play the last half is conducted in the succession of encounters and in the climax in a way very like Milton's, but in *Polietto* all is set to display the unflinching certainty of the protagonist and in *Samson Agonistes* all is to show grace in process. Bartolomei does not have the gift, perhaps, but also he does not have the intent to show how what works within the soul, and the ways in which it works, may be understood to conform to the logic of the passions when it is the passions that are understood as the matter of God's workings.

The differences also help us guess why Milton in the foreword to *Samson Agonistes* spoke of his work as an imitation of the passions; I think this is because he conceived of the affections and energies of man's nature as in themselves possessing the disposition to obey God. He wanted to show that there are ways of understanding how a man who has been reduced to all but mere sensibility could take human form again, could take the direction of manliness and even heroism. He would present this growth as drama, and as drama leading in the nature of things to a conclusive deed, but the work itself will be given over to showing the stages by which his character and will and energy were reordered. The play would not treat of an event and its consequences as the imitation of an action, but, rather, the way in which, through a series of repressions and challenges, a sentient being is raised from depression to purposefulness, partly in the mere response of the body and the nerves to the challenges that pain it, partly through the inexpugnable desire to serve God, and partly mysteriously. We are shown a man being restored to strength as he asserts himself to hold off whatever else is being brought forward to deceive him, to delude him, and to enthral him. He responds to all such efforts as to goads. Thanks to the ineradicable conviction of the existence of goodness and the indeflectible determination to face the truth, the goads move him to shame and anger and resolution and wholeness. If this is not drama precisely speaking, it may be characterized as the representation of the process of the passions as they move towards their end in the character of a particular man, a fulfilment that is at once an act and a submission.[34]

Samson Agonistes might be called a Biblical tragedy, not so

strictly humanist in its exclusion of doctrinal implications as
Buchanan's *Baptistes*, say, nor, of course, with the specific
introduction of Christian matter one inevitably finds in plays
that are declaredly based upon the life of a saint, as *Polietto*
is.[35] Nevertheless, it is certainly a play that expresses not only
the faith of a humanist, or something like the quality of the
ancient Hebrew mind; it expresses Christian faith as Corneille
said any Christian re-creating a story from the Bible must
express it, as if Milton were setting out to accomplish just this:
'Nous devons une foi chrétienne et indispensable à tout ce qui
est dans la Bible.'[36] Milton's Samson is thus the hero who has
become a saint: 'The desire expressed in the introduction to
Book IX of *Paradise Lost* to sing "the better fortitude of
patience and heroic martyrdom" is fulfilled by the portrayal of
a divine pattern in *Paradise Regained. Samson Agonistes* is its
nearest possible fulfillment in the life of mortal man.'[37]

There is much in this that is Puritan and Protestant. In the
development of Christian tragedy it was to be expected that
Catholics would make use of saints' lives where Protestants
might be reluctant to, and in *Samson Agonistes* we have a
martyr who is at most an approximation of the 'type' of Christ
rather than a hero who suffers a conversion and who requires
baptism, even if it is only as in *Polietto* the baptism of blood.
We may at the end reflect upon the perfection of Samson's
submission to God's will, finding in it the certainty of sanctity,
but we shall not discover in him even then any suggestion of
his identification with the incarnate God.

This, I think, is the first meaningful point to make in contrasting Milton with Bartolommei and Corneille, and the next
is that in representing the working of grace as that which
ultimately will transform the exaltation of tragedy into a
loving compassion, Bartolommei and Corneille will do so in conceiving of their works as imitations of an action with the intent
of making use of every device to make their plays stageworthy,
and Milton's play is more a poem than a play: it is not meant
for the stage, and I believe, as his own words give warrant for
supposing, it is more an imitation of passions than of an action.
It proceeds lyrically rather than dramatically. In some ways it
conforms more to the methods the Biblical tragedy of the

humanists had followed from the very beginning. 'La tragédie humaniste est un drame pathétique qui tire l'émotion non de la vue directe, mais de la plainte des victimes.'[38] And he was doing so because this way—which he nevertheless modified profoundly—better served his intention of affirming how God works directly with the individual soul, mingling in the very turning of his consciousness. Bartolommei and Corneille stressed the importance of dreams as vehicles of God's communications, and Milton, following the Bible, relates those that have foretold Samson's mission. But in Bartolommei and Corneille the dreams do not only communicate, they foretell what the play itself will verify—they become devices in the drama as they do not in Milton. In Milton they harmonize with the movement of the speeches in revealing states of mind, and with the climactic speech of the messenger in relating the great event no one else has seen, calling attention to what is still more important as well, what is neither seen nor to be seen, the inwardness of the witnessing of the martyr.

The drama of *Polyeucte*, as Professor Marc Denkinger remarked, is not in the tying and the untying of a knot but in the weaving of strands together, the tying of the knot, and then the locking of it. Like *Samson Agonistes*, it culminates in the perfection of the protagonist's resolution, but when we observe the different means by which Corneille leads us to the admiration of so similar an end I think we may come to an understanding of the special considerations in Milton's mind that led him to modify the traditional tragic structure as he did. What happens to Polyeucte happens because he is tied to others—his friend, his wife, his father-in-law—and as they are caught up in his plans and themselves influence them, his life moves forward as grace would have it move, and the lives of these others come to their completion in the completion of his. Paulina's conversion and the astounding timing of the conversion of Félix are inseparable from what is working to the martyrdom of Polyeucte. And so there is drama because we are witnessing not simply the means of the operation of grace but result after result. In Corneille's play there is the drama that is absent from Milton's, the sequential representation of deeds, and their consequences in still other deeds.

III

The necessities of melodramma

Miss Ellis-Fermor was right, I believe, in making so much of
the fluency of *Samson Agonistes*, but I think Milton's inspiration and the manner in which he ordered his work owe more
to music than Miss Ellis-Fermor had in mind, more to music
and to musical drama in general, and in particular quite
possibly more to Monteverdi's works, or at least to works that
were part of a movement of which he was the most remarkable
spirit.

In addressing the possibility of such a relationship one must
remark first of all on what Mr. D. R. Roberts once studied,
the musical nature of Milton's verse everywhere. As he spoke
of it, he wanted to establish the validity of his 'intuition', that
the music of Milton's verse was achieved in following a
principle Monteverdi also followed, what he called the imita-
tive principle.[39] In support of this insight he offered some
investigations into metrical matters, compared Milton's
rhythms with those of certain madrigals, but, most of all, by
a sensitive commentary on some of Milton's effects he hoped
not so much to offer a proof as to establish the justice of his
insight and praise. He made no reference to Monteverdi's own
critical remarks, although it is in these as it happens that he
might have found a strong reinforcement to his own percep-
tions. For Monteverdi did indeed consider imitation to be the
primary work of the composer, imitation that he thought of in
a Platonic sense, and his special intention for his own music
was that it should be an imitation of the passions of humans.
His language is clear, the doctrine is both consistent and profound, and were that all, one would be sufficiently struck to
observe that Monteverdi was phrasing a critical doctrine in the
precise terms Milton employed in characterizing tragedy. But
the more significant fact is something else. It is not the doctrine
but the achievement that has ever since been taken to be
Monteverdi's glory, the perfecting of a form of expression for
the stage in which human passions might be faithfully and

exquisitely represented. The music and the libretto were joined to this effect, and in this Monteverdi was bringing to completion the first stage in the history of opera.

An understanding of something of what is involved in this may serve to advance the ideas of Mr. Roberts, and also help considerably in the consideration of *Samson Agonistes*. The argument, however, is a long one.

One may commence with the wonderful remark of Angelo Solerti that towards the end of the sixteenth century in Florence a group of humanists and composers, setting out to reconstruct Greek tragedy, discovered opera.

'There were in those days in Florence'—Giovanni Baptista Doni was telling the story—'a certain Giovanni dei Bardi and his friends who used to meet in his house, forming a kind of Academy they called the Camerata. The young noblemen assembled there in order to pass their time decently, in virtuous exercises and learned discourse, and in particular they very frequently discussed matters relating to music, and how to bring back the modes in use in ancient times, so much praised once, and valued, and in these days, and for so many centuries now, quite extinguished.'[40] The account makes it all seem almost casual—it sounds very like the young lords in *Love's Labour's Lost* planning their academy. But among these Florentines were men of learning and accomplishment, and as the years passed some of them produced works that were to become famous.

The problem had two parts—to learn how the Greeks put on their plays and to discover the system of Greek music. For this latter part there was so little to go on that there was very little success in reconstructing music in the ancient manner. With respect to the production of plays, some of the questions concerned how much instrumental music there was to be, and here experiment was possible. For many years music had already accompanied drama on the Italian stage, and there had been musical scenes offered as *intermezzi*. The songs for Poliziano's *Orfeo* were set to music, and when the classical kind of tragedy was reinstituted with *Sophonisba* (in 1514) music accompanied the choruses, which were sung or chanted. There were also other kinds of representations of sacred stories in a somewhat limited dramatic form that also made use of music, and in an early time, according to Doni, the *favola pastorale*, by reason of the kind of thing it was, might be sung entirely.[41] It seems that music most quickly invaded the forms where the classical unities were least called for. But the transformation of works in which music was supplementary into productions in which words, dramatic action, and music were integrally composed depended first of all on one of the chief inventions of the Camerata—compositions for a single voice, either singing or reciting, with an instrumental background. 'From this point on it was a only short step to the linking together of several self-contained songs of this character (monodies) into a poetic and logical whole, and the eldest type of melodrama was complete.'[42]

Sometimes called *musica parlante*, the *recitatif* established styles of vocal composition in which ordered melodies, rhythms, and metres were largely disregarded in favour of an imitation of inflections natural to speech. Syllables were set to music in conformity with accent and inflection without being forced into a regular musical phrase or into a predetermined musical structure. Choruses, too, were homophonic rather than polyphonic.[43]

The aria might still be used for an extended soliloquy, but the *recitatif* served for narrative and dialogue. It served the needs of declamation, expatiation, and comment. The music, in following the sequences of dialogue and chorus, took on the obligation of characterizing situations and actions. In short, the music itself was used to serve the purpose of drama.

To us it now seems that these innovators did not wholly understand the changes to which they were contributing so much, and that they were participating in movements not so purely of a humanist character as they supposed. For one thing, harmony was displacing polyphony and counterpoint in other styles of composition also, and for another a whole new conception of tonality was coming into being. But when all that has been said it is still important to remember that the occasion, at least, of many of the experiments came out of an interest in rediscovering ancient modes, and one of the incentives for the development of monody was the conviction that it had been the preferred form of ancient composers.[44] But whether a discovery or rediscovery, Jacopo Peri devised the art of *recitare cantando*[45] and the way to a new form was prepared. Had he so chosen, Mr. Roberts might have extended his intuition to include this consideration when he referred the music of Milton's verse to a principle of imitation to be defined as Monteverdi did. There is certainly much more in common here than a principle governing the sequences of sound; there is also all that is involved in the initial intent to establish a proper relation between music and drama, and particularly between music and tragic drama.[46]

Peri's *Dafne* was first performed in Florence in 1594 and his *Euridice* was given in 1600. In that same year Giulio Cassini's *Rapimento di Cefalo* was performed in Florence for the marriage of Maria de' Medici and Henry IV, and in 1603 Caccini's *Euridici* was produced, also in Florence.

Monteverdi's first *favola in musica*, the *Orfeo*, was performed in the royal palace in Mantua in 1607 under the auspices of the *Accademia degli Invaghiti*, and the new form achieved its greatest success. One can never explain all the grounds for the perfection of a revolutionary work, but in this instance, at least, one can discover something of what is most significant through Monteverdi's own statement, and in the principles he stressed as the key principles in the composition of musical drama.

Monteverdi spoke insistently of his work as imitation, and as imitation of the passions.[47] In his conception of imitation he is following Plato rather than Aristotle, even though it is drama he has to do with. He does not speak of imitating nature or action so much as he speaks of imitating the passions, and in music and musical drama he is imitating these because, as he sees it, it is the passions of humans that are inherently affecting as such: 'My dear sir, how could I imitate the speech of winds since they do not speak? How could I use them to move the passions! Arianna is affecting because she is a woman, and Orpheus because he is a man, not a wind!'[48]

In accordance with the nature of the *recitatif* Monteverdi regards the words as of primary importance, and the music

must serve them. In this he was in agreement with the
Camerata, that the music imitated the sense of the text not in
imitating the sense of single words but in imitating the sense
as a whole.[49] He possessed an especially fine feeling for the use
of words in drama, as well as in oratorio and cantata and song,
but his peculiar triumph goes beyond this. He evidently composed music of which it was possible to say that it was indeed
a poignant expression of the affections, and that, even apart
from words, it communicates the idea that the life of the passions is the very life of the soul. Passion is for him no longer
merely energy and possession and attack. It is the source of
aspiration and nobility, of what is most divine in human life.
Here, too, music is participating in some of the most profound
reorderings of the Renaissance, concentrating upon the inner
life of man as a thing in itself, and once again it is doing so in
the effort to re-create ancient modes, and, in this instance,
ancient drama.

The fact that it is drama that gave the special occasion to
Monteverdi is evident in another fact here. For the *recitatif*
serves not merely the dramatic as such, it is formal and
elevated in the way appropriate to speech that is to be made
public.[50] It is in this as it were public quality of the language,
and of the music serving it, that the librettist and Monteverdi
achieve their most remarkable effects, for in their opera the
music, as Romain Rolland observed, first came to occupy its
proper domain, it established its possession of the inner life of
man, 'the life of which the declamation, and the recitative
song itself are but pale reflections'.[51]

How profoundly the drama was 'inward', how profoundly
psychological, one may judge from the characterization that
has been made of the libretto of *Arianna*, that it is indeed
Racinian.[52] The completeness of this orientation—in Monteverdi's words, 'ad un sol fine'[53]—is illuminated by his statement that the central mover of the *Orfeo* was a prayer, and
the single mover of the *Arianna* a lament.[54] A prayer and a
lament—matters notably as private as anything can be—and
at the heart of these dramas which take their beginnings as
drama in the fact of declamation, of the *recitatif*.

By whatever means the earlier composers had thought their

compositions were co-ordinated, this doctrine, as he understood it, was what 'bore him along'. He believed that in
imitating the passions he was treating with truth. Peri in the
preface to his *Euridice* had similarly spoken of the merging of
words and music 'according to the affections',[55] but the special
authority of Monteverdi's music is indeed in the display and
the ring of truth, the note of 'the conquest' of the inner life.
It is this that accounts for the power we still feel in his work,
the affections that we recognize as our own—'you are to
believe,' he says, 'that the modern composer constructs his
work upon the foundations of truth'.[56]

The 'lament' and the 'prayer'—if they are, as he said, the
motive power of those first operas—came from the single passion of grief, and its transfiguration. Whatever the elements
of his experience that provided the motive for the tragedy of
Orpheus, by the time of the *Arianna*, in 1608, Monteverdi
knew the further sorrow of the death of his wife. But in both
operas it is precisely the personal weighing of the sorrow that
gives the power and the charm; there is no transmuting of it
of the kind one supposes in Shakespeare when grief for the
death of his son weighs upon him. In a certain respect Monteverdi's is the characteristic Italian way, the character for whom
any song, whether of grief or joy, is, so to speak, natural. The
common observation—that the *Arianna* is the testimony of
Monteverdi's descent into Hell—makes the point superbly.
But so was the *Orfeo*.[57]

It is here, I suppose, that it becomes apt to speak of
Monteverdi's music as baroque, a term that does help characterize what we mean by the 'truth' in his imitation of the
passions, the 'truth' of these *favole in musica*, these *melodrammi*, and especially pointedly since they end, not in
catharsis, but *con lieto fine*, with a happy ending. For it is
here that come into the consideration of *melodrammi* certain
of the most significant elements of tragic theory and most
particularly the consideration of the idea of catharsis, in
works that are composed as imitations of the passions. All
the debates that arose with the development of the pastoral,
tragi-comedy, *tragedie di lieto fine* and *tragedie miste* also
enter here.[58]

The idea of the happy ending in *melodramma* was not always taken as a radical modification of tragic convention if for no other reason than at the beginning *melodramma* was not uniformly characterized as tragedy, even though it may have taken shape as a result of the investigations into the history of the ancient kind. Besides the *favola pastorale* and the *sacra rappresentazione* which had special status, works were entitled *favola in musica, dramma musicale, dramma per musica, opera rappresentata in musica*. The terms *tragedia, tragedia musicale,* and *tragi-comedia* were not generally applied. Monteverdi's *Orfeo* bore the title *favola in musica*. The *Arianna*, however, was a *tragedia*. Both end in prospects —for certain fortunate persons—of glory. Indeed, the joy of the conclusion of the Monteverdi *melodramma* is inherent in the initial intent of the words as founded in truth and in the imitation of the affections—translation, or metamorphosis, into a divinely beautiful life is the outcome to be anticipated in the very course of nature, it appears, given such subjects for imitation and such an idea of the nature of imitation.

In the *Orfeo*, in the place of the terrible ending Poliziano preserved—the killing of Orpheus by the maenads—after Orpheus has forfeited his chance of bringing Euridice back to life on earth, he himself is taken to Olympus by Apollo. This is partly because he is who he is and partly because his love is of the quality it is, and partly it is as a compensation for his loss. Apollo appears at the end in his most glorious guise, the music tells of apotheosis and, in some sense, triumph. Yet in the music as in the story the audience necessarily continues to feel the weight of the suffering, and a continuing pathos, the sense of a sorrow that cannot be put aside. Were it not for the simple beauty of the scene one might not know if it were love or suffering that was being celebrated:

> sopra l'altar del core
> lo spirto acceso in sacrifizio offersi.[59]

However happy the ending the tragic idea remains.

In the *Arianna* there is another happy ending. There, although abandoned by Theseus as he resolves the conflict of love and honour in his affairs, Ariadne herself at the end is married to the god Dionysus. What under other circumstances would have led to a tragic catastrophe here leads to transfiguration, and again the glory of the descent of the god is deepened by the pathos, the compassion we feel for the suffering of the humans and for what of the human has been irretrievably lost—perhaps even sacrificed. The pathos must persist for us, I am sure, even while we are being thrilled by the thought of the removal to Olympus. We are obliged to judge of this from the book—most of the music being lost— but the matter and the quality of the emotion evidently parallel those of the music of the other works.

Towards the end of his life, in the *Incoronazione di Poppea*, Monteverdi reached another perfection, this time in the creation of a secular and historical drama. Mythology plays an extraordinary part in it, but the idea of historicity is very powerful. The goddess Amore protects Poppea from her husband's revenge, and at the end, accompanied by a chorus of *Amori*, she blesses the union with Nero, and assists at the deification of Poppea. And this outrageous event, outrageous and yet as breath-takingly beautiful as the very appearance of Apollo when he comes to take Orpheus to Olympus, retains even here, in the words of the earlier play, the idea of 'l'eterno orrore'.

In musical drama Doni recognized two kinds of tragicomedy: the pastoral, which was almost always about amorous subjects, 'poetic and abstract', and melodic throughout; and the *rappresentazioni spirituali* (like the *Sant' Alessio*) showing the triumph of heavenly love.[60] The different types have their distinctive means and ends, of course, but it is proper to observe in the happy endings of the Monteverdi *drammi* some of the intrinsic qualities and inspirations of both the pastoral and the spiritual plays—the golden beauty and the saintly. The deification of Monteverdi's lovers, the happy ending to his tragedies, are the evidence of the original reordering of tragedy that the very idea of the imitation of the passions requires in the late sixteenth and early seventeenth centuries. And quite as much as in Racine it is the conception of the pastoral perfection that is allowing tragedy to direct itself towards ends that are almost dreamlike in their beauty.

If among the ancients there was anything that approached an emphasis of the kind we know in *melodramma*, I think we should find it in the plays of Euripides, in the poignant lyric direction his prologues often provide, in his treating of surrenders to passion, and in the spectacular use of the *deus ex machina*. But as far as one may come to a just idea of antiquity, it seems that certain primary attitudes of the ancients were so unlike those of the humanists that what is different even from Euripides counts for more than what is like. The humanists and the modern composers were caught up in quite other views of humanity and the human situation, and none, I think, could have entertained so profound a conviction of the power of fate as was almost second nature with the Greeks. The moderns might at times agree with the ancients on the pervasiveness of divine influence, however different the emphasis in their conception of the divine and the demonic, and they might also regard the passions of men as divine and divinely ordered, and yet still they would be far from conceiving of the power of fate to overrule all other divinity. Like Euripides, these dramatists might make human passion the primary object of imitation, but then the essential difference makes itself known: their plays would move inevitably towards tragic effect in the display of what might be ordered or divine within the nature of humanity, and the conflicts of humans with fate or with the gods would never be represented as conflicts with embodied deities. At the end of the *Medea* the divine powers rescue the enchantress, yet this was no act to show how their nature responded to a quality in hers—they acted out of friendship, answering to no necessity other than their inclinations offered. The composers of opera, on the other hand, were deeply rooted in the experience of Christianity and, thanks to the psychology that Christianity had fostered, they will always say that it is from within their own natures that Orfeo and Euridice and Teseo and Arianna and Nerone and Poppea—in this respect not unlike Milton's Samson—learn to treat with the divine. It is from within Arianna's breast that

si fiero stral crudo destin saetta.[61]

In this conception the *deus ex machina* brings rewards and offers a most un-Greek, un-Roman salvation. Out of the urgencies of their natures the characters show not merely the force and beauty of passion but they gain the approbation of the gods—Pluto and Proserpina return Euridice to life, Orpheus is transported to Heaven, and Dionysus takes Ariadne in marriage. In Monteverdi they go to a Heaven where it is not so much virtue as it is love that gains glory for them and the release from strife. And the glory like the destiny had its seeds within the mind. 'And love, the rulership of Amor, emerging, in every disguise of the ancient myth, story, or legend, as the main, if not exclusive, theme of the new music drama came to be the condition of the tragic. Human passions unbridled and ambitions unbound surging to their peak caused suffering, violence, and conflicts which when resolved showed the tragic to be a momentary constellation, and not of lasting continuance.'[62]

The intervention of the gods is beneficent, gracious, the perfection of lovingness, and when it is represented upon the stage we see it embodied in all the radiance and splendour and wonder that the theatre can create. The gods offer their blessings and their love, as if they were themselves what is golden in the love of humans. There is very little of an ancient Fate in these providental interventions, and there is only a little of Christian ideas of Providence and Grace. But that little is probably determining the most significant quality of the happy ending. If the translation does not signify a return to the Earthly Paradise, there is yet about it something of the pastoral innocence. Like that scene of Shakespeare's Delphos, 'the climate delicate, the air most pure'. To match 'l'eterno orrore' there is the idea of the beauty of suffering, and if not of its restorative or redeeming power, the idea of suffering, like the idea of love, as a state so pure that it deserves to be requited by benediction and beatification, so pure that it seems part of the life of the soul in the state of innocence as pastoral poetry conceived of that.

As the story presents it the play ends in blessing a horrible happening, putting aside or buying off the complaints of the suffering. Which is another way of saying that in such a resolu-

tion the idea of justice is obscured because neither the claims of
reason nor of custom are allowed to be heard. It appears that
we are to believe that when it is the passions that are 'the
fundamentals of truth', death will show itself to the most perfectly passionate persons not only as benevolent but as full of
promise.

Just as the very notion of a lament and a prayer keeps
before us the value of what has been lost, or of what is hoped
to be restored, now, or in another life, so these courteous and
solicitous divinities taking the passionate lovers to their world
assure us that what we hope for is what we have already known;
that love is not, as some others in the play have cause to think,
rude, bloody, and fully of blame. It is rather the very paradise
the fortunate lovers are taken to, and indeed what they have
already known as the paradise within.

I think what finally excludes from these operas the revul-
sion that Racine always stirs comes from the dominance of the
sense of the theatrical, the sense that this is all imagined and
contrived and staged not only as part of a fantastic history, but
with the kind of exaggeration, the heightening and amplify-
ing, that is required for entertaining a large public. The
spectacular character of the presentation both simplifies and
falsifies the urgency and power of the passions we are being
brought to admire, and as Busenello and Dryden both say,
love is to be admired precisely because it is a painted fire.

These plays reach their completion not in the effecting of
catharsis, but in the display of beauty and of the divinity even
within suffering, and in the conclusion to the prayer and the
lament in the evocation of the divine consolation.

Such a conclusion deprives the audience of the catharsis
tragedy effects, and instead it leaves us with solace and even
happiness, relief at being brought back from the edge of the
most awful fear and the most painful sympathy, relief, too,
from being forced to purgation. But above all there is the
pleasure of contemplating a power so triumphant within the
compass of love that in the midst of betrayal and subversion it
can still show itself golden and idyllic, beautiful beyond the
ordinary consciousness of mortal existence. As Nerone sings to
Poppea—

Per capirti ne' gli occhi
il Sol s'impiccioli,
per albergarti in seno
l'alba dal Ciel parti,
e per farti sovrana a donne, e a Dee,
Giove nel tuo bel volto
stillo le stelle, e consumò l'Idee.

(Lines 1554–60)

Love has escaped the world of violence—its enemies are scattered to the remotest parts of the world. The lovers themselves, with the blessings of the gods, are free from the consequences of their own acts. Tyrants and murderers, they are nevertheless rewarded with felicity. The plays become imitations not of action in its effects, as tragedy conceives the effects of action to be, but imitations of passions and alliances that by their own urgency are allowed to receive benediction.

A considerable part of the power of *melodramma* depends on the use of subjects from pagan mythology and secular history. The appeal of the psychology is secular even while it is the secular that it takes to be credited with unearthly excellence. The exclusion of the specifically Christian and the Biblical and the hagiographic derives in part no doubt from an obligation to the original intent, to renew the tragedy of antiquity, using ancient stories and legends, and this would also have been consonant to so much of the character of humanism as it attempted to re-establish the honour of ancient history. However much of necessity the ancient values must suffer from translation into the language of Christian culture, the humanists, and the composers, would continue their explorations of the pagan and secular. And in a certain way their art at least would gain in poignancy and pathos—not only in Monteverdi is the grief of Orpheus the more pathetic for the absence of the Christian consolation.

But composers also made works from Christian material—

out of the Bible and the lives of the saints, and out of the tradition of medieval allegory. It is an extraordinary fact that what we call opera would at this time so nearly exclusively take subjects from pagan antiquity, and that the Christian and Biblical subjects would so generally provide the subjects for oratorios and cantatas. At first glance the ancient crux would seem to suggest the answer—that a Christian tragedy might be a contradiction in terms, and that *melodramma*, in aspiring to tragedy, avoided the dilemma. There is possibly something to this. It is also possible that the requirements of another kind of musical progression better suit this other material—not merely an un-tragic but an un-dramatic progression. Narrative music, as the oratorio surely is in its origins, and as the cantata may be, certainly allowed legends and biography to be related in their historic ordering. And there is still another factor— and this all but eludes comment. It is to be recognized in the observation that the *melodramma* is Florentine, the oratorio Roman; the music of the one is 'representative', of the other 'descriptive'.[63]

In the history of music the forms managed to keep their distance, but when they do approach each other, what they lose as what they gain is evident. Arcangelo Spagna in speaking of his oratorio *Debora* (1656) called it 'un perfetto Melodramma spirituale'.[64] He had dropped the formal introductory narrative characteristic of early oratorios, and this in part justified his use of the term *melodramma*. All the same the epithet 'spirituale' shows that a modification is to be understood. Or again, as has been said of the famous *Jephte* of Giacomo Carissimi, 'the Latin oratorio became a *melodramma*, but it lost its religious character'.[65]

The oratorio and the *sacra rappresentazione*—as in the *Rappresentazione di Anima et di Corpo*—were formed by an idea and an argument that moved towards its conclusion in a sanctification. The *San Alessio* is a *sacra rappresentazione*, but Romain Rolland and others have called it an oratorio in the tradition of the *Anima et Corpo*. In such works the allegorical and the hagiographical count for more than plot; the interest is in the facts, in the succession of significant moments, whether in narrative or argument, and in the summation which is also the consummation. In the ordering of the matter the idea of the dramatic unities, and most especially the idea of unity of action, loses importance in the face of the main consideration—to establish the conviction of the truth of what is being represented, truth according to Scripture and the known legends, but also to establish the conviction of spiritual and psychological verisimilitude—in short, all that will support the conviction of faith. In the first half of the seventeenth century the idea of psychological truth would get a fuller play in *melodramma* than in oratorio, and this was made possible in part through the use of monody. Vincenzo Galileo had foreseen this and he was right. But it would also be, I should think, because *melodramma* continued to aspire, as these other forms did not, to comprehend within itself the substance of tragedy.

Milton, too, was to make his tragic poem an imitation of passions; he, too, was to conduct his work towards a *lieto fine*. His purpose was also to support the teaching of Scripture and even to tell of the making of a saint. For reasons very much like those confining the range of the oratorio and the cantata the idea of the dramatic in *Samson Agonistes* as well as the idea of the tragic catharsis was to be narrowly restrained.

IV

Samson Agonistes *and the differing means of tragical effects*

It seems to me that *Samson Agonistes* is in the line of drama that leads to Racine—it presents 'the wily suttleties and refluxes of mans thoughts from within'.[66] In the searching out of Samson's mind, in his testing, in his raging, in the way in which he comes to redirect himself, the play proceeds as a discovery of his affections and the movements of his mind. As an imitation of what Samson was enduring and learning, and in making this the subject of the work, Milton was not only diverging from the idea of tragic drama Aristotle outlined, he was following another, the line the writers of *melodramma* were also following, although of course in not quite the same way. Racine was also to imitate the ancients and most often independently of the support of musical composition, but his exploitation of psychology was to be devised to hold the stage. Milton's poem was for the reader.

I think *declamation* as a term helps characterize the verse of *Samson Agonistes*. It helps describe its tone, its use in the progression of argument, and in what else determines why one speech is to follow another. Most often these are speeches that do not rise out of the occasions the dialogue of drama depends on, out of the innumerable complexities present to the minds of persons confronting each other in a dramatic situation, where the surface concerns are given expression first and the underlying concerns express themselves through indirection or in the acting. Here each person speaks as if his first need is to speak for himself, and only secondarily for the sake of the other. It is partly dialogue but predominantly a setting up of contrasts. Samson speaks usually only in order to say what he has to say. The others speak most often in opposition, urging or cajoling or contradicting. But even here the point in the sequence is not to conclude an argument or to lead to action or to resolve conflict—the point is to expatiate, to display the full complexities of the human situation as it is and not to lead us through suspense to the anticipation of events.

The progression is somewhat that of the *stile concertante* in the developing opera. One argument, drawing forth another, may receive an answer, but the final purpose of any speech or any sequence is, not to justify, but to reveal 'the suttleties and refluxes'. It is as it were only incidentally that each person addresses himself to another, his primary note is of one saying what he is willing that God, or the people of his religion, should hear him say. It is the note of those who wish to be heard by the true God, only none knows enough of his own truth to know what he should say that would please Him.

As such it is the manner of those who sing. The word *declamation* is also useful here because it helps establish what I take it this play shares with dramatic works composed as *drammi per musica* where the terms are *recitatif* and *recitare cantando.* Like everything of Milton's the verse of *Samson Agonistes* is marvellously musical, but no more to be set to music than it is to be uttered by actors upon a stage. *Samson Agonistes* is offered as a *tour de force*, no matter what one determines to be its genre. But it is also a success, a work of such beauty and fineness that one must believe that here at least words may speak for the passions as perfectly as song or melody or harmony. I suppose that there are several places that are less than superbly musical in this sense—there are times when one may even say this of Verdi—but there are enough scenes where the beauty of the language is enough to assure the success of the whole—the coherence and fluidity of its movement, sound and feeling and thought articulated perfectly, the ascent to the climax, and the resolution in the most exquisite and serene of consolations.

> Blest pair of *Sirens*, pledges of Heav'ns joy,
> Sphear-born harmonious Sisters, Voice, and Verse,
> Wed your divine sounds, and mixt power employ.
> (*At a Solemn Musick*, lines 1–3)

> Denique quid vocis modulamen inane iuvabit,
> Verborum sensusque vacans, numerique loquacis?
> (*Ad Patrem*, lines 50–51)[67]

The verse of Racine, as perfect in its music as the French language has ever permitted, also serves dramatic representation and the presentation of psychology with wonderful felicity. And the contrast of this perfection and subtlety with Milton's does more, I think, to help establish the unique character of Milton's classicism than any other comparison. Racine's characters are carried along by their concerns and passions, and in their appearance before us we are as absorbed as in anything else by what it is they are able to make of their condition. Racine has them translate their feelings, for themselves as much as for us, into the language of politeness, of social consideration, of respect for the community of noblemen. The poetry is in the translation of passion into formality, in the translation of the mere movements of the animal into words that our minds can certify as proper and just. The language of passion has been transformed into the language of the conventional and the judgements of society. In the poetry of Racine we are able to acknowledge both the facts, and the fact of translation.

The words of the characters of Milton's play—when they are under stress chiefly, of course—are utterances in which it seems that speech and judgement have come to simultaneous birth, and there is no need for translation—as if judgement were innate in sensibility and sensibility were one with judgement. Nothing has been translated. This is the lyrical immediacy of a poet who, in Macduff's words, feels as a man. The characters of Racine are first animals at bay, then they remind themselves as they remind us that they are also men and women:

> Je le vis, je rougis, je pâlis à sa vue;
> Un trouble s'éleva dans mon âme éperdue;
> Mes yeux ne vivaient plus, je ne pouvais parler,
> Je sentis tout mon corps et transir et brûler.

> (*Phèdre*, I, iii)

And Samson:
> O that torment should not be confin'd
> To the bodies wounds and sores
> With maladies innumerable
> In heart, head, brest, and reins;
> But must secret passage find
> To th'inmost mind.

> (606–611)

It is instructive to notice the idea of intrusion into a world where Samson will be overheard that Milton exploits in introducing his play with those words that come straight from the heart, without reflection, without censoring, the perfection of the fatigue of a spirit:

A little onward—

The characteristic note of the opening of the classical tragedies approximates the note of proclamations, before a temple or before the king's palace. The contrast with the opening of Milton's play could hardly be greater. The chorus utters the first words of *The Suppliants*—

May Zeus, who guardeth suppliants, of his grace look upon
our company that took ship and put to sea. . . . (*Smyth*)

Athena speaks the first words of the *Ajax*:

> Son of Laertes, ever on the prowl
> To seize some coign of vantage 'gainst thy foes,
> Now at the tent of Ajax by the ships,
> Where he is posted on the flank, I see thee. . . .
>
> (F. Storr)

Euripides commences the *Iphigenia in Tauris* almost like a
public declaration, majestic, certainly, royal, the opposite of
the simply human:

> Child of the man of torment and of pride
> Tantalid Pelops bore a royal bride
> On flying steeds from Pisa. Thence did spring
> Atreus. . . .
>
> (G. Murray)

Sophonisba speaks the prologue in Trissino's play, and she
commences:

> Lassa, dove poss'io voltar la lingua,
> Se non la 've la spinge il mio pensiero?
> Che giorno, e notte sempre mi molesta,
> E come posso disfogar alquanto
> Questo grave dolor, che 'l cuor m'ingombra,
> Se non manifestando i miei martiri?
> I quali ad un ad un voglio narrarti.

In Giustiniano's *Jephte* (1583) an angel speaks the prologue,
but the first scene begins with an exclamation not unlike that
which begins Trissino's:

> Ahi, di nuoua paura il cor me trema,
> Et l'animo pauenta, & nella gola
> Fissa è la uoce, ne dar può la lingua
> A le parole il solita camino.

Nor do I think English tragedy—certainly not Shakespeare's
—ever begins like Milton's, at the heart of the matter.

As for the great French heroic drama, everywhere you turn the speeches have the most obvious character, as dramatic speech, not lyric—Corneille's *Sophonisbe* begins:

Madame, il était temps qu'il nous vînt du secours;

and his *Attila*—

Ils ne sont pas venus, nos deux rois?

The stamp of the interchange between persons in the anticipation of action is there from the beginning. It is much the same in Racine. Hippolyte speaks the first words in *Phèdre*—

Le dessin en est pris: je pars, cher Théramène . . .

And *Esther* commences with words of the most intimate note of conversation—

Est-ce toi, chère Élise? O jour trois fois heureux!

In the books of the early operas, however, one may observe what is to be expected, there is no such tense an introduction into a world where forces are to oppose each other with the concentration of drama; the words are quieter, more self-absorbed, one senses the isolation the words should encourage a singer to cultivate as he comes upon a stage to sing and to hold us with the beauty and charm of the song.

A personification, La Musica, sings the prologue to *La Favola d'Orfeo* that Alessandro Striggio composed for Monteverdi. She begins,

Dal mio Permesso amato a voi ne vegno,
incliti Eroi, sangue gentil di Regi,
di cui la Fama eccelsi pregi,
ne giunge al ver perch'è tropp'alto il segno.

When the prologue ends a shepherd sings:

In questo lieto e fortunato giorno
c'ha posto fine a gli amorosi affanni
del nostro Semideo, cantiam, pastori,
con si soavi accenti
che sien degni d'Orfeo nostri concenti.

Of the operas of the period I have seen the one that begins most nearly in the manner of *Samson Agonistes* is Busenello's

Incoronazione di Poppea. After the prologue, Ottone, whose wife has become the mistress of Nerone, although he does not know this, appears upon the scene before the palace where two of the guards of Nerone are sleeping.

> E pure io torno qui, qual linea a centro,
> qual foco a sfera, e qual ruscello al mare.
> e se ben luce alcuna non m'appare,
> ahi, so ben io, che sta il mio Sol qui dentro.
> Caro tetto amoroso,
> albergo di mia vita, e del mio bene,
> il passo, e 'l core ad inchinarti viene.

This is *recitare cantando* certainly.

The point I mean these comparisons to help make is that the first words of *Samson Agonistes* begin as they would if an actor were to appear on stage and to introduce himself to us singing, and that the manner of his words and what they point to is a play to proceed as *melodramma* does. The responses that will be made, after the first singing, will be as near as may be the responses of song to song.

If instead of likening *Samson Agonistes* to *melodramma* one should compare it to oratorio or cantata, one would do this in order to argue an even greater neglect of the uses of suspense, and in order to emphasize the poem more as a continuing celebration than as a representation. One should not go so far, I think, but the fundamental point that will lead us to the most appropriate likeness is that the deficiency of the poem as drama is commanded by the perfection of the religiousness of the play, by the tyranny of the particular faith it expresses. It is as un-dramatic as it is un-tragic because it is so much an imitation of the passions and of the working of grace, grace mingling with them to transform them. The action of grace is to be known, not seen; the dimensions of its world are unconfined; and its workings are to be made known to an audience not in observing what takes place upon a stage, or in the resolution of persons in conflict with each other, but through certifying the impression of the unseen. It does this partly in moving the affections and partly through narration. To effect such an end the powers inherent in drama as drama must be restrained. In stirring the passions it will be sufficient if the requirements of decorum and verisimilitude are honoured.

The fulfilment of expectation in Monteverdi is characteristically in the ending in glory. The splendour of that is brought to the very scene by the gods themselves, putting an end to all the episodes of grief and suffering and perfidy, and glory is the conclusion in every sense, because we have come to recognize that the suffering we have been witnessing and moved by is a preparation for it. The souls of Orfeo and Arianna and Poppea are ready for it, prepared as athletes are in going forth to battle, anointed and expectant. All that has happened has shown them worthy, they have been faithful, and their passions have grown in strength. And so the gods in approbation, or even as it were enchanted, determine to bless them, or beatify.

Samson's story, too, belongs among the lives of the saints and the preparation for his salvation is made as preparations for Monteverdi's heroes and heroines are, through the divinity that works in vanity and rage and ambition and lust and the very defiance of God, and even in disbelief and betrayal. There is Providence in the fall of a sparrow, and in the fall of Samson and, however variously, in the fall of Orfeo and Arianna and Poppea.

The most obvious difference in the ordering of these dramas from Milton's appears in the greater number of characters, in the more complicated interchanges between them, in the changes of scene, in the reliance on spectacle, and, of course, in progressing through nothing like a single action. More pointedly also, the oppositions within the scenes and the successions of scene are more obviously directed towards playing up to the songs of the central characters, although there are times in Milton's play, as happens also among the ancients, when much seems to be leading up to an especially powerful chorus. But in Monteverdi, as perhaps must always be true in works where so much is lavished upon the beauty of the voice of the singer, the laments and prayers and hymns of the central figures are as important to the ordering of the events as they are to the central inspiration. So much of the whole performance serves to fill out the singing of the main figure, and so much of the drama consists in discovering the passage by which he or she is to pass from happiness to defeat and to apotheosis. The ordering of these matters is substantially like Milton's, but on the other hand there is, I think, no utterance of Samson's that is quite the apex of the play as Arianna's lament or Orfeo's prayer. Milton's and Monteverdi's methods are much more like in the use of central figures who are asked to do so little. Neither Orfeo or Arianna or Poppea does anything. Pluto and Proserpina take action, as do Teseo and Nerone, but the figures who are to be saved do almost nothing— they are prey, passive, captive, and then liberated.

Where the imitators of classical tragedy like Trissino chiefly differed from the successors to the Camerata was in the closeness with which they felt bound to Aristotle. They felt deeply the need to observe the unities, although even at the beginning, in *Sophonisba* itself, they were not all observed. The unities nevertheless represented a compelling ideal, as important as the principles of verisimilitude and decorum in asserting their authority. The writing of *melodramma* commenced with a similar respect for ancient theory, but by 1616—that is, in less than two decades—the librettists had broken free from dependence upon any of them.[68] Milton's obvious exploitation of the concentrated effects that the unities serve is largely in contrast with the later practice of *melodramma*. *L'Arianna* in the earlier period of the development of the form did make effective use of the unities of action and time and evidently for reasons very like those that appealed to Milton and Racine. The entire action takes place very shortly before the catastrophe, there is a minimum of distraction, and the movement of the work proceeds in simple coherence. But as time passed the writers of *melodramma* judged that what they were working for, the culmination of beauty in the sequences of musical drama, were as well or better effected through composition arranged according to other orders than those to be determined by the sequences required in a unified action. For indeed it was not action that chiefly concerned them, and the considerations relevant to a requirement for unity of action are not relevant to a work that is presented as primarily an imitation of the passions.

Milton, doing without music as well as foregoing the idea of production in a theatre, may have chosen to observe the unities of time and place if for no other reason than that the episode from sacred history he was representing involved so few persons. And since indeed the matter is an episode rather than a plot, simplicity belonged to its very nature and there was required little of that complex manipulation of the relations of messengers, the bringing forth of characters out of the distant past, and the meshing of coincidence that are involved in the contrivance of unity for a truly dramatic action. At any rate, his work was to proceed not as a sequence of events but of encounters. His purpose was to effect a climax through the steady intensification of the meaning of Samson's burden and suffering, in the expression of what he is feeling, in all the reflection to be brought to bear upon that, and in the gradual bringing into our understanding, as the pathos and significance of Samson's state becomes more and more embracing, that what we are present at is the revelation of the working of grace in the very concourse of the passions. His means is the marriage of sound and sense, sustained and developed by argument as that took its occasion in the shiftings and settlings of passion. And the conclusion, the climax, is not in the act of pulling down the pillars, nor in the account of it, but rather in the discovery of the formalities of consolation and benediction, in the most perfect beauty of speech and through that beauty in the communication of the faith that speaks of blessedness.[69]

Professor Schrade has concluded that tragic catharsis is not to be expected of musical drama: 'We take compassion as a guide in the labyrinth of passions, and if we are unwilling to concede that insight into the mysteries of the passionate nature of man matches the Aristotelian catharsis, we nevertheless must admit that the spontaneous revelation of human nature conveys a blissfulness at least congenial to the awful intelligence of tragedy.'[70] A similar qualification must be provided, I believe, for *Samson Agonistes*. As a progressive representation, ending in the relation of a violent action and comments on it, and that action made possible by a succession of changes in Samson's disposition, and through mysterious impulsion, the play by its nature cannot attain effects achieved through the contemplation of events. At the end the audience feels that it has been freed in imagination from a great trouble, anxiety has been allayed, terror has subsided in a decent and gratifying awe. The famous eulogy characterizes perfectly the state of our feelings in the ending of it:

Nothing is here for tears.

This is the formula of funeral benediction rather than of the terrible state of the purged.

It is Tasso, I think, who hits upon the significant point. Aristotle had said that a tragic plot should be resolved from within the very action it was imitating, and that it was a defect to bring about a solution through an external device. Tasso, however, believed that the *deus ex machina* could be allowed in the solution because he believed that under certain circumstances the same action can be both marvellous and true, most especially since Christians had been brought up from earliest childhood to just such an acceptance. 'But this method of joining the true with the marvellous is not open to those poems in which the deities of the pagans are introduced.'[71] In short, a poet's obligation to truth and versimilitude could not permit the intrusion of the false in the solution of tragedy.

But there is here a distinction to be made that is not so simple as one in which the pagan deities are made equivalent to untruth and Christian deity to truth. Euripides, too, employed the *deus ex machina*, and for the modern audience at least the question has to do not so much with the actuality of the pagan deities as with the nature of their intercession, and whether, in the light of the need for verisimilitude, the matters at issue in the play are being obscured.

In the *Iphigenia in Aulis* as in the *Iphigenia in Tauris* deity intervenes to save those it has loved from death. But the salvation is not to immortality, nor to the fulfilment of the long-lasting purposes of the Omnipotent. The audience marvels, but it is not being asked to consider any system of divine rewards and punishments. The powers-that-be befriend those they love, otherwise the occasions for wrong and suffering continue as before.

For the audience there is relief and awe and joy, but, I think, nothing like reconciliation or resignation or the peace that would come through the thought that we too might be included in the amnesty. For a little the claims of pity and terror have been accompanied by a vision that is truly wonderful. And that is all. The tragedy is forestalled, not transcended.

The triumph and glory with which Monteverdi ends is also mixedly happy—happiness for Orfeo's happiness, relief that he has been rescued from pain. But as it is with Euripides, where we know that the fates and the furies and all evil are only for the time unheard from, so in the world of Monteverdi, in the world of the happiness of love there is even at the end the reminder of the persistence of the rage:

> Evohè liete e ridenti
> te lodiam, padre Leneo,
> or ch'abbiam colmo il core
> del tuo divin furore.

Like the composers of *melodramma* who were also more committed to the imitation of passion than of action, Milton differed from them, it appears, in holding that it was still the tragic catharsis his work was to effect. Instead of matching deed with deed, violence with violence, he matches suffering with the acceptance of suffering. And then, at a certain point, deity intervenes to end the suffering and reward the *Agonistes*. The reward is death, and it is also salvation. Because the reward is according to nature and is represented as wholly faithful to the idea of verisimilitude—as Tasso would have it—it may be thought not to diminish the requirements for catharsis. And because the salvation achieved is the salvation of the true God, the marvellous being true, it does not lesson, it might even intensify the catharsis, since the fears that tempt and taunt the Christian are the worst of all.

And there is something else. For the *deus ex machina* of this play is the *deus ex machina* of Scripture and of history. He is not seen in the play. He performs nothing that is to be seen. He performs from within, like some wonderful unseen spirit governing the very passages of the blood and mind. The God who acts from without acts from within. As Professor Woodhouse said, *Samson Agonistes* ends 'in something that is more like triumph than mere relief: death is indeed relief—but death is swallowed up in victory'. In Samson's religious experience, and, hopefully, in the experience of the play, is 'the silent operation of grace'.[72]

V

The manner of the progress of Samson Agonistes

When Milton writes of imitating the passions and allaying fear and pity, he writes with his characteristic piety. He is always striving 'to know God aright', and for him the catharsis of tragedy may also serve that purpose. When Monteverdi writes of imitation it is out of as serious a dedication, but towards a somewhat different end. He is closer to Tasso than to Michelangelo, and while he shares with Milton complete respect for clarity and objectivity and philosophy, for magic and drama and for the classical manner, he can feel at rest in the presence of the simply human, and the passions of Euridice and Orfeo and Arianna shine in the glory they possess of themselves. Only he takes more joy within the physical representation of the divine.

The passions in *Samson Agonistes* are most especially exhaustion, shame, reproach, resentment, vainglory, lust, hate, contempt, fear, arrogance, humility, pity, and dedication. They are made known to us in the conduct of a war between nations and priests. Presiding invisibly over the warring, as definitively as the sky itself, is Jehovah. The whole scene is given meaning by the sense of the elevated, divine presence, and if there is no *deus ex machina* of the conventional kind, yet the whole of the representation is directed to show how finally God will work in some other than an arbitrary way.

Although a play *con lieto fine*, the resolution is not to be so obviously staged as *The Winter's Tale*, where the tenderest aspiration finds the most joyous satisfaction; or in so spectacular a way as in the *Orfeo*, where Apollo himself appears to astonish us with his splendour. The ending of this play lacks the beauty the stage can give, but it nevertheless moves us greatly, with the sense of wonder and belief, for in what we learn here God is powerfully acknowledged and His presence is stunningly felt even though He acts as it were invisibly, and this, too, judged to be true only on reflection, after the event.

In the drama of the century war and love provided the main subjects for the theatre, but there is little enough of love here. It gets a hearing from time to time, and it has contributed to Samson's downfall, but it is neither the impelling cause nor a continuing concern. Treachery on one side and folly on the other brought him down, and avarice or ambition could have served quite as well as love or lust the particular needs of this story. It is true that for the poetry, and for the imagined stage, there is an attractive lavishness in the portrayal of Dalila—in the excellent phrase, 'stylo lussurians theatrali', and the idea of the power and intricacy of sensuality certainly enriches the quarrel. Still, there is nothing in the character of Samson's love as love that is particularly important in contributing to his defeat. This is not Adam's radical uxoriousness. Nor is it, as far as I can tell, the conflict of love with religion so much as weakness that brings him down, a deficiency of understanding that undermines his dedication. He does not well understand what it means to have been chosen by God, and he is deficient in allegiance and obedience. He regains his strength not through controlling or overpowering love but in learning to trust.

As the ideas of service and betrayal come to be defined in the progression of scenes, it is interesting to observe that the theme grows more embracing without the aid of the philosophizing that grows into so many branches in *Comus* and *Lycidas* and *Paradise Lost*. There is no Platonism. There are no explorations of the nature of Fate. In this work the imitation of the passions signifies also the exclusion of ratiocination from the substance of the work. It is not the interest of philosophy that will finally dominate our attention but a rather simpler kind of wonder finally, as we come to see that the play is showing an example of God's working. The play offers an example, and the proof, of God's goodness, and the aim is edification, not simply in observing episodes in the life of a saint but in observing the way of life of one who finally justifies his election by God for God's service. Everything leads not to some such attention as we pay to reasoning in the Epilogue to *Comus*, but to imagining that we are seeing what is happening at the end, in contemplating and reflecting upon an act we imagine we are seeing. We are being led to contemplate a theatrical image as if it were an historical event.

From a slightly different point of view we may say that everything leads to the device at the end, as a theatrical device, whose effect depends in part upon our recognition of it as a contrivance. Samson will pull down the pillars out of our sight, and so we are able to imagine the extent of the destruction as beyond what could appear upon a stage. And we value the contrivance as such because it allows us to think with less distraction upon the significance and consequences of this final effort, and especially since there is something mysterious about it.

Then there is the subsidiary theatrical device which is at least as important here: the account of the event by a messenger allows for the other effect that is unique to drama, establishing the relevance of that which happens away from the stage to that which we actually can see, and by extension relating the life the play tells of to life outside the theatre. Those on the stage hearing of the event are at that moment in the same position as the audience; both are learning what each most wants to learn, and so, at the ending moment of the play, are one in sharing the concern and enlightenment and comfort of the resolution. Manoa and the Chorus and ourselves become one, one imaginary onlooker at the great and wonderful exertion. The events of the play thus seem to merge with the life we ourselves are living. The device is worthy of Bernini.

In substituting a dramatic form for the narrative of the Book of Judges, Milton apparently meant to give the story another kind of power, whether in making it more instructive

or more moving. Excluding a narrator, he could concentrate on
the envisioning of the scene and on the confinement of the
action in ways that make for drama. His first step, then, was to
transform the narrative in order to gain for the story and the
doctrine another kind of acceptance than is to be effected by the
narration even of sacred history. He sacrifices the authority of
the sacrosanct for the charm of dramatic representation. But it is
not only through drama as such, but through drama as a form
of poetry that he means to implant in the reader the conviction
of the miraculous nature of the changes in Samson's mind—our
intuition of the nature of the changes in his thought and that
God works with them according to the very nature of Samson's
mind. The effort, in short, is the typical humanist undertaking,
bringing the whole of human experience into the realm of
understanding.

But because this has been made into a poem with the most
complex articulation, we are led to think of what is before us as
not merely intelligible but as moving and beautiful. From the
first words all Milton's art is giving beauty to the sound of the
suffering man. In his suffering and his indignity this rather
ordinary giant—no Caesar, no Coriolanus—comes to gain the
kind of beauty Brunelleschi and many others have given to a
crucified body, The beauty, as always in such works in the
Renaissance, as it is, too, in Shakespeare's embodying of Lear,
is not only in the grandeur of the conception, or in the music
of the verse, it is in the very idea of the beauty suffering
confers when the sufferer is strong enough not to fight it.
And in Milton at least the dignity is partly Samson's and partly
God's—in Samson's willingness to subordinate his suffering to
patience, and in God's indeflectible determination to make
use of this wretched man.

Such, then, as I see it, are some of the effects Milton gains
in transferring the Scriptural story to the imagined theatre.
There are other effects as well, and other means Milton uses
as an artist, and there is no need to try to exhaust them. But
in the effort to establish the character of *Samson Agonistes* by
comparing it most especially with musical dramas like those of
Monteverdi, it may be useful to mention one other matter. In

the nature of things, when making this into a dramatic rather than a narrative poem, Milton was obliged to set a certain tone for the words, the tone of a writer who is thinking of his audience as a public gathering rather than as a solitary reader. The reader of a narrative naturally takes the story to himself, into his own silence, as if it were somehow meant only for him, and the tone of the words is expected to be quiet and even private. But the reader, to say nothing of the spectator of a drama, loses sight of his peculiarly intimate interests, the sort he knows when he identifies himself with a narrator. He subordinates the lyric identification to what he partly recognizes as public concern. And so, with the words:

A little further on—

Milton strikes the note of general charity along with the note of poignancy. He has gone beyond the manner of *Lycidas* where he sets the tone of objectivity, considering even himself as a remote person. Here the tone is that of one who is identified sympathetically with a figure whose renewal is taking place in the public view.

The marvel is that the sense of beauty, so winning and so conducive to the notion that sense and sentiment are uniquely personal, has become public and is none the less affecting. But perhaps this is precisely the difference between the lyric expression of the seventeenth century and our own; and perhaps it is also characteristic of the manner of the classicizing opera.

In the first speech Samson is setting the scene. If this is not the stage of a theatre it is imagined as such: he seems to point— 'yonder bank—there am I wont to sit'. This evident staginess we accept as no distraction because it fits with Samson's blindness, and it also serves the immediate situation of the play in which a blind man is groping his way to take a place upon the stage where we can see him well.

As he goes on he speaks of himself with a detachment that compounds the irony with which he is continuing to speak in accordance with the conventions of the stage. He seems to be saying: this is the place in which you, the audience, are to see

this person, me, take my place. And he continues in this
noticeably odd manner, speaking of himself in the third person:

> Why was my breeding order'd and prescrib'd
> As of a person separate to God . . .
> Ask for this great Deliverer now . . .
>
> (30–40)

When he speaks of himself in the first person—the mingling of
first and third is continuous—he seems to want to distinguish,
for himself and for us, between what he is and what he was. It
is partly because, in speaking of himself in the past, he feels so
painfully how different he now is, and it is partly because in
speaking of himself in the present, he is speaking of someone
he is not quite used to, some new person who is a stranger to
him:

> But peace, I must not quarrel with the will
> Of highest dispensation . . .
>
> (60–61)

He is also speaking as if he were looking at himself from a
distance, and from a height:

> Light the prime work of God to me is extinct,
> And all her various objects of delight
> Annull'd, which might in part my grief have eas'd,
> Inferiour to the vilest now become
> Of man or worm . . .
>
> (70–74)

The conventions of monologue and soliloquy in part account
for the artifices:

> But who are these? for with joint pace I hear
> The tread of many feet stearing this way—
>
> (110–111)

and they are of a piece with Samson's staging of himself, his
staging of his history, and his staging of his grief. In the
directions he is providing, in the mingling of tenses, in the
hinting of the presence of others, he is expressing the fundamental structure both of the irony and of the beauty of the

play—this man who speaks the wholly unrestricted truth is a man who has lost not only his physical bearings but his inner direction. His truth is that he has lost touch with the saving truth.

This irony, if that is the proper word for it, comprehends the idea of the entire production as the drama we are to imagine—the mingling of the present with the past, the utterance of truths that are partly the evident truths of history and psychology and partly mysterious, the portrayal of blindness that is but a shadow of real blindness, and suffering graced with beauty.

I think it is in part Milton's adaptation of the manner of the *recitatif* in *melodramma* that is working with his religious purpose to extend and complicate the irony, and in what distinguishes the effect of his play from the ancient tragedies. What happens in musical drama happens in developing the import of the preceding events according to a sequence independent of causal linking to them. What happens in tragedy happens because it has to.

What happens in musical drama happens in the way of contrast or variation or recapitulation—it fills out. Doing this, each declamation mingles the past with the present in such a way that what is most immediate is often half descriptive. What happens in tragedy happens because force is being brought to bear, and the audience is held by the anticipation of the event, for before our eyes something is happening that is pregnant with the future, something is forcing someone to an act. In musical drama all actions are ways of repeating something, and we look to the future only as that in which the hindrances to the consequences of the past have been removed.

The end of *Samson Agonistes* holds us with the wonder at what has been working in Samson to bring this final deed about. For the future we are given hope. Yet it has all been arranged for the sake of our knowledge, the catharsis is proposed as a service to religion, we are being given hope because we are being moved to the strengthening of faith, in the acceptance of God's ways and in rejoicing in them.

In *Samson Agonistes* something is leading towards a single deed, and this comes about without anyone forcing anything, nor indeed do we see, or understand, what is leading towards it. After a while—but only towards the end—there is anticipation, but even this is moderated by the more important sense, assurance. For we are being prepared to understand that there is need neither for suspense nor for surprise at the event we are to learn of. The substance of faith, the substantial interest of the development in the progression of the speeches, continues to disperse the possibility of the dramatic. And the catharsis is the purification of the passions of a man in his suffering, and who in the end has surrendered himself not to necessity but to the mysterious God. His single act in the play derives from no rationally intelligible cause. And we have been brought, as we see that Samson has, to rest in admiration and in love.

NOTES

[1] From the biographical account of his nephew, Edward Phillips, printed as a preface to *Letters of State, Written by Mr. John Milton*, London, 1694 (*The Life Records of John Milton*, edited by J. M. French, Vol. 1, New Brunswick, 1949, p. 415).

[2] The title-page of the 1671 edition reads:

> *Samson Agonistes*
> A Dramatic Poem
> *Aristot. Poet. Cap.* 6
>
> Τραγωδία μίμησις πράξεως σπουδαίας, etc.
> *Tragœdia est imitatio actionis seriæ*, etc. *Per misericordiam et metum perficiens talium affectuum lustrationem.*

The title of the preface is: 'Of that Sort of Dramatic Poem Which is call'd Tragedy.' I suppose that Milton is careful to use the phrase 'dramatic poem' for the very reason that he is willing in the preface itself to allow the word tragedy to be applied to the Book of Revelations—for however one might divide that into acts, even less than his own poem was it intended for the stage.

In the analysis that follows Milton interprets catharsis in the therapeutic sense, an interpretation he could have taken from Italian criticism of the previous century. I have not discovered, however, that in the criticism of ancient tragedy the Italian critics ever spoke of the imitation of the passions as Milton did. Trissino in the preface to *Sophonisba* in 1514, in the play that was to initiate the renewal of classical tragedy, spoke of the business of such plays as the imitation through the means of pleasing speech of 'una uirtuosa, e perfetta attione'. The plot itself, however, is not like that of the *Oedipus* or the *Iphigenia in Tauris*, but is in the category of the plot of Sophocles' *Ajax*, which Aristotle calles 'a tragedy of suffering'. (See M. T. Herrick, *Italian Tragedy in the Renaissance*, Urbana, 1965, p. 46.)

At first glance it might seem that in this characterization of a kind of tragedy Aristotle provides a basis for Milton's definition, but that possibility seems not to be supportable. As G. F. Else interprets πάθος in Aristotle, this signifies not passion, but the tragic deed, and he argues that the kind of tragedy which Aristotle calls παθητική [1455b32] is dominated by the tragic deed—which must be, he believes, a deliberate act: in the *Ajax* it is the act of suicide. 'But παθητική does not get its definition merely from the dominance of the πάθος. It is also defined in part by the two neighboring 'kinds' [of tragic play]; for as against "complex" it suggests a simple plot-structure, and as against "moral" it connotes an unhappy ending. Such a nexus of ideas is hard to render by any single English word. The best I can suggest is "fatal".—"Bloody" would be crude but perhaps expressive.' (*Aristotle's Poetics: The Argument*, Cambridge, 1957, p. 532.) Certainly, *Sophonisba* is dominated by action quite as much as the *Ajax*, and its plot is not reduced to an ordering governed chiefly by the requirements of decorum and verisimilitude.

Nevertheless Italian criticism provides several notions that help explain and to an extent justify Milton's modification of the definition of tragedy even as he continues to sanction the use of the words *imitation* and *catharsis*. The problem centres on what the nature of action is considered to be. Francesco Bonciani in 1578, in writing on Aristotle, is very conscious that action in drama is not the same as action in life and it is with the sense of this that he derives a definition which he finds supported in Aristotle's *Rhetoric*; in dramatic represen-tation 'a person by means of words represents the form and the nature of a thing and gives it motion'. (Translated by Bernard Weinberg, *A History of Literary Criticism in the Italian Renaissance*, Chicago, 1961, p. 581.) The idea is more fully developed by Francesco Buona-mici: the actions represented in art are only the signs of true actions, and imitation consists in representing the nature of things. (The summary of his position is also given by Weinberg, pp. 689–99.)

But apart from the criticism of tragedy, and of drama generally, there were Italian critics who deliberately transferred the idea of the imitation of action to an imitation of passion, particularly in account-ing for the nature of lyric poetry. Professor Baxter Hathaway quotes a passage of Benedetto Varchi that does this in order to characterize special kinds of imitation: 'Just as sculptors and painters imitate principally exteriors, that is, bodies, so poets imitate principally in-teriors, that is, the minds, or rather the passions of the mind like love, hate, anger, sorrow, joy.' (*The Age of Criticism. The Late*

Renaissance in Italy, Ithaca, 1962, p. 82. The quotation is from
Varchi's *Lezzioni*, Florence, 1950, p. 583, where Varchi is in part
following Alessandro Lionardi, *Dialogi della inventione poetica*,
Venice, 1554, p. 50.) Tasso sometimes interpreted 'action' rather
broadly, but it is Alessandro Guarini who in 1599 goes the farthest in
testing the paradox, arguing that a lyric poet 'in imitating a series
of passions could be said to be forming a "fable", and hence an action'.
(*Compendio della poesia tragicomica*, translated in *The Age of Criticism*, p. 58.) Professor Hathaway observed that this is a position very
much like Sir Richard Blackmore's in the eighteenth century in
proposing that Job might be considered a passive rather than an
active hero. (*The Age of Criticism*, pp. 58–59). Agnolo Segni had
limited the proposition—lyrics imitate passions or *mores*. (*Ragiona-
mento sopra le cose pertinenti alla poetica*, Florence, 1581, cited in
The Age of Criticism, p. 48.)

Another difficulty in interpreting Aristotle's doctrine arises from
the observation that in drama it is the agents as well as what they do
that hold our attention. It is the very obviousness of this that led
Segni (1573) to make Aristotle himself the authority for the idea that
the objects of imitation in drama are not restricted to human actions,
but include characters, passions, and thoughts. (Weinberg, p. 302.)
This kind of interpretation is the basis of Robortello's quite original
notion, and the one that seems to me to come closest to Milton's: 'If
you think of [imitation] in terms of the poet who writes, then we may
say that the principal end of tragedy is to imitate the nature of souls
and the characters of men [*imitari habitum animi, & mores hominum*]
through written words, through which description it is possible to
discern whether men are happy or unhappy. If you assume it to
refer to the actor as he acts, then we may say that the greatest and
most powerful end is that very action as a result of which men are
judged to be happy or unhappy.' (Translated from *In librum
Aristotelis de arte poetica explicationes* (1548) by Weinberg, p.
393.)

In short, among the Italians I find no writers upon tragedy who
would fully authorize Milton's transformation of Aristotle, even if
one attempted to limit the scope of his change in the light of a statement he makes in the *De Doctrina Christiana* that 'action and passion
are relative terms'. (Bohn edition, IV, 177.) For although the arguments of Bonciani and Buonamici might open the way to such a
reconciliation, the tragic works themselves universally exemplify the
more usual idea of the nature of action.

At this point it is useful also to take account of Professor P. R.
Sellin's explanation of Milton's use of *Agonistes*, in which the idea
of 'acting' in that word is shown in Renaissance commentaries to
signify dissembling, assuming a mask, playing a part, and he therefore argues that the term applies particularly to Samson's behaviour
in going forth to participate in the games of the Philistines. And he

further shows that this is the interpretation of Giovanni Diodati in his translation of Judges XVI, 25. ('Milton's Epithet *Agonistes*', *Studies in English Literature*, IV (1964), 157 and 161–2.)

[3] W. R. Parker, *Milton's Debt to Greek Tragedy in Samson Agonistes*, Baltimore, 1937, p. 57.

[4] H. D. F. Kitto, *Greek Tragedy, A Literary Study*, London, 1961, p. 31.

[5] *Ibid.*, p. 44.

[6] *Ibid.*, p. 58.

[7] *The Frontiers of Drama*, London, 1945, pp. 17–24.

[8] *Ibid.*, p. 31.

[9] *Ibid.*, p. 30.

[10] An effort—unsuccessful, I think—has been made to show that *Samson Agonistes* does possess the middle Dr. Johnson thought it did not have, and that it does therefore conform to the usual interpretation of Aristotle. (M. E. Grenander, 'Samson's Middle: Aristotle and Dr. Johnson', *University of Toronto Quarterly*, XXIV (1955), 377–89.)

[11] It seems that there are some points in which Milton would have found more examples among the Italians than among the Greeks— the occasional use of a chorus for ornament or spectacle, but not speaking or chanting, the play ending in a short observation of the chorus's (rhymed often by the Italians), and certain commonplaces that were frequently the substances of the choruses in the plays of the Italians. But the sources of what is unique in *Samson Agonistes* are apparently not to be discovered in this body of writing.

Mr. F. T. Prince has made an effort to relate certain elements in the composition of Andreini's *L'Adamo* to *Samson Agonistes*, partly in accordance with his conviction that the Italian journey made all the difference in Milton's handling of verse generally: 'Both its monostrophic choruses and its use of intermittent rhyme in semi-lyrical dialogues provide parallels to Milton's use of rhyme in his choruses; and, since Milton knew *L'Adamo* at the time when he first seriously meditated on subjects for tragedies, it may well have contributed to his views on methods of imitating the Greek Chorus. When he came to write his tragedy he had long left behind any intention to emulate the *sacre rappresentazoni* and fixed upon the strict dramatic ideal of Greek tragedy; in his realization of this ideal in *Samson* any lingering notions left by Andreini's dramatic poem were caught up into much more closely controlled and highly organized verse-forms.' (*The Italian Element in Milton's Verse*, Oxford, 1954, pp. 154–5.)

Mr. Prince is here stating more an impression than an argument and his conclusion suffers from not taking into account the more substantial and comprehensive if not conclusive arguments of Mrs. G. L. Finney in 'Chorus in *Samson Agonistes*', *Publications of the Modern Language Association*, LVIII (1943), 649–64, and the very useful study of Marguerite Little, *Some Italian Elements in the Choral*

Practice of 'Samson Agonistes,' a doctoral dissertation (1946) at the University of Illinois.

Some most interesting observations have been made by Miss Edith Buchanan, showing correspondences from among the Italian plays with some of the plans for tragedies Milton put down in his Commonplace Book. (*The Italian Neo-Senecan Background of Samson Agonistes*, dissertation (1952) at Duke University.)

12 Herrick, *Italian Tragedy in the Renaissance*, p. 289.
13 See M. T. Herrick, *Tragicomedy*, Illinois Studies in Language and Literature, Vol. 39, Urbana, 1955.
14 Gustave Lanson, 'L'Idée de la Tragédie en France avant Jodelle', *Revue d'Histoire Littéraire de la France*, XI (1904), 561.
15 From George Sandys's translation, *Christs Passion. A Tragedy*, London, 1640, pp. 72, 73.
16 *Tragoedia Sophompaneas*, Amsterdam, 1635, p. 54.
17 K. L. Johannessen, *Zwischen Himmel und Erde*, Fredrikstad, 1963, pp. 94–95.
18 *Domitien, suivi de Joseph à Dothan*, Paris, 1959, p. 288.

I have had the help of Professor Clarence Pott with the Dutch, and it is clear that Giono's adaptation brings into the language imagery and modifications that are not in Vondel—for example, this speech is not addressed to God. Giono has extended the interpretation of Professor Smit—'Joseph à Dothan nous fait si clairement entrevoir dans Joseph, aujourd'hui misérable, le futur vice-roi du pharaon que l'exitus infelix' perd toute puissance de conviction'. (W. A. P. Smit and P. Brachin, *Vondel (1587–1679)*, Paris, 1964, p. 39.) His own elaboration is certainly effective and I am convinced that it is wise. The doubt all this raises, however, concerns the possibility that the contemporary audience might not have seen past the ending complaint to a satisfying remembrance of the Christian promise. I have myself been won over to this interpretation, but I hope some time to see the whole matter thoroughly reviewed.
19 Translated by Watson Kirkconnell, *That Invincible Samson*, Toronto, 1964, p. 141.
20 The doctrine is Augustine's: 'Nor is Samson acquitted of guilt on any other plea, inasmuch as he crushed himself by the collapse of the house along with his enemies, than the plea that the Spirit who through him had been working miracles had secretly ordered this.' (*The City of God*, I, xxi.)
21 *De Tragœdiæ Constitutione Liber* . . . *Editio auctio multo*, Leyden, 1643, pp. 104–6. (Printed first in 1611.)
22 *Poeticarum Institutionum, Libri Tres*, Amsterdam, 1696, II, xiii, §30 and §31. (The original printing was in 1647.)
23 'Sources of Milton's Catharsis: A reconsideration', *Journal of English and Germanic Philology*, LX (1961), 712–30.

The idea of 'a milder purification', however, does have a considerable history in Italian criticism from the mid-sixteenth century, and it has been argued that it was this earlier Italian criticism rather than Heinsius that gave Milton his lead. (Martin Mueller, 'Sixteenth-Century Italian Criticism and Milton's Theory of Catharsis', *Studies in English Literature*, VI (1966), 139–50.

[24] Kosta Loukovitch, *L'Evolution de la Tragédie Religieuse Classique en France*, Paris, 1933, p. 231.

[25] F. M. Krouse, *Milton's Samson and the Christian Tradition*, Princeton, 1949.

[26] *The Life Records of John Milton*, edited by J. M. French, Vol. I, Rutgers, 1948, p. 409. Bartolommei was also present at a meeting of the Academy on June 28, 1638, when Miss Edith Hubbard suggested Milton might also have been present (*Life Records*, V, 385), and indeed he seems to have attended most of the meetings that summer.

[27] 'Un Précurseur Italien de Corneille, Girolamo Bartolommei', *Annales de l' Université de Grenoble*, IX (1897), no. 1, pp. 557–77. Loukovitch is persuaded that there is indeed an obligation here, but he does not demonstrate it. (*L'Evolution de la Tragédie Religieuse en France*, pp. 231–4.)

[28] *Tragedie de Girolamo Bartolommei*, Rome, 1632, sig. a7^v.

[29] Sigs. b9^r—b12^v.

[30] *Tragedie* (1632), sig. b7^r; *Tragedie di Girolamo Bartolommei, Già Smeducci. Ricorrette, ed Accresciute. Impressione Seconda*, Rome, 1655, sig. d3^v.

In Heinsius the definition goes; 'Tragœdia est seriæ absolutæque actionis, & quæ justæ magnitudinis sit, imitatio; sermone, harmonia, & rhythmo, sauiter condita. ita vt species singulæ singulis in partibus habeant locum. quæque non narrando, verum per misericordiam & horrorem, eorundem expiationem affectuum inducit.' (*De Tragœdiæ Constitutione*, p. 18.)

[31] Sig. c1^v.

[32] Sigs. e2^v—e3^r.

Bartolommei speaks of catharsis in homoeopathic and therapeutic terms and draws certain distinctions. He varies somewhat in his analysis of what is being purged—the passions generally or the man himself—but he clearly means to emphasize the purging of the whole man: 'intendere, che l'huomo si purghi, e non la Commiserazione, e 'l Timore' (1655 edition: sig. d3^v).

He characterizes tragedy as 'Medica degli affetti disordinati' (c3^v), and he says that the result of the purging is well-being and a moderation of the passions: 'Forse questa purgazione riesce di tanto giouumento all' huomo, che da essa gli resulti la salute, el il totale moderamento degli affetti' (c3^r). It is partly because he does not believe that there can be such a thing as an excess of compassion that he wishes to insist upon the health of the whole man as the aim of the purging, and somewhat as Milton does he allows himself to speak of the moderation of passions generally ['and such-like passions'], where one may suppose that moderation is indeed a good.

It is on this account that he refines the idea of the analogy with medicine: 'la purgazione, che si procura a' corpi si opera con medicamento, che tenga vna certa simpatia, e naturale domestichezza, con l'vmore peccante; a fine che egli in tal maniera per forza d'vna occulta affinità seco la traggia, si come la Calamita il ferro, l'Ambra la paglia; tuttuaia conseruano qualche diuersità di spezie fra di loro l'vmore, e 'l medicamento; ne si vede, che l'vna bile purghi l'altra bile; ma si bene vn'Agrarico, vn Riobarbaro, che si confaccia con l'vmor da purgarsi, il che proporzionalmente altresi nella cura degli animi debba auer lougo; non parendo verisimile, che la Commiserazione purgar deua la Commiserazione, e 'l Timore il Timore' (d_1^r). Tragedy works, then, to inculcate these emotions which thereafter by their very nature temper such other passions as are disorderly.

He likens the tragic catharsis to medicine in the way that he does because he is convinced that Aristotle did not mean that it was pity and fear that were being purged. He interpreted Aristotle to be saying that these were the means of purgation, that the tragic works stimulated these passions in the audience in order to effect the moderation of other passions. He was supported in part in his interpretation by the conviction that an excess of compassion is impossible. There are many passions that in excess are particularly harmful to the State, and it is these that must be governed. Tragedy, he said, treats of great personages and in the great the common excesses of pride show themselves in 'l'insolente alterigia' and 'la fastosa insolenza' (d_2^v). Tragedy must purge those in the audience who aspire to greatness, 'il che venga a fare mediante la Compassione, e 'l Timore' (d_2^v—d_3^r). Tragedy therefore deserved its name 'come salutifera moderatrice degli affetti de' più grandi Personaggi' (d_2^v).

[33] Loukovitch, L'Evolution de la Tragédie Religieuse, p. 34.
[34] In this analysis, I am, of course, deeply obliged to Una Ellis-Fermor's essay on 'Religious Drama' in The Frontiers of Drama.
[35] 'To say that Samson Agonistes is a classical tragedy with a Christian theme and outlook does not completely define the effect or the meaning used to attain it; but it puts us, I think, on the right track.' (A. S. P. Woodhouse, 'Tragic Effect in Samson Agonistes', University of Toronto Quarterly, XXVIII (1959), 222.)
[36] From the Examen to Polyeucte.
[37] J. H. Hanford, 'Samson Agonistes and Milton in Old Age', reprinted in John Milton's Samson Agonistes, edited by R. E. Hone, San Francisco, 1966, p. 181.

Certain similarities between Samson Agonistes and Polietto must be remarked on.

The two heroes are warriors in behalf of their people and their religion—Samson is God's 'faithful Champion' (1751), Polietto is 'campione di Cristo' (1632 edition, sig. n_6^r). The lives of both are greatly affected by dreams that came from God. Both—under very different circumstances—find themselves alone in the midst of their enemies when they are moved to destroy, in one case, images, in the other, a temple, Both die—again under very different circumstances —as martyrs, and in their deaths both are said to be affording examples for generations to come. Both show the working of the grace of God in much of their lives.

The similarities are, of course, in large part the similarities in the actual lives of the martyrs. There are other similarities that belong to the various accounts of the lives of the two men. And there are certain similarities in the dramatic management of these sources to point to, not only in order that we may form an opinion about what might be generically similar in plays based on the lives of martyrs, but in order that we may determine whether either of these writers knew the other's work. I may say that I find the similarities tantalizing, but nothing enables me to certify that Milton knew Bartolommei's play or that Bartolommei knew Milton's.

Polietto, like Samson, was chosen by God to be His champion in warlike exploits:

> O se gli effetti
> Nascan conformi a' detti, eletto Io Duce
> Nella santa Milizia, a cui mi chiama
> L'alta grazia di Cristo: Egli 'l Sourano
> Celeste Imperator, cui mi consacro,
> Pronto a seguir sua Trionfante Croce.
> O s'egli mi circondi del lucente
> Adamantino scudo di sua grazia. . . .
>
> (1655 edition: Act III, scene 2; p. 288)

> O wherefore was my birth from Heaven foretold
> Twice by an Angel, who at last in sight
> Of both my parents all in flames ascended
> From off the Altar, where an Off'ring burn'd,
> As in a fiery column charioting
> His Godlike presence, and from some great act
> Or benefit reveal'd to Abraham's race?
> Why was my breeding order'd and prescrib'd
> As of a person separate to God,
> Design'd for great exploits? . . .
>
> (23–32)

Polietto has been inspired by dreams. We hear of the importance of dreams in Samson's life, but not that he was inspired by any. On the other hand, he himself remarks on a certain turbulence that we are led to interpret as a divine thrusting on:

> I begin to feel
> Some rouzing motions in me which dispose
> To something extraordinary my thoughts.
>
> (1381–3)

Similar 'rousings' are indicated in Bartolommei's play:

> Ben veggio, ò Polietto, che 'l tuo zelo,
> E 'l generoso ardir, che 'l sen t'infiamma,
> E nuovo affetto della diua grazia,
> Ch'a magnanime imprese ti trasporta.
>
> (II, 2; p. 289)

> Vn' assidua tempesta di pensieri
> Nella mente mi muoue.
>
> (IV, 1; p. 299)

One such impulse moves Polietto to an act of destruction:

> Dimmi s'approui,
> Che nel pubblico Foro, ou' attaccati,
> Gli empi Editti di Decio furo dianzi,
> Zelante Io m'appresenti, e m'appalese
> Cristiano ad alta voce; a corso poi
> Fra gl' idolatri Tempi, abbatta, e calchi
> Di Gioue, e Marte i simulacri indegni.
> Forse l'esemplo mio render potria
> Piu d'vno ardito a palesar la Fede
> Di Cristo apertamente, e a porre 'n fondo
> L'antico Culto de' bugiardi Dei.
>
> (III, 2; p. 289)

Another scene of destruction has similar elements:

> Cui di repente la ridente scena
> Faro cangiarne 'n funerale pompa,
> Tramutati in Cupressi i Lauri attesi,
> Gli applausi in onte, e scherni, e forse ancora
> La cara visa in tormentosa morte.
>
> (III, I; p. 283)

The Messenger described Samson's destruction in these words:

> Those two massie Pillars
> With horrible convulsion to and fro,
> He tugg'd, he shook, till down they came and drew
> The whole roof after them, with burst of thunder
> Upon the heads of all who sate beneath,
> Lords, Ladies, Captains, Councellors, or Priests,
> Thir choice nobility and flower.
>
> (1648–54)

A rival and enemy of Polietto's took part in a certain procession:

> I tonanti Tamburi, e le canore
> Trombe precorser nunzie della festa,
> Ch'ordinata seguio; si che nel mezzo

Alle Milizie sue il nuovo Duce
Movesse il tardo piè, severo in fronte. . . .
Ed ecco intanto risonar si sente
L'aer de suoni, e voci; ecco 'l superbo,
E feroce Artaban, Censor nouvello,
Che guida seco in procession gli Dei
Inchinò tosto l'universa Gente
A' sommi Numi riverente 'l piede,
E Giove, e Marte n'adorò prostrata. . . .

(V, 2; p. 315)

Samson once moved with comparable insolence:

is this the man,
That invincible *Samson*, far renown'd,
The dread of *Israel's* foes, who with a strength
Equivalent to Angels walk'd thir streets,
None offering fight; who single combatant
Duell'd thir Armies rank't in proud array,
Himself an Army, now unequal match
To save himself against a coward arm'd
At one spears length.

(340–348)

And when the time came he moved forward into as festive a celebration:

This day to *Dagon* is a solemn Feast,
With Sacrifices, Triumph, Pomp, and Games.

(1311–12)

The morning Trumpets Festival proclaim'd
Through each high street . . .
. . . before him Pipes
And Timbrels, on each side went armed guards,
Both horse and foot before him and behind
Archers and Slingers, Cataphracts and Spears.
At sight of him the people with a shout
Rifted the Air clamouring thir god with praise,
Who had made thir dreadful enemy thir thrall.
He patient but undaunted where they led him,
Came to the place.

(1598–1624)

At the death of both heroes the chorus and others take consolation in the manner of the death, and that of Polietto had been foreshadowedi

Vn bel morire
Tutta la vita onora, e la corona.

(I, iii; p. 249)

I with what speed the while
(*Gaza* is not in plight to say us nay)
Will send for all my kindred, all my friends
To fetch him hence and solemnly attend
With silent obsequie and funeral train
Home to his Fathers house: there will I build him
A Monument, and plant it round with shade
Of Laurel ever green, and branching Palm,
With all his Trophies hung, and Acts enroll'd
In copious Legend, or sweet Lyric Song;
Thither shall all the valiant youth resort,
And from his memory inflame thir breasts
To matchless valour, and adventures high.

(1728–40)

And these are the last words of Bartolommei's play:

Ma tempo, che mouiamo al sacro Tempio
A dar del Martiri Santo alle beate
Reliquie sepoltura, Voi Fedeli,
Che miraste di Lui l'opre preclare,
Restate d'esse forti imitatori,
Costanti sempre della Fè Cristiana;
Pugnate ardenti, posti in Dio la speme,
Contro 'l Mondo, e Satan; qui breue guerra
Partorisce nel Ciel perpetua pace.

Towards the end of both plays there is a prophecy of a kind of
immortality for both heroes, expressed in part through the image of
the phoenix:

Anzi si mira
Ben tutto giorno vn tal miracol vago,
Oprato da Natura, ond' altri apprenda
Da somiglianze di bell' opre sue,
Ch' impossibil non è, che l'huom risorga
Da morte a nuova vita. Il Sol, che nasce
Lucente nel mattin, forse la sera
Nell' Occaso non more, e non discende
Fra l'ombre a seppellirsi 'n grembo all'onde?
Tomba vitale, onde rinato sorga.
Nè men di lui mancò l' argentea Luna,
E non men d'esso suo Fratello, al foco
Ringiouinita s' avvisò, ripreso
Dal suo fine il principio. Il simil forse
Nell' aurata Fenice non s' ammira?
Madre, e Figlia a se stessa, che si rende
Sparso de vario odor, nido l' sepolcro,
Nutrici le fauille, e 'l cener seme,

Cui torni a germogliar vinta la Morte,
Sorgendo dal suo tumol fortunata,
Splendida più che mai, e trionfante,
Tra vaga schiera di seguaci Augelli,
Suo corteggio esultante. E non sia vero,
Ch' Autor della Natura il vero Dio,
Da volontaria morte a immortal vita
Risorger vaglia? mentr' vn tale effetto
Nell' opre sue create egli dimostra?

(V, 5; p. 322-3)

But he though blind of sight,
Despis'd and thought extinguish't quite,
With inward eyes illuminated
His fierie vertue rouz'd
From under ashes into sudden flame. . . .
So vertue giv'n for lost,
Deprest, and overthrown, as seem'd.
Like that self-begott'n bird
In the *Arabian* woods embost,
That no second knows nor third,
And lay e're while a Holocaust,
From out her ashie womb now teem'd,
Revives, reflourishes, then vigorous most
When most unactive deem'd,
And though her body die, her fame survives,
A secular bird ages of lives.

(1687-1707)

I shall omit a great number of similarities in language and in imagery, for here, as in the comparison with Vondel's *Samson*, it is easy to get lost where so much is surely a manner common to the age. I must observe, however, what I find quite inexplicable, that *Polietto* has nearly as many references to blindness and to the inner light as Milton's play.

I think we are obliged to believe that Milton spoke with Bartolommei and that he knew of his work. I think we must believe that he was familiar with reasonings like his about the nature of tragedy and sacred tragedy. I think that what he learned of this was of use to Milton in forming his play, and in forming it differently and to an important degree to a different end.

The preface to *Samson Agonistes* speaks of tragedy in some of the same terms Bartolommei uses, but more briefly, and, I think, unclearly and even confusedly. The common interest is certain, but Milton's idea of catharsis is far from clear, and Bartolommei's is quite clear, and quite impressive.

A plot is worked out in *Polietto*, as it is not in *Samson Agonistes*, the characters are more complexly involved with each other, and the chief factors in the resolution of the plot are events. In *Samson Agonistes* the chief factors in the movement of the play are internal, changes in Samson's mind. And this I think to be the most significant point—Bartolommei conceives of the life of his saint as indeed taking place in a world of rival religions and gods, in which God intervenes in miraculous events and in sacraments, and in which the miracle of the Incarnation is the continuous reference. And in *Samson Agonistes* God and man are treating with each other privately. Milton's play is unmistakably Protestant, his humanism is serving the idea of the solitary walk with God. Bartolommei's humanism is subordinate to his intent to honour the miraculous and the sacramental.

I think that if Bartolommei's work meant anything to Milton it meant—as I think the works of Monteverdi and Rospigliosi and Mazocchi also did—that he would learn from this use of classical forms how to put these same forms to the uses of Protestant piety.

I must remark finally that in a volume published in 1657, *Dialoghi Sacri Musicali*, Bartolommei presented still another form of composition. These are short pieces, to be produced but without scenery. One of these is *Sansone Vittorioso*, perhaps less than two hundred lines. The work proceeds in exchanges between individuals as well as between choruses, 'del modo recitativo ne' soliloqui' (p. x). I see no similarities between this and Milton's work except perhaps in the versification.

38 Gustave Lanson, as quoted by Loukovitch, *L'Evolution de la Tragédie Religieuse*, p. 32.

39 'The Music of Milton', *Philological Quarterly*, XXVI (1947), 328–44.

40 *Trattato della Musica Scenica*, in *Lyra Barberina . . . Accedunt Eiusdem Opera, Pleraque Nondum Edita*, Florence, 1763, II, 23.

41 *Trattato della Lyrica Scenica*, in *Lyra Barberina*, II, 15.

42 H. F. Redlich, *Claudio Monteverdi, Life and Works*, translated by Kathleen Dale, London, 1952, p. 95.

As Doni put it: 'In ogni tempo si è costumato di frammettere alle Azioni dramatiche qualche sorte di cantilena, o in forma d' Intermedi tra un Atto, e l'altro, o pure dentro l'istesso Atto, per qualche occorrenze del soggetto rappresentato. Ma quando si cominciassero a cantare tutte le Azioni intere, fresca ne è ancora la memoria.' (*Trattato della Lyrica Scenica*, in *Lyra Barberina*, II, 22.)

43 Doni shows how the use might be extended: 'Le Monodie, ò melodie d'una sola aria, e per un solo cantore; e parimente per le Chorodie, cioè canti d'una sola aria, per cantarsi à core all' unisono, ò all' ottava.' (*Compendio del Trattato de' Generi e de' Modi della Musica*, Rome, 1635, p. 68.)

44 *La Camerata Fiorentina; Vincenzo Galilei*, ed. Fabio Fano, Milan, 1934, p. xxxvi.

45 Marco da Gagliano is the authority for this in the preface (1608) to his *Dafne*, reprinted in Angelo Solerti, *Le Origini del Melodramma*, Turin, 1903, p. 81.

⁴⁶ Milton linked music and poetry habitually, and in such a way that it seems as if he could not conceive of their separate existence. When he writes to his father he reasons as if his life were involved in the point: 'What pleasure is there in the empty modulation of the voice without words and meaning and the rhythm of eloquence?' (*Ad Patrem*, lines 50–51.) And in the extraordinary judgement he made upon the Book of Revelations he shows how vividly he imagines the union of music and tragedy: 'And the Apocalyps of Saint *John* is the majestick image of a high and stately Tragedy, shutting up and intermingling her solemn Scenes and Acts with a sevenfold *Chorus* of halleluja's and harping symphonies. . . .' (*The Reason of Church-Government Urg'd against Prelaty*, Book II [*Complete Prose Works of John Milton*, ed. D. M. Wolfe, Vol. I, New Haven, 1953, p. 815].)

⁴⁷ Monteverdi once speaks of the three principal passions, or affections, of the mind as wrath, temperance, and humility, and in discussing their expression in music he cites Plato's *Rhetoric*, book III: 'Suscipe Harmoniam illam quae ut decet imitatur fortiter euntis in proclium, voces, atque accentus.' (From the preface to *Madrigali Guerrieri, et amorosi. Libro ottavo*, 1638, reprinted in G. Francesco Malipiero, *Claudio Monteverdi*, Milan, 1929, p. 89.) At the same place he also cites Tasso's poetry as an example of the kind of imitation he himself is undertaking.

In a letter that used to be thought to be addressed to G. B. Doni he again credits Plato with the authority for his own practice: '. . . ho provato in pratica che quando fui per scrivere il pianto del Arianna, non trovando libro che mi aprisse la via naturale alla imitatione nè meno che mi illuminasse che dovessi imitatore, altri che Platone per via di un suo lume rinchiuso così che appena potevo di lontano con la mia debil vista quel poco che mi mostrasse; ho provato dicco la gran fatica che sia bisogno fare in far quel poco ch'io feci d'immitatione, et perciò spero sij per non dispiacere ma rieschi come si voglia alla fine son per contentarmi d'essere più tosto poco lodato nel novo, che molto nel ordinario scrivere. . . .' (October 22, 1633, as printed in Malipiero, p. 293.)

The doctrine had already been developed in Vincenzo Galilei's *Dialogo della musica antica e della moderna* of 1581: 'The highest function of music is a naturalistic expression—the "imitation of nature" in so far as human passions are a part of nature.' (Armen Carapetyan, 'The Concept of *Imitazione della Natura* in the Sixteenth Century', *Journal of Renaissance and Baroque Music*, I [1946], 57.) 'Music must recapture the primitive elements, both of expression and use, such as existed with the ancients, and it must unabashedly return to the candor of human passions' (p. 65).

⁴⁸ From a letter of December 9, 1616, reprinted in Malipiero, *Claudio Monteverdi*, p. 166.

⁴⁹ 'Dovendosi imitare tutto il senso, e non le parole spezzate.' (G. B. Doni, *Compendio*, p. 79.)

50 'Recitativo . . . s'intende oggi quella sorte di melodìa, che può acconciamente, e con garbo recitarsi, cioè cantarsi da un solo in guisa tale, che le parole s'intendono, o facciasi ciò sul palco delle scene, o nelle Chiese, e Oratorii a foggia di Dialoghi, o pure nelle Camere private, o altrove.' (G. B. Doni, *Trattato della Musica Scenica*, in *Lyra Barberina*, II, 29.)

There is this further pointed criticism:

'Basically, recitative is almost a play spoken: which is why the operas have no musical structure apart from the structure of the drama. If we cannot understand the words these early operas are meaningless and tedious, except in so far as, when the voices speak in passion, the recitative is liable to be heightened to lyrical intensity—to become arioso. . . . In Monteverdi's early operas (as in his madrigals) music begins to become dramatic, and drama to approach the condition of music. . . .

'Yet the theory behind Monteverdi's early operas is still that the play is the thing, embodied in the musically heightened speech of recitative, as Shakespeare's play is embodied in his poetically intensified dialogue. And counterpoised against the recited play is the instrumental and occasionally choral dance music, which is a direct transference of the social ritual of the masque. The sung speech is the drama of the personal life; the dance music is the communal values of the public life. Opera, as we know it, was the gradual interpenetration of these two forces: which happened from both directions.' (Wilfred Mellers, *Harmonious Meeting*, London, 1965, p. 152.)

51 *Musiciens d'Autrefois*, Paris, 1908, p. 92.

52 Xavier de Courville, 'L'Arianna de Monteverdi', *Revue Musicale*, October 1921, as cited by Henri Prunières, *Monteverdi, His Life and Work*, translated by M. D. Mackie, London, n.d., p. 79.

53 From a letter to Alessandro Striggio, the writer of the *libretto* of the *Orfeo*, December 9, 1616 (Malipiero, *Claudio Monteverdi*, p. 167).

54 'La favola tutta poi quanto alla mia non poca ignoranza non sento che ponto mi mova et con dificolta anco la intendo, ne sento che lei mi porta con ordine naturale ad un fine che mi mova. L'Arianna mi porta ad un giusto lamento; et l'Orfeo ad una giusta preghiera. . . .' (*Ibid.*, p. 166.)

55 Reprinted in Solerti, *Le Origini del Melodramma*, pp. 56–57.

56 '. . . credete che il moderno Compositore fabrica sopra li fondamenti della verità.' (From the preface to the *Quinto Libro de' Madrigali a cinque voci*, 1605, reprinted in Malipiero, *Claudio Monteverdi*, p. 72.)

At this point I am particularly happy to rely upon the observations of Mr. Leo Schrade: 'When at the beginning of his dramatic work Monteverdi sounded out the human tragedy of Ariadne, he admitted that he had none to instruct him and no musical guide to lead him through the secrets of expressing human passions in music, save Plato's doctrine of imitation. And when late in his life, close to the time of the *Incoronazione di Poppea*, he wrote that he was engrossed in the philosophic research of natural science, he confessed that this inquiry into the nature of man served him better than any professional guidance, and what he harvested from these studies went, as he said, into his artistic work. None had been greater than Monteverdi in bringing to the fore the conflict of demonic passions, profound melancholy, and tragic suffering. Dio of Prusa said that the artist must be none other than *mimetes tes daimonias physeos*, the imitator of the demonic nature. This precisely concurs with what Monteverdi regarded as the business of the artist.' (*Tragedy in the Art of Music*, Cambridge, 1964, p. 67.)

There is also this thoughtful and apt consideration of how music and the idea of the discovery of truth go hand in hand in Monteverdi: 'Con la sua opera il Monteverdi scrive il suo mirabile *Traité des passions de l'âme*, mentre i filosofi del secolo per vincere l'isolamento intellettuale e sentimentale in cui l'uomo era venuto a trovarsi cercano di reinserirlo metafisicamente mediante l'istituzione di un nuovo rapporto col mondo. Ora, persino dal Descartes l'agire dell' uomo è visto sotto il dominio del sentimento, cosicchè la stessa ragione deve trasformarsi in sentimento per commuoverci e muoverci all'azione. Le passioni sono i moti dell'anima e le mobili musiche monteverdiane ne sono la sensibile trascrizione musicale, nell'ultima fase creativa portata alla massima evidenza scenico-teatrale attraverso esperienza che culminano nel *Ritorno di Ulisse in patria* e nell' *Incoronazione di Poppea*.' (Luigi Ronga, 'La Musica', in *La Civiltà Veneziana nell'Età Barocca*, ed. *Centro di Cultura e Civiltà della Fondazione Giorgio Cini*, n. d., p. 133.)

[57] '. . . quelli che sostengono la parte delle Monodie dicono che la perfettione della Musica consiste nel bello e gratioso cantare; e nel fare intendere tutti i sentimenti del poeta . . . non essendo il fine della Musica il Diletto; ma le commotione de gl' Affetti.' (G. B. Doni, *Compendio*, p. 103.)

It seems to me also that what Doni says of what is to be expected of soliloquy in musical drama characterizes the very quality of much of the verse of Milton's play, perhaps most finally Samson's beginning words: 'Da questo si può raccogliere, che dovunque l'Attore parla seco stesso in scena con qualche commozione di affetto, allora se gli convenga il canto, e che quello dice, sia veramente un Cantico.' (*De' Trattati Musica . . . Tomo Secondo*, p. 10.)

And again: 'Ma che gli affetti veementi siano potenti incentivi della Musica, e che dove si rappresentavano in Scena, ivi massima-mente si richegga la melodio' (p. 11).

[58] Battista Guarini said the business of a tragi-comedy was 'to imitate through a stage spectacle an invented action, combining all those tragic and comic parts which can be put together in a verisi-

milar way and with decorum, organized under a single dramatic form, to the end of purging by means of pleasure the sadness of the listeners'. (Translated from *Il Verrato* [1588] by Bernard Weinberg, *A History of Literary Criticism in the Italian Renaissance*, Chicago, 1961, p. 661.)

[59] Alessandro Striggio, *La Favola d'Orfeo*, lines 600–1, in *Drammi per Musica dal Rinuccini allo Zeno*, edited by A. Della Corte, Turin, 1958. All my quotations of *libretti* are from this volume.

[60] *Trattato della Musica Scenica*, in *Lyra Barberina*, II, 14–15.

[61] *L'Arianna*, line 764.

[62] Schrade, *Tragedy in the Art of Music*, p. 57.

[63] Guidi Pasquetti, *L'Oratorio Musicale in Italia*, Florence, 1914, p. 198.

[64] 'Discorso Dogmatico sugli Oratorii', reprinted in Giuseppe Calabrese, *Origini del Melodramma Sacro in Roma*, Gravina, 1907, p. 249.

[65] Calabrese, p. 186.

It is at this point that I think it proper to say that I subscribe to the conclusion of F. M. Krouse: 'And when one has explored the region which encloses all of *Samson Agonistes* not related to Greek tragedy, one returns to the poem convinced that only in *form* are the bonds of similarity significant; the content of *Samson Agonistes*, insofar as it can be distinguished at all from form, has much stronger bonds with regions in which Greek tragedy is a mere pin-point on the map.' (*Milton's Samson and the Christian Tradition*, Princeton, 1949, p. 82.)

[66] *The Reason of Church Government Urg'd against Prelaty*, II, introduction (*Complete Prose Works*, I, 817).

[67] 'And now, to sum it all up, what pleasure is there in the inane modulation of the voice without words and meaning and rhythmic eloquence?' (Translated by M. Y. Hughes.)

[68] Ulderico Rolandi *Il libretto per musica attraverso i tempi*, Rome, 1950, p. 60.

[69] The earlier Italian critics and playwrights had also acknowledged how according to the use of the supernatural in the concluding events of tragedy catharsis might be modified in its very nature. Robortello, Minturno, and Cinthio were among those who added admiration to pity and fear in accounting for the pleasure to be derived from works in which the intervention of a deity provided an ending to some degree happy. (See Herrick, *Italian Tragedy in the Renaissance*, pp. 81 and 88 particularly.)

[70] *Tragedy in the Art of Music*, pp. 73–74.

[71] 'Discourses on the Heroic Poem', 14, translated by A. H. Gilbert, in *Literary Criticism: Plato to Dryden*, Detroit, 1962, p. 481.

[72] 'Tragic Effect in *Samson Agonistes*', *University of Toronto Quarterly*, XXVIII (1959), 217.

Professor Woodhouse's judgement was to the contrary effect:

'And calm of mind all passion spent.

And as if to confirm this reading of the lines, they again culminate in a formulation—perhaps the most famous in all literature—of the Aristotelian *katharsis*. Clearly Milton supposed that, with his basic Christian assumptions, he had still produced a genuinely tragic effect. Nor will the reader who clears his mind of prepossessions, and allows the poem to have its full effect, be likely to demur' (p. 216).

The argument I have presented, of course, brings into question the very possibility of catharsis in Aristotle's sense in this work except as it becomes modified by the substitution of passion for action as the subject of imitation. It may very well be that this is still an appropriate word to characterize the effect of the play, as Milton would appear to want it, if for no other reason than that it is the only word available.

Professor Roy Daniels would hardly concur, I judge, with Professor Woodhouse's characterization of the ending effect of the play, for he insists on an unresolved tension in the play that continues into the conclusion—and on this point I am wholly in agreement with Professor Woodhouse in finding an unclouded resolution: 'The new rationalism supplies another unifying agent. . . . The miraculous elements in Samson's story are not stressed; his feats of strength are made reasonable: his acts, however strange, are rationally accounted for. At the centre of the drama is Samson's will, and it is the part of reason to bring his will into alignment with the will of God.

'Milton has realized with complete success that Baroque quality which critics refer to as tension of opposites, as ambiguity or paradox. Much of it comes easily out of the fundamental paradox of biblical material and classical form. Samson to the seventeenth-century reader is irresistibly reminiscent of Hercules, the strong man who coped with all enemies yet at the same time Samson is a type of Christ who by his own death destroyed our enemies. Samson is also a martyr, whose function it is to witness and to suffer, and simultaneously a divine avenger who invokes and brings down wrath upon his enemies. It has already been shown that he was regarded as a saint, from which category Milton was careful not to remove him. Yet he committed suicide, an abhorred crime. Within the structure of the classical drama Samson must function as the hero, with a 'flaw' that leads to his tragic end. The lament for *Samson Agonistes* is, as we have pointed out, both classical and Christian. And the philosophic conclusion is similarly ambivalent.' (*Milton, Mannerism and Baroque*, Toronto, 1963, pp. 215–16.)

While I agree with Professor Woodhouse that the play, so far from ending in tension, ends in the perfection of composure, I myself believe that in the culmination of feeling it is more in accord with the tradition of expressions of consolation than it is with the conclusions that follow from the catharsis of tragedy. For expressions of consolation may also be dearly bought and perhaps as profoundly expressive. As in Homer's 'Nothing is ever accomplished by yielding to wild lamentation' (*Iliad*, XXIV, 524), and more than once and better still in Plutarch: 'For no good man, after he is dead, is deserving of lamentations, but of hymns and songs of joy' (*Letter to Apollonius*, 114D), and again: 'Here, we must not merely marvel, we must remember' (*De Tranquilitate*, 474D).

Bibliographical Note

David Masson's description of Milton's travels in his *Life of Milton* has been the finest and the most thorough study we have had of the society Milton encountered. Individual monographs like Artur Egel's *Milton und Italien* (1940) have added some details to our knowledge but the most valuable sourcebook is J. M. French's *Life Records of John Milton*, reprinting all that is known and almost all that has been suggested concerning the incidents of Milton's life. There remain, of course, many gaps in our knowledge and many points that are obscure. We know almost nothing of Milton's visit to Paris, his meeting with Grotius, and his apparently leisurely journey through France. Milton's mention of Alessandro Cherubini suggests that in passing from Florence to Rome and in stopping at Siena he would have met there members of the Cherubini family who were such important patrons of music, but if there are any records to certify this they have not been brought to light. We do know that he visited Lucca for several days, that the Diodatis were deep in the academic life of that city, one that at this time was particularly dedicated to producing dramas, but there our knowledge ends. (The minutes of the academy that would have most likely entertained Milton, the Oscuri, are mutilated, and those that would have covered the time of Milton's visit are missing.)

But even the knowledge we have is inevitably scanty. When Milton or someone else does give us something particular to go on, or when we try to find the basis for a legend—that he stayed at the Gaddi house in Florence or that he played on the organ at Vallombrosa or that he did in fact witness a production of *L'Adamo*—we find nothing of the circumstantial testimony biography requires.

On the other hand there are many excellent guides to the life of the times that are of the greatest use in helping us recreate the quality of the society Milton was moving in. The first volumes of the *Dizionario Biografico degli Italiani* are of course improving upon works which nevertheless still possess great authority: Salvino Salvini's *Fasti Consolari dell' Academia Fiorentina* (1717), Giulio Negri's *Istoria degli Fiorentini* (1722), and Tiraboschi's *Storia della Letteratura Italiana* (1772–95). The *Enciclopedia dello Spettacolo* is marvellously rich and the contributions to it by Pier Maria Capponi are invaluable.

Then there are the landmarks of scholarship—von Pastor's history of the Papacy, Molmenti's histories of Venice, Favaro's commentaries on Galileo, Loewenberg's *Annals of Opera*, Maylender's *Storia delle Accademie d'Italia*, Cardinal Ehrle's works on the topography of Rome, E. S. De Beer's edition of John Evelyn's *Journals*. As for the study of the history of ideas and expression—in music and painting as well as in literature and philosophy—Croce, in his own writing and through his vast influence, has done most to characterize the unity in diversity in this most various age.

The diversity is extraordinary, and many figures, in literary life especially, who are now judged to be most minor, have not been much written about although it is certain that they played important parts in the dominant movements. There are good studies of Dati, inadequate ones of Manso, and nothing or almost nothing on Gaddi, G. B. Doni, and Loredano. I know of nothing that gets at the heart of the differences between Salvatore Rosa and Bernini that would reveal most vividly the character of the intellectual life of Rome in the 1630s. One of the most notable gaps is the absence of studies on the ardent collaboration of Mazarin and the Barberinis in their musical and theatrical ventures although there is surely material, perhaps in the archives of the French Embassy, that would solve particular questions about Milton's visit to Rome.

There are fortunately some first hand sources of the greatest value easily accessible. Many of the papers of the Svogliati survive in the collections of the Magliabecchiana in Florence, several of those of the Incogniti of Venice have been printed as have some of those of the Otiosi of Naples. Of special authority are three contemporary journals—André Maugars, *Response faite à un curieux sur le sentiment de la Musique d'Italie, Escrite à Rome le premier octobre* 1639, ed. Er.

Thonain, Paris, 1865; J. J. Bouchard, *Journal*, MS. 502 in the École Nationale Supérieure des Beaux-Arts, Paris; and Giacinto Gigli, *Diario Romano* (1608–70), ed. Giuseppe Ricciotti, Rome, 1958. There are also the *Avvisi di Roma*, accounts of daily happenings in the official life of the city chiefly, to be found in manuscript.

Meanwhile modern scholars are continually bringing forward knowledge of much of the buried material—G. B. Parkes, Lytton Sells, F. T. Prince, Mrs. Clara Dentler among those writing in English—and Sergio Baldi is editing Milton's Italian poems. Paolo Portoghesi and Maurizio and Marcello Fagiolo-Dell 'Arco are contributing most valuably to the study of the baroque in Rome.

Index

Index

Campanella, T., 71, 98, 101
Capaccio, G. C., 106 *n7*
Capello, B., 117
Carapetyan, A., 200 *n47*
Caravaggio, M. Da, 75
Cardoyn, C., 123 *n12*
Carducci, G., 49 *n46*
Carissimi, G., 167
Cary, J. P., 69, 91 *n37*
Castelli, B., 43 *n1*, 46 *nn16, 18*
Castelli, O., 84
Catullus, 105
Cavalieri, E. Del, 49 *n47*
Cavalli, (P.) F., 55, 118, 120, 124 *n26*
Celano, C., 106 *n6*
Chapelain, J., 38
Charles I, K. of England, 74, 75
Charles V, Emp., 40
Chaucer, 27
Cherubini, A., 54
Chiabrera, G., 13, 22, 23, 29
Chimentelli, V., 12, 25, 44 *n10*
Christine, Q. of Sweden, 83
Cicero, 92, 102
Cifra, A., 122 *n1*, 129
Cinthio, G., 134, 203 *n69*
Clementi, F., 85
Coblenz, Pr. of, 66
Colagrosso, F., 91 *nn33, 36*
Colonna family, 62, 73, 90 *n22*
Colonna, V., 117
Coltellini, A., 7, 17, 18, 23, 25, 26, 44 *n10*, 48 *n44*, 124 *n16*
Columbus, C., 97
Copernicus, 3, 37
Corneille, P., 47 *n39*, 136, 139, 145, 147, 148, 149–50, 153–4, 173
Cortona, P. da, 52, 76, 83
Coryat, T., 109, 110–11, 122–4
Courville, X. de, 201 *n52*
Cowper, W., 49 *nn48–50*, 50 *nn51–53*, 55
Crashaw, R., 26
Cristina di Lorena, 46 *nn14, 16*

218

Henrietta Maria, Q. of England, 74
Henry IV, K. of France, 158
Herrick, M. T., 188, 191 *nn13, 14,* 203 *n69*
Hobbes, T., 3
Holstein, L., 20, 53–54, 69, 74, 81 *n2*–82, 83, 89 *n18,* 90 *n24,* 94
Homer, 204
Hondedei, Z., 91 *n31*
Hone, R. E., 193 *n37*
Horace, 105, 108 *n30*
Howell, J., 109
Hubbard, E., 44 *n10,* 192 *n26*
Hughes, M. Y., 203 *n67*

Ivanovich, C., 125 *n27*

Johannessen, K. L., 191 *n17*
Johnson, S., 38, 116, 131, 132, 190 *n10*

Kitto, H. D. F., 131, 190 *n4*
Krouse, F. M., 192 *n25,* 203 *n65*

Lami, G., 48 *n45*
Landi, S., 69, 76
Lanson, G., 139, 191 *n14,* 199 *n38*
Lassels, R., 109, 112–13, 122 *nn9, 10*
Leonardo da Vinci, 20, 75
Leopold (son of Ferd. II) ,44 *n9*
Liljegren, S. B., 45 *n10*
Lionardi, A., 189
Little, M., 190 *n11*
Locatelli, S., 123 *n12*
Loewenberg, A., 85 *n2*
Loredano family, 117
Loredano, G. F., 115–17, 118, 122, 123 *n16,* 124 *n16*
Loredano, L., 115
Lorenzo, M., 7
Lorrain, C., 71
Loukovitch, K., 192 *nn24, 27,* 193 *n33,* 199 *n38*
Lovejoy, A. O., 50 *n56*
Lucullus, 102
Lungo, I. del, 43 *n1,* 45 *n12*
Lupis, A., 123 *n16,* 124 *n20*

222

---

222 INDEX

Ricciotti, G., 88 *n11*
Roberts, D. R., 155, 156, 158
Robertello, F., 148, 189, 203 *n69*
Rolandi, U., 203 *n68*
Rolland, R., 74, 84, 159, 167
Ronga, L., 202 *n56*
Rosa, S., 6, 15, 62, 88 *n10*, 94
Rospigliosi family, 62
Rospiglioni, G., 13, 56, 71, 76, 77–78, 85, 199 *n37*
Rovai, F., 23, 45 *n10*, 46 *n23*

Salviati, D. of, 22, 40
Salviati, F., 3, 40
Salvini, S., 46 *n25*
Salzilli, G., 90 *n24*
Sandys, G., 191 *n15*
Sannazaro, J., 102
Sarpi, P., 110, 120, 122
Sarto, A. del, 20
Saviotti, A., 91 *n31*
Scaliger, J. J., 143
Scrade, L., 177, 201 *n56*, 203 *n62*
Segni, A., 189
Sellin, P. R., 144, 189
Shakespeare, 109, 160, 164, 172, 183, 201 *n50*
Silvagni, D., 83
Simon, Father, 79
Sirluck, E., 44 *n7*
Sixtus V, Pope, 63, 70
Smeducci, B., 28
Smit, W. A. P., 191 *n18*
Solerti, A., 156, 199 *n45*, 201 *n55*
Somerset, Lord J., 68
Sophocles, 188
Southey, R., 49 *nn48, 49*
Spada, Governor, 84
Spagna, A., 167
Spenser, E., 105
Spongano, R., 45 *n13*
Stoye, J. W., 123 *n15*, 125 *n28*
Striggio, A., 173, 201 *n53*, 203 *n59*
Strozzi, Giovanni B., 18